Effective Support and Education
of Autistic Young People

Effective Support and Education of Autistic Young People

Educational Psychology Perspectives

Edited by
Judith Gainsborough

Foreword by Robyn Steward

Sub-editors: Laura Cockburn, Ursula Cornish, Erik Dwyer,
Ken Greaves, Charlotte Hatton, Laurence Hime, Diana Loffler

Jessica Kingsley Publishers
London and Philadelphia

First published in Great Britain in 2022 by Jessica Kingsley Publishers
An imprint of Hodder & Stoughton Ltd
An Hachette Company

3

A CIP catalogue record for this title is available from the
British Library and the Library of Congress

ISBN 978 1 78775 820 9
eISBN 978 1 78775 821 6

Printed and bound by CPI Group (UK) Ltd, Croydon, CR0 4YY

Jessica Kingsley Publishers' policy is to use papers that are natural,
renewable and recyclable products and made from wood grown in sustainable forests. The logging and manufacturing processes are expected
to conform to the environmental regulations of the country of origin.

Jessica Kingsley Publishers
Carmelite House
50 Victoria Embankment
London EC4Y 0DZ

www.jkp.com

Contents

About the Contributors

Bola Abimbola is Chief Executive Officer and Founder of Soulspace Healing. She is a Business Clarity and Emotional Freedom Coach who empowers those ready for deeper inner congruence to cultivate emotional intelligence, the understanding and managing of our emotions for self and for relationships in business and personal life. With a BSc degree in psychology and over 20 years in the field of trauma, disability, psychology, health service, policy, politics and stress management, Bola developed the SMITT™ system for emotional intelligence, incorporating mindfulness, neuroplasticity, psychology and trauma recovery. She is a certified trauma recovery coach and teacher at the International Association of Trauma Recovery Coaching (IAOTRC). She can be reached via her website www.soulspacehealing.com.

Alyssa M. Alcorn is an interdisciplinary researcher working across psychology, human–computer interaction, education and design. Much of her work has focused on developing and evaluating technology-based tools for use in school settings with autistic pupils, including participatory design of new technologies with children and teachers. At the time of writing, she is a postdoctoral researcher at the Salvesen Mindroom Research Centre, University of Edinburgh, developing resources for teaching about neurodiversity in primary schools. She received her MSc and PhD from the University of Edinburgh, and was previously a researcher at the Centre for Research in Autism and Education (CRAE) at UCL Institute of Education.

Owen Rhys Barry currently works as Deputy Principal Educational Psychologist in a local authority in Wales. He has supported educational settings with the needs of children, young people, families and educators with autism for 11 years. Owen has also worked closely with a neurodevelopmental service in a local health board in Wales to provide diagnostic assessments and support for neurodevelopmental conditions. He joined the Educational Psychologists' Autism Special Interest Group (EP-ASIG) Management Committee as a trainee member in 2013–15 and then continued sitting on the committee as a qualified member until 2018.

Dr Jennifer Baulcomb is Principal Educational Psychologist and Clinical Neuropsychologist in Children's Neurosciences at Evelina London Children's Hospital. She has worked in primary and tertiary autism services for over a decade and is passionate about developing interventions for children and young people with autism. She has contributed to national committees, guidelines and charities (NICE Developmental Follow-up for Children and Young People Born Preterm, the Childhood Stroke Association). Jennifer is currently part of a national clinical research programme to prospectively study the natural history of SCN1A-related epilepsy and Dravet syndrome in the UK.

Dr Luke Beardon has worked for over three decades in the autism field in a whole range of positions, starting as a volunteer aged 14 and from a hands-on support worker all the way through to his current role as a senior lecturer in autism at Sheffield Hallam University's Autism Centre, where he is the course leader for the Postgraduate Certificate in Autism and Asperger Syndrome. With multiple autism-related awards, inspirational teaching awards, four books to his name, and several other publications, Luke is passionate in trying to make the world a better place for the autistic community through teaching and other forms of knowledge transfer.

Venessa Bobb is the founder of the social enterprise A2ndVoice and a member of the All-Party Parliamentary Advisory Group on Autism. She has spoken at two EP-ASIG study days: the 2014 Day on Autism and the Criminal Justice System (CJS), where she spoke about parental experiences of the CJS; and at the 2018 event entitled 'Reflections on EP Practice When Working with Autism and Black, Asian and Minority Groups'. Venessa talks about her perspective as a Black parent.

Phil Christie is a consultant child psychologist who works on an independent basis and with colleagues as part of Autism Associates. He was Director of Children's Services for a regional autism charity for 30 years; this included overseeing a specialist school for pupils with autism. Phil was also lead consultant at the Elizabeth Newson Centre, which had a particular specialism in clinical and research work around pathological demand avoidance (PDA). He was elected as Chair of the Advisory Council for the Autism Education Trust and, since 2016, has been Vice-Chair of the programme board.

Dr Laura Cockburn, an educational psychologist who is employed by the London Borough of Haringey. Previously, Laura worked for the National Autistic Society (NAS) UK, where she was the head of the Lorna Wing Centre in Chigwell, Essex, one of two diagnostic centres in the NAS. She worked as a clinical diagnostician together with a team of other specialist professionals. Laura developed a specialism in autism while working in both the UK and in South-East Asia. She has a particular interest in understanding culture and ethnicity as a result of working in Singapore with the local population and international schools. Laura continues to learn a great deal from her neurodivergent family.

Ursula Cornish is a senior educational psychologist. In 1979, she convinced Westminster Council that it had to establish a unit for adults with autism within the newly established Social Education Centre for adults with learning disabilities at Lisson Grove. She used all her energy as a teacher and psychologist to provide the local authority (LA) with sufficient evidence that autism was real and required special provision for the adults within the Centre. Eventually, the LA agreed to provide funds. She contributed full time in LAs to the lifelong, social, emotional and cognitive well-being of autistic children and young people.

Laura Crane is Associate Professor at University College London (UCL) Institute of Education's Centre for Research in Autism and Education. Her research focuses on understanding the educational experiences of autistic children and young people, and identifying evidence-based ways to support pupils, their families and their educators. Central to all of Laura's work is a commitment to the involvement of the autistic and broader autism communities in the process of research. Laura also chairs the Pan London Autism Schools Network Research group (PLASN-R), a collective of autism special schools and academic researchers aiming to bridge the gap between autism education research and practice.

Erik Dwyer is Assistant Principal Educational Psychologist with the London Borough of Hammersmith and Fulham. He has a keen interest in how psychology can support the education and development of autistic young people and has been the lead EP for the borough in this area for several years. In collaboration with a colleague, he recently developed a new mechanism for target setting and tracking progress within the key areas of autism, based within the Social Communication, Emotional Regulation and Transactional Support (SCERTS) intervention framework, which is now being rolled out in schools across three London boroughs. Erik has been a member of the Autism Special Interest Group (ASIG) since its inauguration.

Annie Etherington is a practitioner tutor on the distance learning MA in Autism at Birmingham University. In addition, she works as an independent consultant and trainer both in the UK and internationally. She has written a number of papers and articles for specialist publications including the journal *Good Autism Practice*. Her experience in autism has involved leading a local-authority specialist autism-outreach team, as well as teaching across the age range, from preschool to adult, and in a range of settings – mainstream, specialist, day and residential – as well as working with autistic children and their parents/carers in their own homes.

Sue Fletcher-Watson is a developmental psychologist who aims to apply rigorous methods from psychology to questions with clinical, educational and societal impact. She has a particular focus on autism and on development and evaluation of technologies for autistic users, and she strives to achieve meaningful partnerships with community representatives and to support neurodivergent leadership in research. Sue holds a Chair in Developmental Psychology at the University of Edinburgh and is Director of the Salvesen Mindroom Research Centre.

Judith Gainsborough is a retired principal educational psychologist and Associate Fellow of the British Psychological Society. In her local authority work, she led multidisciplinary initiatives to involve parents and the voluntary sector in developing high-quality autism provision for all children who required it. In 2006, she was instrumental in the setting up of a home-based service for autistic preschool children in her local authority. Judith has been Chair of the EP-ASIG Management

Group for several years and has worked as part of the diagnostic team at the Lorna Wing Centre in Chigwell. She is Chair of Trustees of a multi-academy trust.

Juliet Gittens has worked in the education sector for more than 30 years. When her autistic son became involved in the criminal justice system, there was a huge and long-term impact on Juliet and her family. She has overcome many challenges to ensure that her son and the rest of her family receive the consideration and support that they need.

Dr Carrie Grant MBE (hc) is a BAFTA award-winning broadcaster, vocal coach and advocate. Her TV and music career has spanned 35 years. Awards include a MOBO, a BASCA, two doctorates and an MBE. She has the biggest-selling vocal coaching book and online course in the world. Carrie presents for BBC's *The One Show* and co-hosts Radio London's *Saturday Breakfast Show* with David Grant MBE. Together they have four children – three birth, one adopted, and all neurodivergent and they run a support group for over 150 families. Carrie is President of the Unite Union supporting school nurses and health visitors.

Scot Greathead is a consultant speech and language therapist. His research has focused on understanding better the experiences of children with special educational needs and their families. He has also hosted multidisciplinary action research groups in partnership with the Centre for Research in Autism and Education at University College London. These groups have explored the effectiveness of the SCERTS model in fostering greater classroom engagement through building children's socio-emotional skills. Scot currently works as Assistant Head at Five Acre Wood, a special school in Maidstone, Kent, and is a director at Speech Therapy Services Ltd.

Dr Ken Greaves has been a practising educational psychologist since 1989 and is strongly committed to applying psychology from a perspective that promotes equality of opportunity. He has worked as part of the diagnostic team at the Lorna Wing Centre and as a specialist senior EP with responsibilities for autism. Ken is a member of the Association of Black Psychologists and co-founded the EP-ASIG, and has worked in an advisory capacity to numerous organizations including the National Autistic Society and Cambridge University. He is a Senior Associate of the Royal Society of Medicine and has contributed to media publications about autism, ethnicity and culture.

Dr Jennifer Greene is an educational and child psychologist with ten years' experience, working in the public sector in the UK, prior to relocating to Singapore in 2017. She also tutored on the Doctorate in Educational and Child Psychology Programme at University College London. Jennifer currently works as a consultant educational and child psychologist supporting local and expat children and families in Singapore. She has a special interest in the autism spectrum and neurodevelopmental differences, a passion that has been a thread throughout her career. Jennifer is also a published author and an editor of the journal *BPS Debate*.

Dr Charlotte Hatton is a Tavistock Clinic-trained educational psychologist with experience working in various London authorities. Charlotte has provided both training and support for autistic children and young people, as well as their families and school staff, in several specialist autism provisions. She has a particular passion for the transition into adulthood for autistic young people and those who support them, which she has explored further through her doctoral research.

Laurence Hime is Principal Educational Psychologist for an inner London borough and has a special interest in autism. As part of delivering an EP service to local authorities, Laurence has responsibility for specialist autism provisions and has delivered accredited training in autism in this country and abroad. He was seconded to child and adolescent mental health services (CAMHS) to manage a home-school initiative for young people with severe learning needs and autism, and believes in the importance of meaningful links and shared understanding with parents. Laurence has been a member of the EP-ASIG Management Committee for over ten years and has a postgraduate qualification in autism.

John-Paul (JP) Horsley received a diagnosis of autism at the age of 38 and is the parent of two autistic children. He was a pop star at the age of 22. JP became a one-to-one for autistic children and is currently working with autistic adults at the National Autism Unit at Bethlem Royal Hospital. He believes that there is reason for optimism after diagnosis and that parents need to show their autistic children as many different experiences as possible because there are no barriers to what they can achieve.

Clare Hughes has worked at the National Autistic Society for over 19 years and has worked exclusively in autism and the criminal justice system since 2013. This has included leading on a number of projects in prison and probation, as well as projects involving young people who may be at risk of getting into trouble. Clare has also been involved in the development of a number of resources and journal articles on this topic and has helped Autism Accreditation programme at the National Autistic Society to develop quality standards for criminal justice agencies.

Dr Alexandra Lewis is a consultant forensic child and adolescent psychiatrist, specializing in neurodiversity. She is a national clinical advisor at NHS England and NHS Improvement, contributing both to work related to young people at risk of being or already within the criminal justice system, and to improving recognition and responsiveness to neurodiversity across the CJS. Alexandra contributed to an award-winning project, undertaken in partnership with the National Autistic Society, to develop standards improving support of autistic people within the adult and youth secure estates. She has also provided expert witness evidence in many Crown Court cases involving neurodiverse defendants.

Diana Loffler is a specialist educational psychologist in autism who worked for a long period in the London Borough of Hounslow. She was involved in developing and supporting provision for autistic children, training for school staff, supporting parents and delivering programmes, as well as working directly with autistic children and young people, individually and in groups. Diana was also part of the local child development team involved in diagnosing preschool children.

Dr Katie Maras is a senior lecturer in psychology and Deputy Director of the Centre for Applied Autism Research at the University of Bath. A main focus of Katie's research is on autistic people's experiences within the criminal justice system and the adaptations that police and other professionals can make to accommodate their differences. Katie works with police and other legal professionals to provide evidence-based policy, guidance and training when working with autistic people, and has particular expertise regarding police interviewing techniques.

Dr Heather Moran has worked with young people and their families for 40 years; she has been a residential social worker, a special school teacher and an educational psychologist. Heather has been an NHS clinical psychologist for 22 years and has a professional interest in young people with relationship difficulties, many of whom have attachment problems and/or autism/attention deficit hyperactivity disorder (ADHD). Her podcast (*Drawing the Ideal Self*) and website offer free continuing professional development to professionals (https://drawingtheidealself.co.uk.) Heather has fostered children with emotional and behavioural problems and has adopted four children with various strengths and difficulties. Although not intentional, these experiences have been useful to her as a psychologist.

Lynne Moxon has been an educational psychologist for 40 years, for local authorities and charities, specializing in working with autistic people, and was a senior lecturer at Northumbria University, running the Master's in Autism course. Lynne is now retired apart from some training sessions in the field of sexuality and autism; she studied this area while devising and teaching Aspects of Adulthood (socio-sexual skills, behaviour self-management and citizenship) weekly, to groups of autistic young adults and also through training with parents and support staff. Lynne has always used psychoeducation – the process of providing education and information to those finding life testing.

Adam O'Loughlin is a police inspector with 20 years of experience. Adam joined the police aged 24 and was diagnosed as autistic in 2016 when he was 39. He enjoys talking about his experiences and is a national and international speaker on autism and criminal justice, with the aim that more people will feel able to be open about their own neurodiversity and see that there are places for them to thrive. Alongside his busy full-time career, he can usually be found telling terrible 'dad jokes' on Twitter at @autisticcop.

Lindsay Panton began her career as a primary school teacher and subsequently trained as an educational psychologist at Nottingham University, which specialized in autism. The most complex cases were referred to the team, providing invaluable experience. She practised as an EP in Norfolk for several years before working for the National Autistic Society as a project development officer to set up support for families with children with autism. Later, as a private EP, Lindsay specialized in assessment, training and tribunals. Her passion and enthusiasm for understanding and supporting those affected by autism continues.

Dr Jane Park is Specialist Practitioner Educational Psychologist with Telford and Wrekin EPS. Her primary area of professional interest is in the field of supporting young people with complex needs in the post-16 age range. Jane's work has recently been published in the book *Applied Educational Psychology With 16–25 Year Olds* (2018), by the British Psychological Society's Division of Educational and Child Psychology, and in an academic paper, 'Using the Grid Elaboration Method (GEM) to investigate the transition experiences of young autistic adults', published in March 2020 (*Educational Psychology in Practice*).

Billy Parker has an interest in various areas of science, including biology and biopsychology, and has a general appreciation for different scientific fields of study. He has channelled these interests into academic work and is currently studying for a degree at Royal Holloway, University of London. Billy enjoys learning in-depth information about topics of interest, and pursues knowledge about those given subjects with curiosity and passion. Outside these activities, he is also a frequent swimmer and enjoys following a balanced schedule of discipline and leisure that is fulfilling, rewarding and enjoyable.

Liz Pellicano is a Professor at the Macquarie School of Education at Macquarie University in Sydney, and an Australian Research Council Future Fellow. She is a developmental cognitive scientist committed to transforming autism science so that it more accurately reflects everyday autistic life. Liz trained at the University of Western Australia before becoming a Junior Research Fellow at the University of Oxford. In 2009, she joined the newly created Centre for Research in Autism and Education at UCL Institute of Education, and then became Director of the CRAE in 2013 and Professor of Autism Education in 2015.

Dr Prithvi Perepa is a lecturer in autism studies at the University of Birmingham. One of his research interests is the cultural interpretation of autism, and the experiences of autism in different cultural groups. He has authored journal articles, book chapters and a book on this subject; his book, *Autism, Ethnicity and Culture* (2019), is one of the first books to explore the intersectionality of autism and ethnicity. Prior to working in higher education, Prithvi worked for the National Autistic Society, where his role was to make the services provided by the organization culturally inclusive.

Carol Povey has worked with autistic people and their families for over 40 years, lately as the Director of the Centre for Autism at the National Autistic Society, where she still works on a part-time basis, with a particular focus on the Autism Education Trust. Most recently, she has become a special educational needs and disabilities (SEND) tribunal member and has advised foreign governments and UK organizations on their autism services. Carol has contributed to a number of publications and has trained and presented at conferences nationally and internationally.

Dr Irina Roncaglia is a chartered practitioner psychologist who is Health and Care Professions Council (HCPC) registered, and an Associate Fellow of the British Psychological Society. She has worked for the National Autistic Society for over 18 years at the Sybil Elgar School and more recently as a clinical lead principal psychologist. Irina sits on the editorial board of *Psychological Thought* and the *Journal of Dance Medicine and Science*, and is a member of the International Association of Dance and Medicine (IADMS) and of One Dance UK. Her research interests include transitions, lifespan models, resilience, coping processes and strategies, and performing arts. She completed her doctoral research with Birkbeck, University of London, investigating the retirement transitions in elite performers.

Zaffy Simone has struggled throughout life with health, sensory, social and learning issues, and has put a lot of time and energy into learning the reasons why. He has learned how to manage his health by linking up the multiple layers between mind and body, which hold our wellbeing. Zaffy says, 'Each diagnosis has played its part in finding the pieces to my puzzle; my aim now is to help others by raising awareness and understanding through sharing my experiences'. He uses his art to give a visual representation to his experiences as well as openly discussing his personal journey.

Dr Vicky Slonims is Senior Consultant Speech and Language Therapist in the service for children with complex neurodevelopmental disorders at Evelina London Children's Hospital (Guy's and St Thomas' NHS Foundation Trust), and Visiting Reader in Complex Communication Disorders in the Child and Adolescent Psychiatry Division of the Institute of Psychiatry, Psychology and Neuroscience, King's College London. She is Chair of the Language and Communication Study Group, a national autism research network (Discover) supported by the charity Autistica. Her research is closely aligned to her clinical interests in intervention for children with autism spectrum disorders and work with children with severe communication impairments and challenging behaviour.

Robyn Steward is autistic (diagnosed aged 11). She delivers training for professionals, parents and young people, and is an ambassador for the National Autistic Society and SNAP (Special Needs and Parents) charity in Essex. She has written three books: *The Independent Woman's Handbook for Super Safe Living on the Autistic Spectrum* (2014), *The Autism-Friendly Guide to Periods* (2019) and *The Autism-Friendly Guide to Self-Employment* (2021). Robyn co-hosts the BBC Sounds podcast *1800 Seconds on Autism* as well as hosting *The Autism Journal Podcast*. She is a research associate at University College London.

Dr Rhiannon Yates is an educational psychologist who trained at the Institute of Education, University College London. Within her work, she has a particular interest in how pupil and family voice can shape school experiences and foster emotional well-being. Rhiannon's past research projects have looked at how to engage children with severe and profound learning difficulties in play together, the friendship experiences of autistic girls, and understanding the experiences of pre-verbal children in residential schools.

Nicola Yuill is Professor of Developmental Psychology and Director of the Children and Technology Lab (ChatLab) in the School of Psychology, University of Sussex. She is Co-Director of the Autism Community Research Network Sussex (ACoRNS) and has published research into the topics of children's collaboration through technology, children's social cognition, autism and technology, social behaviour, and children's text comprehension. Nicola is the author of *Technology to Support Children's Collaborative Interactions: Close Encounters of the Shared Kind* (Palgrave McMillan, 2021).

Foreword

Robyn Steward

I first met Ken Greaves when I was 20. I wanted to know why I had struggled all through education with reading and writing and needed an educational psychologist (EP) who also knew about autism. (I'm autistic.) Ken wrote a detailed report that has been influential in my life. It gave me a greater understanding of my spiky profile – lots of ability and difficulty rather than an average level of competency at most things.

I really liked Ken and admired his work. Over the last 14 years, we have become friends. When he invited me to speak at a study day for EPs who wanted to learn more about autism, I was thrilled. It was so nice to be talking to a group of professionals who could make a real difference to autistic children and young people, and who recognized that we all need to keep learning and taking in new perspectives.

This book is like a capsule containing information on the key themes which need to be considered by all of us – professionals, parents and autistic people. You'll hear the voices of autistic people and parents. You can read the book cover to cover or just dip into it when you want to know about a particular topic. You'll also see lots of academic paper references, which you can follow up.

In the last few years, intersectionality has become a word that is used a lot. It means when one or more things affect each other. An example could be a faulty traffic light that causes traffic jams in all the roads in the area. Similarly, a person's culture, gender, sexuality, disabilities and abilities, and access to appropriate technology and support, can all affect how a person is able to cope in school, and well beyond into adult life.

The field of educational psychology is sometimes only looked at as something that helps children, but actually it can help everyone, because we are all still learning, and in fact carrying on learning may help reduce the risk of conditions like dementia.[1]

Also, we need to keep learning throughout our lives, for instance, when we change job or come across a new problem. If you have a deep understanding of how you learn and what your particular abilities and difficulties are, you can work out how to use your abilities to compensate.

I hope you will gain insights which will positively impact you or the people whose lives you support.

---

1   Youssef, F.F. & Addae, J.I. (2002) 'Learning may provide neuroprotection against dementia.' *West Indian Medical Journal, 51*(3), 143–147.

Acknowledgements

We would like to thank Chris Alders for his unswerving support and cheerful encouragement as well as for reading chapters diligently and providing feedback. Irvine Gersch and John Hutchings also responded generously to our requests for feedback. We are very grateful for their advice. We would like to thank Linda Miller, Sue Shepherd, Annette English and Nick Peacey, who all supported the founding of EP-ASIG in 2007. Later on, the Centre for Research in Autism in Education, led by Liz Pellicano and then Anna Remington, allowed us space for our meetings and booked conference facilities for us. Without their support, we would not have been able to hold EP-ASIG study days and we are extremely grateful to them. Judith would particularly like to thank Martin Conway for all the love, infinite patience and intellectual generosity without which this book would never have been created. She would also like to thank Diana Diamond for her constant emotional support and faith in her daughter's abilities. We would like to thank all those people who have spoken at EP-ASIG study days since 2007 for their magnificent contribution to furthering our knowledge about autism. Lastly, we are indebted to all the autistic individuals we have worked with over many years for inspiring our passion.

Introduction

The Story of the Educational Psychology
Autism Special Interest Group (EP-ASIG)

Judith Gainsborough

There were five Friday afternoons spaced through the year, sacrosanct to our small but perfectly formed Educational Psychology – Autism Special Interest Group (EP-ASIG), when we would meet together at the Centre for Research in Autism in Education (CRAE), Gordon Square, in Central London, in what must have been a rather splendid drawing room in another era. Part of the meeting was set aside for the planning of arrangements for that year's study day. The remainder of the meeting was given over to a much broader purpose – the sharing of experience on issues around autism, the issues which we were all dealing with in our professional lives. Such issues could be on a number of levels. Someone might be seeking a new perspective on an individual case and the relative merits of certain interventions. Someone else might have attended a conference and heard a particularly inspiring talk. A third might be expressing concern about a gap in provision in their local authority, and so on. Such opportunities to share ideas with other educational psychologists, equally passionate about the needs of autistic children and young people and their families, were highly valued. The study day itself offered an opportunity to around a hundred EPs from around the country not only to hear the most prestigious speakers in the field of autism, but also to network with other EPs and garner information and share ideas which would support them in their professional lives.

Since its inauguration in 2007, EP-ASIG has held a free study day every year at the University of London Institute of Education for EPs from all around the UK. The group has had an impressive membership including three principal EPs, several senior specialist EPs in autism, the manager of the Lorna Wing Centre for Autism in Chigwell, and trainee EPs from several courses around the country. There was initial support and funding from the Special Educational Needs Joint Inservice Training (SENJIT) and, when this was no longer available, Liz Pellicano, the then Director of the Centre for Research in Autism in Education (CRAE), took over support for EP-ASIG, organizing rooms for meetings and a conference room for the study day. Support from CRAE, now under the Directorship of Anna Remington, has continued to the present.

The development of an idea

The idea for this book grew from a tiny kernel after one study day's effusive feedback, warmed by a bottle of wine in one of the public houses a short walk from the Institute of Education and nurtured through some months until early 2020. The restrictions following the Covid-19 pandemic forced the group to abandon their plans for the 2020 study day and led to an opportunity to develop some thinking about a book, which would offer practical information on what to do to help children and young people with autism and their families with some of the most challenging and overwhelming issues of life today.

Contributions to the book were invited from those who had previously spoken at study days, representing the leading edge of developments in the field. Each chapter offers a range of perspectives, from leading-edge research and evidence-based interventions, to overviews from professionals and personal reflections from parents and autistic young people. There are chapters on issues such as sexual gender/identity for autistic adolescents struggling to understand how to fit into peer society; the minefield of the criminal justice system (CJS) for youngsters who exhibit odd, disruptive or violent behaviour without deliberate intent to harm; and the complexity of cultural perspectives and autism where, for instance, a family might view the manifestations of autistic behaviour as something evil.

We have also included chapters on the challenges for parents in developing relationships with their autistic children and further chapters on the huge area of behaviour that is perceived to be challenging, as well as understanding anxiety and well-being. Transition to adulthood is an enormously difficult time not only for the autistic young person, but also for the family and professionals involved. Chapter 6 explores the challenges and suggests some ways forward, and Chapter 10 covers the innovations of information technology to support autistic individuals. These are everyday issues for practitioners desperate for some information that can provide a clearer way forward, a toolbox of evidence-based interventions and a much-needed description of what it feels like to be autistic or to be the parent of an autistic child. Laura Crane and Liz Pellicano have co-written Chapter 2, which covers some of the current research in the area with relevance to those working in education, and Chapter 1 provides a personal view of the trajectories of the role of the EP and the developing knowledge of autism.

It has been an illuminating journey for the editors, collating these perspectives and, in particular, giving space for the voices of autistic people and the parents of autistic people to be heard. Many individual struggles are described in these pages; what has become clear to us is that every journey is a unique one, and solutions, strategies and ways forward seem to be almost instinctive and come from within each person, truly part of their personalities and life choices. In examining these personal stories, we have reflected on Jordan and Jones's 1996 review of interventions which concluded that no one intervention was found to be the most appropriate for all autistic young people and that an individually planned approach, drawing on the interventions that best suit that young person, would always be the most sensible course of action.

We hope that this book offers a unique approach, exploring a range of views and experiences in each area, offering a wealth of information, cutting-edge research and evidence-based interventions as well as inspiring life stories from parents and autistic people. This is a book which can be read in its entirety or dipped into to provide advice, practical support or comfort when needed. We believe that this book may be valuable to a wide range of readers, certainly not only EPs, but also all professionals working in the field of autism, including clinical psychologists, teachers, speech and language therapists and social workers. We particularly hope that this book will be a helpful source of information and practical advice for the parents and carers of autistic children and young people and for autistic people themselves.

Terminology and use of language

Many of the contributors have used identity-first language (e.g., 'autistic child/young person/adult/individual') rather than person-first language (e.g., 'person with autism') in accordance with the views of many autistic people and their families, as reported by Kenny *et al.* (2016).[1]

'Neurodiversity' is a term that has been used throughout the book and refers to the concept that all human minds and brains are different. Being autistic is a form of neurodivergence. 'Neurotypical', an abbreviation of 'neurologically typical', is a term that describes people with 'typical' brains. It is often used in the autistic community to refer to people who are not on the autism spectrum. The term 'allistic' has a similar meaning and is also to be found in the book.

Although we have tried to follow the majority view in use of language in this book, the range of contributors is diverse and the choice of language and terminology may at times reflect that.

References

Jordan, R. & Jones, G. (1999) 'Review of research into educational interventions for children with autism in the UK.' *Autism, 3*(1), 101–110.

Kenny, L., Hattersley, C., Molins, B., Buckley, C., Povey, C. & Pellicano, E. (2016) 'Which terms should be used to describe autism? Perspectives from the UK autism community.' *Autism, 18*(7), 794–802.

All royalties from the sale of this book will be donated to an independent charity – Resources for Autism, and a community interest company – A2ndVoice, both of which work with autistic children and adults and their families.

---

1   Kenny *et al.* (2016) reported that 60 per cent of autistic respondents in their survey approved the use of identity-first communications. However, more than 30 per cent approved person-first, that is, 'a person who has autism', and 25 per cent approved 'a person who has autism/Asperger syndrome', or 'person with autism/Asperger syndrome'.

CHAPTER 1

Autism and Educational Psychology: Two Developing Stories

Judith Gainsborough and Laura Cockburn

Introduction

In this chapter, we will contrast the changing histories of autism and the role of educational psychologists, charting the course of the increase in prevalence of autism, since the 1980s (Elsabbagh *et al.* 2012), alongside our views on the developing role of the EP.

We believe that autistic children and young people have some of the most complex needs that EPs will encounter in their working lives. The combination of their psychological knowledge and direct work with schools, children and young people and their families, in addition to training and research skills, offers EPs a unique opportunity to support the needs of autistic individuals. We hope that this book will be useful for a broad range of professionals and parents. EP-ASIG was founded in order to support EPs who wanted to develop their skills and knowledge in the field of autism and thereby provide better support to individuals and their families together with the systems around them, such as schools and other professionals. Therefore, this chapter will aim to explore how EPs can offer a unique perspective to the field of autism and how this has developed over time.

A brief history of autism

The needs of autistic children and young people and their families is a predominant theme for EPs practising today, as it is for a wide range of practitioners, particularly those working in education (McConkey 2020). This of course was not always the case. When the present writers of this chapter began their careers in educational psychology in the mid-1980s, autism was discussed infrequently and they received barely a handful of referrals per year of children who were thought to have an autism spectrum condition (ASC). Judith remembers, at the start of her career as an EP, that preschool referrals to her educational psychology service would include very few children per year who were on the path to a diagnostic assessment of autism. By the early 2000s, referrals had increased massively.

Thinking back to her own teaching experience in the early 1980s, Judith can recall a number of children on the fringes of the social group who displayed behaviour which, at that time, was perceived as 'odd'. Take Timothy, for instance: five years old, a mop of astonishingly snowy white hair, thick glasses shielding pale blue eyes, preferring to stay in the classroom with her rather than to venture into the playground melee. His preferences included building high towers with bricks, and looking at pictures of mechanical diggers. He was generally compliant and attentive, socially isolated and quite passive in social groups. At the first sign of a change of routine, Timothy would drop to the floor, crawl under a table and start making a series of deep throaty growls. Strategies such as the use of visually structured supports, warnings before changes of activity and opportunities for alternative activities at break-times helped to make Timothy's day more manageable for him and he began to make good academic progress. Children like Timothy, maybe ten years later, might have received a diagnosis of ASC or Asperger syndrome. Such children often struggled through their school years, being thought of as 'odd' and rarely receiving any help or support. There are echoes of this kind of childhood experience in some of the contributions by autistic people such as John-Paul Horsley in Chapter 7 and Zaffy Simone in Chapter 8.

Through the ensuing few years, there was to be a massive increase in the awareness and understanding of autism alongside a rapidly increasing prevalence. Wing and Gould (1979) published their findings on the prevalence rate of autism among children with special needs in the London Borough of Camberwell. There were nearly five per 10,000 children who fitted Kanner's original profile (1944), known as 'early infantile autism'. In addition, however, Wing and Gould were able to identify a larger group of about 15 per 10,000 who were experiencing what they referred to as a 'triad of impairments', namely, difficulties with social interaction, social communication and social imagination. It was clear that the narrowness of Kanner's original profile was excluding a much larger group from getting any recognition of possible issues and help for their difficulties. Wing (1981) described the profiles of a small group of youngsters in her paper 'Asperger's Syndrome: A Clinical Account' and continued to argue for the expansion of the category of autism, linking it to other developmental disorders. Wing later adopted the term 'autism spectrum', a reference to the colours of the rainbow, thus reframing thinking in order to celebrate difference and diversity (Silberman 2015).

Many researchers in the field of autism have thought that the global rise in the prevalence rates of autism diagnoses through the 1980s and 1990s (Elsabbagh *et al.* 2012) cannot be explained completely by the broadening of the category. Wing and Potter (2002) suggested the significance of some other factors including the broader knowledge of practitioners, sharpened skills in identification and more efficient assessment tools and processes. Estimates of the numbers of autistic people varies around the world for many different reasons. According to the National Autistic Society website, 700,000 people are on the autism spectrum in the UK. There is no official count of people with autism, but this is a well-established estimate and possibly an underestimation of the true numbers. This number represents more than 1 per cent of the population. McConkey (2020), in his survey of referral rates in the UK, has reported that the rise in the numbers of school pupils with autism has continued through the last decade.

The National Autistic Society website defines autism as 'a lifelong developmental disability which affects how people communicate and interact with the world'. The definition of autism has changed over the years and continues to do so with our increasing understanding and a shifting of perspectives and priorities for researchers and practitioners alike, as both begin to prioritize the views and needs of autistic individuals. Fletcher-Watson and Happé (2019) describe the swing in the last 20 years away from characterizing autism in terms of a deficit or impairment, such as theory of mind (false-belief understanding), executive function (planning, prioritizing, inhibiting inappropriate impulsive actions, and cognitive flexibility) and cognitive coherence (making sense of meaningless patterns) towards considering a pattern of differences, which present both advantages and disadvantages in relation to neurotypical social norms and expectations. In Chapter 2, Crane and Pellicano will explore in more detail some of the current priorities for research as a consequence of this shift.

'Autism' is a medical term, and diagnosis should be completed by a specified multidisciplinary team (National Institute for Health and Care Excellence Guidance 2011; updated 2017). The diagnostic criteria have been updated on a number of occasions in recognition of the changing understanding of autism. Diagnosis now includes assessment of social and communication skills and other behaviours, focusing on features consistent with the criteria given in the *International Classification of Diseases (ICD-10)* (World Health Organization 1995) or the *Diagnostic and Statistical Manual of Mental Disorders, Fifth Edition* (DSM-V) (American Psychiatric Association 2013). Most notable additions to recommended diagnostic practice include an acknowledgement of the importance of having the different perspectives of a multidisciplinary team for assessment and taking account of the voice of both the person and family.

The developing role of educational psychologists

For the purposes of this book, it will be helpful to explore the role and perspective of EPs and how they contribute to the understanding of children and young people within school systems as well as diagnostic frameworks linking to autism.

When the present writers of this chapter were embarking on their careers as EPs, many members of the profession were beginning to rethink traditional ways of their practice. This included issues such as the reliance on psychometric assessment and also a school visiting approach based solely on individual referrals. Additionally, there was a growing awareness of the need to take account of cultural and linguistic differences in assessment practices. Gillham edited *Reconstructing Educational Psychology* in 1978, a collection of chapters that explored new and exciting ideas for fundamental changes of the EP role. In fact, a chapter in Gillham's book by Dessent (Chapter 2, 1978) described Cyril Burt's appointment by the London County Council as the first educational psychologist in 1913 and how he saw his work as 'essentially that of a scientific investigator and researcher' (p.28), something which we believe remains central to the role of the EP to this day.

Gillham's book described how EPs were located within child guidance clinics in the 1950s and 1960s, where there was little opportunity to practise Burt's interactionist approach to assessment, which advocated collecting information from the school and the home environment as well as an individual assessment of the child. The role of the EP at that time could be described as highly medicalized and dominated by psychometric testing.

Since that time, EPs have moved away from a medical model, where the perceived problem was within the child, and have developed new ways of working based on theoretical frameworks which had little to do with the medical professional community. While EPs contribute to diagnostic assessment and help to make sense of developmental differences, they tend to use a more social constructionist theoretical framework where inclusion and the social model of disability is important in their work. They are influenced by Bronfenbrenner (1974) who recognized the multiple aspects of a developing child's life that interact with and affect the child. His work looked beyond individual development and considered wider influencing factors within the context of development. Social learning theory (Bandura 1977) and sociocultural theory (Vygotsky 1978) where the environment is explicitly or implicitly considered are also theoretical frameworks that underpin the work of educational psychologists. That is, to improve understanding and support for children and young people, EPs see child development as a complex system of relationships, impacted by the environment, family and school, in addition to broad cultural values.

The practice of educational psychology acknowledges the importance of understanding the profile of the young person and promoting inclusion. Inclusive education upholds the importance of opening access to a wide range of educational and social opportunities for all children, not only those with disabilities or identified special educational needs (SEN). More recently, Besic (2020) has discussed how the concept of intersectionality can help to identify the interaction of multiple factors that lead to discriminatory processes in schools towards different student groups. This is important to recognize when developing more understanding of autism and highlighting the issue that 'one size does not fit all'. As Stephen Shore famously commented, 'If you've met one individual with autism, you've met one individual with autism.' Further chapters in this book will explore the importance of understanding the different profiles of behaviour and communication within any diagnostic work in autism and the extent to which issues such as adoption, culture and context can affect how professionals and parents understand children and young people. Venessa Bobb's account of her experiences as a Black parent struggling to get some recognition of her son's special needs provides a stark example of the need for professionals to consider a complexity of factors related to culture and ethnicity.

Recent developments in our understanding of autism

Our knowledge and understanding of autism continue to develop, and there is more recognition about the importance of describing the overall profile of an autistic person – recognizing both their strengths and what may be challenges. EPs work within a context where they stress the importance of understanding the child or young person's family and social context (Bronfenbrenner 1974), which also contributes to making sense of the profile of needs.

The term 'profile' is used a great deal in the context of an assessment of needs. Some of the autistic contributors to this book have referred to the findings of a 'spiky profile' when talking about their own assessments. Hong-Hua *et al.* (2020) describe an uneven cognitive developmental profile in autistic children and the relative impacts of autism severity, age and gender at a developmental level. The Autism Education Trust website, which provides online resources for teachers, describes a number of sensory profiles in order to support observations of children and identify their specific sensitivities. Phil Christie in Chapter 4 will discuss pathological demand avoidance (PDA), which is increasingly understood as one of the profiles on the autism spectrum requiring further research.

What has become clear is that it is vital to develop an understanding of the profile of an autistic person in order to understand their strengths and challenges and identify the most appropriate interventions. This has always been a fundamental part of the practice of an EP's assessment of special educational needs and the consequent design of appropriate learning programmes, for instance for Individual Education Plans (IEPs) and Education Health and Care Plans (EHCPs). There continue to be discussions about whether autism is a disability and about how it should be described. The medical model of disability tends to look at within-person deficits and might focus on what the person cannot do as compared with what they can do. The social approach to disability proposes that the experience of disability is contingent on environmental, social and cultural factors (Norwich 2002). EPs work together with schools, parents and the children themselves to ensure that an overall understanding of the child's profile of needs is understood, including strengths and difficulties together with appropriately matched interventions. Rees (2017) talks about how this has encouraged the use of the diagnostic 'label' in a positive way. Thus, an understanding of new autistic profiles would appear to be a crucial part of ensuring an optimum educational experience for all autistic children.

There is also awareness of how the profile of autism in different communities is being further understood and this will be explored in Chapter 9. It is evident that the more we take account of the issues affecting autistic individuals and their families in terms of government policy and educational practice as well as culture, class and gender, the better will be our understanding of the needs of autistic individuals.

New terminology has helped us to reframe previous concepts. The concept of neurodiversity is beginning to shift thinking about research priorities, as will be seen in Chapter 2. It has inspired a move away from looking at the causes of autism to looking at ways in which autistic people and their families can lead happier and more fulfilling lives. It is also shifting thinking about the school and workplace environment, in fact in every walk of life. Understanding neurodiversity can be seen to be the foundation for a new world 'suited to the needs and special abilities of all kinds of minds' (Silberman 2015, p.516).

In acknowledgement of the approach that EPs tend to adopt, the term 'neurodiversity' is used throughout the book and refers to the recognition that all human minds and brains are different. This term is increasingly being used by autistic people and professionals; it was first used by Singer (1999) and advocates a complete reframing of attitudes to disability, in favour of a celebration of difference. As Silberman (2015) notes, neurodiversity should be seen as 'a valuable part of humanity's genetic legacy while ameliorating the aspects of autism that can be profoundly disabling without adequate forms of support' (p.511). By contrast, the term 'neurotypical', an abbreviation of 'neurologically typical', has been adopted by many in the autism community, and more recently by many professionals and practitioners, as a label for people who are not autistic, although this has been replaced by some with the term 'allistic'.

One of the most important developments in the field in recent years has been the understanding of autistic girls and women and how they were being underdiagnosed. Happé, Ronald and Plomin (2006) suggested that girls may have a different profile to boys, that their behaviour is often misinterpreted and also that they are overlooked for support. Dean, Harwood and Kasari (2017) described autistic girls as having a tendency towards 'masking' such that they might rely on copying the behaviour of other girls. Carpenter, Happé and Egerton (2019) reported on how autistic girls might hide their difficulties and described the psychological impact such that they can be at a higher risk of developing a range of mental health problems. The account in Chapter 8 of Zaffy Simone's experiences as a young girl suffering from anorexia and then alcohol abuse is one such distressing example. There is a need not only for further research in this area, but also for practitioners to develop their knowledge and awareness of this profile to ensure that girls receive a timely and appropriate intervention.

The impact of legislation on the EP role and changing frameworks to support EP practice

Legislation and changes to the training of EPs have to a large extent shaped the nature of the EP role and led to competing tensions for EPs in terms of the different demands on their time (Boyle, MacKay & Lauchlan 2017). The present writers worked in a context where new opportunities to be involved in such areas as practitioner research, presenting training for schools and groups of parents, or providing some individual interventions had to be balanced with the demands of statutory work and its deadlines. The Every Child Matters (ECM): Change for Children legislation (Department for Education and Skills 2004) signalled significant changes in the delivery of educational psychology services. There was to be an increased emphasis on multiagency working as well as a move to being part of an integrated children's services working for the community rather than predominantly in schools.

Although EPs have had to balance the demands of multiagency working with the continued SEN statutory responsibilities, there were very many exciting opportunities for them to use their psychological knowledge and skills in working with a diverse range of professionals on a completely new set of issues. A Department for Education and Skills report (Farrell *et al.* 2006) found that EP involvement in this new context was much valued by others. The researchers recorded multiagency working with 'social workers, educational welfare officers, residential support workers, child psychiatrists, child clinical psychologists, paediatricians, a variety of CAMHS [child and adolescent mental health service] workers and therapists, speech and language therapists, YOT (Youth Offending Team) staff, Connexions workers, parent partnership workers, school teachers, specialist teachers and special educational needs coordinators, police officers, portage workers, specialist nurses, physiotherapists and occupational therapists, [and] voluntary sector professionals' (pp.38–39). In fact, research indicates a subsequent reduction in the volume of requests for SEN statutory assessment for some years following the ECM legislation (Marsh 2014). Such developments were observed to have facilitated support for autistic children and young people in a number of different ways and enabled EPs to put into practice the vision of the Department for Education and Employment Working Group (Department for Education and Employment 2000). The group had proposed that EPs were well placed to offer 'a clear and unique role to multidisciplinary working in terms of the application of psychological methods, concepts, models, theories and knowledge' (*ibid.*).

The 2014 Children and Families Act also developed EPs' responsibilities to extend their involvement with children and young adults from 0 to 25 years of age. We believe that this was a very significant opportunity for EPs to utilize their skills to support a highly vulnerable group of young people transitioning to adulthood. Chapter 6 will detail such issues and opportunities for practitioners with regards to autism.

Many of these changes in legislation impacted the role of EPs and can be seen to have broadened and developed their practice, enabling them to work at different levels. Over time, EPs increasingly began to use frameworks that would facilitate a more wide-reaching role, encompassing the application of psychology at the organizational level as well as the individual child level. MacKay (1999) described a model for EP services in Scotland that detailed five core functions, namely consultation, assessment, intervention, training and research, and at three different levels: individual child and family, the school or establishment and the local authority (LA).

The Interactive Factors Framework (Frederickson & Cline 2009) and the Monsen Problem-Solving Model (Monsen & Fredrickson 2008) are examples of frameworks used to guide a consultation process that became fundamental in EP practice. This approach assisted EPs to work together with parents, schools and other professionals at different levels in order to clarify a problem, generate hypotheses, test interventions and evaluate outcomes. Added to this was the increasing acknowledgement of the importance of evidence-based practice and the assertion that EPs were well placed to identify appropriate interventions and strategies in order to resolve problems (MacKay, Boyle & Cole 2016).

EPs have become more involved in both assessment and diagnosis as well as interventions, often working together within multidisciplinary teams. These developments can be seen to have resulted in supporting the work of EPs as members of multidisciplinary professional groups as well as working with the people themselves and their families. In recent years, the concept of formulation has attracted increasing interest across both psychiatry and psychology, including EPs. The term 'formulation', which is discussed in Chapter 3, is increasingly being used by EPs with the aim of helping to understand and make sense of different behaviour and profiles of need rather than providing a more categorical definition. Johnstone and Dallos (2014) provide detailed understanding of formulation, noting in the preface of their second edition that it 'draws upon psychological theory in order to create a working hypothesis or "best guess" for a client's difficulties, in the light of their relationships and social context and the sense they have made of the events in their lives.' Formulation links closely together with the way EPs work and their theoretical frameworks, and is listed as a skill in the Health and Care Professional Council (2021) regulations for all psychologists and in the curriculum for psychiatrists' training in the UK (Royal College of Psychiatrists 2010).

In the latest standards of proficiency, all practitioner psychologists in the UK, including EPs, are expected to be able to use psychological formulations to plan appropriate interventions that take the service user's perspective into account (Health and Care Professions Council 2021).

The EP role in supporting autistic children and young people and their families

On reflection, increased expectations and opportunities for multidisciplinary working and also for working at different levels can be seen to have helped pave the way for a much greater involvement for EPs with autistic children and their families. The recognition of the efficacy of a multidisciplinary approach in identifying needs and a team approach to supporting families could be seen to be very important in helping to understand children and young people and to contribute to a diagnostic team. The NICE (National Institute for Health and Care Excellence) guidelines on autism first published in 2011 and updated in 2017 recommended that the autism diagnostic team should include or have regular access to an EP, thus ensuring that there was a professional on the team who could advise on all issues to do with the child's education and their individual needs.

The present writers recently collated the views and experiences of their colleagues on the EP-ASIG Management Group who had responsibilities for autism in their roles, working in different contexts such as LAs, charities and independent practice. Data from the group indicated that many of them were being asked to provide advice on autism provision at different levels. At the child and family level, for instance, EPs reported that they were involved in developing further understanding on the assessment of a child's special educational needs as well as providing support and advice on managing learning and behaviour at home. At the next level, EPs described working with schools to recommend a range of evidence-based interventions across all phases and to help develop an autism-friendly ethos, generally to effect improvements in behaviour and attention levels. Some EPs worked closely together with parents at an individual level and offered parent training and support groups. These interventions were aimed at involving parents in the education of their children, providing them with opportunities to develop further understanding of their child as well as building knowledge of home-based strategies. As discussed further in Chapter 3, this helped to highlight the importance of understanding children and young people both at home and at school as well as providing parents with a much-needed opportunity to share their concerns, anxieties and problems.

At the organizational level, EPs reported that they were advising LAs on gaps in provision. For instance, one EP chaired a working group on autism with representatives from education, health and social services, voluntary agencies and parent bodies. The overall brief was to identify, and disseminate to schools and professionals, examples of best inclusive practice and to provide advice to the LA on developments in provision.

This working group identified an urgent need within the LA to improve the autism diagnostic experience for families, coordinating input from the education, health and social care services and, crucially, offering at the point of diagnosis an LA-wide home-based intervention ensuring that all preschool children had equal access to high-quality support. Before this, a small number of children with a diagnosis of autism were receiving a range of private interventions, which had been commissioned by families, frustrated by the lack of provision. SEN tribunals set up by the 1994 Education Act had enabled families to propose that such interventions were the financial responsibility of the LA. It was hoped that a new proposed LA-led provision of support would ensure an equality of access to special expertise for all the families living in the LA. It should be noted that this was a very unusual opportunity. Services across the country varied significantly depending on the ways in which LAs prioritized their resources.

The new service was set up by the EP and an autism advisory teacher. It offered a multidisciplinary approach including professionals from EP, occupational therapy, speech and language therapy, advisory teacher services together with specialist teaching assistants called 'facilitators', who were trained to implement a tailor-made programme in the home, working with parents and carers (Gainsborough 2011). The educational programmes were based on SCERTS (Social Communication, Emotional Regulation and Transactional Support) (Prizant *et al.* 2005), at the time a new and exciting US-based framework for intervention, which addressed many of the core challenges faced by autistic children. It focused on building competence in social communication and emotional regulation as well as defining the kind of support from key adults around the child, namely transactional support. This will be explored further by Scot Greathead and Rhiannon Yates in Chapter 4 and Annie Etherington in Chapter 5. The service also used a range of other interventions that were identified as evidence-based. These included PECS (the Picture Exchange Communication System) (Bondy & Frost 2001), TEACCH (Treatment and Education of Autistic and Related Communication-Handicapped Children (Mesibov, Shea & Schopler 2004) and Intensive Interaction (Hewitt 1996). There was an evaluative study of the service by the University of Swansea (Reed *et al.* 2013) which found that children on the programme showed progress which compared favourably to several other interventions in terms of adaptive behavioural functioning, language skills, decreasing parental stress and improving parental perceptions of their own abilities.

EPs' specialist knowledge in autism

Research into the effectiveness of autism interventions (such as Jordan & Jones 1999) and training resources for schools such as the Inclusion

Development Programme in Autism (Department for Children, Schools and Families 2009) and the Autism Education Trust standards (Jones, Lacey & Robertson 2012) have been instrumental in supporting a comprehensive knowledge base for all practitioners, including EPs. Robinson, Bond and Oldfield (2018) surveyed the intervention practices of EPs for autistic students in the UK and Ireland and concluded that EPs were involved in the implementation of many of the interventions for autism which are considered to have an evidence base. Such interventions included visually supported materials, Social Stories (Gray 1997), behavioural approaches, prompting, modelling and social skills training. EPs also reported being involved in SCERTS, TEACCH and the National Autistic Society's (NAS) Early Bird and Early Bird Plus support programmes for parents and carers.

However, the research indicated too that there were other interventions with an equally good evidence base that were not being used by EPs. The authors suggested that EPs with their knowledge of individual schools and their scientist-practitioner role were extremely well placed to work with schools and provide advice and support on the selection of the most appropriate interventions. EPs made decisions about the best interventions depending on a number of factors. These included not only an evidence base, but also how feasible the intervention was in the particular context and knowledge about the child's profile. It was vital to take account of the individual needs of the child and family, the resources and staffing available in the school, the allocation of EP time in the school and the attitudes and motivational factors of school staff.

In their analysis, Robinson and colleagues (2018) concluded that 'in order to offer autistic students with ASD the best possible opportunities to meet individualised outcomes, EPs need to ensure that they are familiar with EBI [evidence-based interventions], research for ASD through independent research or CPD [continuing professional development] in specific interventions' (p.18). Related to this is the fact that EPs were being asked increasingly to attend SEN tribunals (established by the 1994 Education Act) as LA representatives. It was important that EPs became knowledgeable about evidence-based interventions together with being skilled in conducting assessments for autistic children. Crucially, there was a role for EPs in working with LAs to examine the effectiveness of developing provision for autistic children living in the locality, and to advise on the most appropriate evidence-based interventions and provisions. This was the context in which EP-ASIG was founded, and meetings had a number of functions. It was recognized that there was a need for a special interest group for EPs where information and experiences could be shared, new ideas developed, and support and advice offered for concerns on a number of levels from individual casework to setting up provisions or a piece of research. An opportunity was offered every year to a Year 2 EP trainee with an interest in autism to join the group. This offered a unique experience for a trainee to work with experienced EPs setting up a study day and sharing knowledge and practice, but also facilitated opportunities for the group to learn about cutting-edge research and innovations in practice.

Chapter conclusion: The way forward

This brief outline of the developing understanding of autism alongside the development of the EP role and, in particular, the special interest many EPs have for autism, highlights the unique role EPs can play in identifying needs and planning interventions at different levels for autistic individuals and their families.

Our book will provide insights into the journeys of a number of autistic individuals as well as several parents of autistic children, charting a 'spectrum' of heartening and challenging experiences, successes and failures, supportive practices and ongoing barriers. We hope that this book may offer inspiration to parents, educators, professionals and researchers to develop their knowledge base and skill set in order to help this very significant number of children and young people with a complexity of needs.

There is much value in EPs continuing to be involved and at the forefront of promoting a developing understanding of the concepts around autism, particularly relating to schools and other educational systems. As discussed earlier, the positioning of educational psychology services nationally within school support, but linked to a wider multidisciplinary field, has led not only to the development of a unique and privileged position as regards EPs' knowledge and understanding of SEN but also to our ability to apply our skills within the contexts that really matter to children and young people.

EPs have in-depth understanding of complex educational systems and how they interrelate with the home, community and other support services. As such, they have a key responsibility in supporting, guiding, listening to and advocating for autistic young people in order to ensure that these systems are responding appropriately to their differences.

It is therefore vital for EPs to continue to keep abreast of research and new developments in order to ensure that autistic individuals under their care have access to the most appropriate and effective support and intervention. The focus on a recognition of the valuable contribution autistic people have made and will continue to make in the future is a key challenge for EPs. They must be cognizant of the voices and journeys of autistic adults and implications for their own practice. Furthermore, they need to continue to develop effective ways to elicit young people's and parents' voices in planning for their futures, identifying appropriate priorities in their learning programmes and supporting independence. There must be continued recognition of some of the difficulties in eliciting the voice of autistic children and young people and the family. Furthermore, much needs to be done to find ways to improve the awareness of the mutual difficulties of understanding between autistic and non-autistic people as described by Milton's 'double empathy problem' (Milton 2012), which will be explored further in Chapter 2. When making recommendations about resources, it is vital to consider those resources within the autism community (that is, the community of autistic people, their families and the professionals who support them) so that we can promote support *by* autistic people *for* autistic people as discussed by Crane and Pellicano in Chapter 2.

Additionally, EPs need to build on their growing understanding of the issues around neurodiversity and to be able to champion a positive and strengths-based approach when planning a young person's future. As we will see in Chapter 2, research continues to identify the significance of a collaborative approach not only with the young person and their family but also with other professionals.

POINTS FOR REFLECTION

☞ The child's voice and that of the parents/carers are central to any assessment of the child's needs.

☞ Consider the use of formulation as a helpful tool in broadening the scope of an assessment.

☞ The extension of the professional's role should include advocacy for autistic young people and adults.

References

American Psychiatric Association (2013) *Diagnostic and Statistical Manual of Mental Disorder, Fifth Edition (DSM-5)*. Washington, DC: American Psychiatric Publishing.

Bandura, A. (1977) *Social Learning Theory*. Englewood Cliffs, NJ: Prentice Hall.

Besic, E. (2020) 'Intersectionality: A pathway towards inclusive education.' *Prospects, 49*, 111–122.

Bondy, A. & Frost, L. (2001) 'The Picture Exchange Communication System.' *Behaviour Modification, 25* (5), 725–744.

Boyle, J., MacKay, T. & Lauchlan, F. (2017) 'The Legislative Context and Shared Practice Models.' In B. Kelly, L. Marks Woolfson & J. Boyle (eds) *Frameworks for Practice in Educational Psychology: A Textbook for Trainees and Practitioners* (second edition, first edition 2008). London: Jessica Kingsley Publishers.

Bronfenbrenner, U. (1974) 'Developmental research, public policy and the ecology of childhood.' *Child Development, 45*(1), 1–5.

Carpenter, B., Happé, F. & Egerton, J. (2019) 'Where are all the Autistic Girls?' In B. Carpenter, F. Happé, & J. Egerton (eds) *Girls and Autism: Educational, Family and Personal Perspectives*. London: Routledge.

Dean, M., Harwood, R. & Kasari, C. (2017) 'The art of camouflage: Gender differences in the social behaviours of girls and boys with autism spectrum disorder.' *Autism, 21*(6), 678–689.

Department for Children, Schools and Families (2009) *Inclusion Development Programme: Supporting Pupils on the Autism Spectrum*. London. HMSO.

Department for Education and Employment (2000) *Educational Psychology Services (England): Current Role, Good Practice and Future Directions (Report of the Working Group)*. London: HMSO.

Department for Education and Skills (2004) *Every Child Matters: Change for Children*. London: HMSO.

Dessent, T. (1978) 'The Historical Development of School Psychological services in Reconstructing Educational Psychology.' In B. Gillham (ed.) *Reconstructing Educational Psychology*. London: Croom Helm.

Elsabbagh, M., Divan, G., Koh, Y.J., Kim, Y.S. *et al.* (2012) 'Global prevalence of autism and other pervasive developmental disorders.' *Autism Research, 5*(3), 160–179.

Farrell, P., Woods, K., Lewis, S., Rooney, S., Squires, G. & O'Connor, M. (2006) *A Review of the Functions and Contribution of Educational Psychologists in England and Wales in Light of 'Every Child Matters: Change for Children'*. Nottingham: DfES Publications.

Fletcher-Watson, S. & Happé, F. (2019) *Autism: A New Introduction to Psychological Theory and Current Debate*. London: Routledge.

Frederickson, N. & Cline, T. (2009) *Special Educational Needs, Inclusion and Diversity* (second edition). Buckingham: Open University Press.

Gainsborough, J. (2011) 'The Barnet Early Autism Model (BEAM) – An account of the development of Barnet's service for pre-school children with a diagnosis of Autism Spectrum Condition (ASC).' *DECP Debate Edition 138*, March 2011.

Gillham, B. (ed.) (1978) *Reconstructing Educational Psychology*. London: Croom Helm.

Gray, C. (1997) *Social Stories and Comic Strip Conversations*. Bicester, Oxfordshire: Winslow Press.

Happé, F., Ronald, A. & Plomin, R. (2006) 'Time to give up on a single explanation for autism.' *Nature Neuroscience, 9*, 1218–1220.

Health and Care Professionals Council (2021) *The Standards of Proficiency for Practitioner Psychologists (14.7)*. Accessed 08/03/2021 at www.hcpc-uk.org/standards/standards-of-proficiency/practitioner-psychologists.

Hewitt, D. (1996) 'How to do Intensive Interaction.' In M. Collis & P. Lacey (eds) *Interactive Approaches to Teaching: A Framework for INSET*. London: David Fulton.

Hong-Hua, L., Wang, C.C., Feng, J.Y., Wang, B., Li, C.L. & Jia, F.Y. (2020) 'A developmental profile of children with autism spectrum disorder in China using the Griffiths Mental Development Scales.' *Frontiers in Psychology, 11*, 570923.

Johnstone, L. & Dallos, R. (2014, first edition 2006) (eds) *Formulation in Psychology and Psychotherapy*. London: Routledge.

Jones, G., Lacey, P. & Robertson, C. (2012) *AET National Standards*. London: Autism Education Trust.

Jordan, R. & Jones, G. (1999) 'Review of research into educational interventions for children with autism in the UK.' *Autism 3*(1), 101–110.

Kanner, L. (1944) 'Early infantile autism.' *Journal of Pediatrics, 25*(3), 211–217.

MacKay, T.A.W.N. (1999) *Quality Assurance in Education Authority Psychological Services: Self-Evaluation Using Performance Indicators*. Edinburgh: Scottish Executive Education Department.

MacKay, T., Boyle, J. & Cole, R. (2016) 'Methods for research in professional educational psychology.' *Educational and Child Psychology, 33*(3), 6–10.

McConkey, R. (2020) 'The rise in the numbers of school pupils with autism: A comparison of the four countries in the United Kingdom.' *Support for Learning, 35*(2), 132–143.

Marsh, A.J. (2014) 'Statements of special educational needs and tribunal appeals in England and Wales 2003-2013 - in numbers.' *Educational Psychology in Practice, 30*(4), 393–408.

Mesibov, G.B., Shea,V. & Schopler, E. (2004) *The TEACCH Approach to Autism Spectrum Disorders*. New York, NY: Springer.

Milton, D.E. (2012) 'On the ontological status of autism: The "Double Empathy Problem".' *Disability and Society, 27*(6), 883–887.

Monsen, J.J. & Frederickson, N. (2008) 'The Problem Analysis Framework: A Guide to Decision Making, Problem Solving and Action Within Applied Psychological Practice.' In B. Kelly, L. Wolfson & J. Boyle (eds) *Frameworks for Practice in Educational Psychology: A Textbook for Trainees and Practitioners*. London: Jessica Kingsley Publishers.

National Autistic Society website. *EarlyBird (under five years), EarlyBird Plus (ages four–nine), Healthy Minds (ages five–11) and Teen Life (ages 10–16)*. Accessed 19/08/2021 at www.autism.org.uk/what-we-do/support-in-the-community/family-support.

National Institute for Health and Care Excellence (NICE) (2011, updated 2017) *Autism Spectrum Disorder in Under 19s: Recognition, Referral and Diagnosis*. NICE guideline CG128. Accessed 10/03/21 at https://pathways.nice.org.uk/pathways/autism-spectrum-disorder.

Norwich, B. (2002) 'Education, inclusion and individual differences: Recognising and resolving dilemmas.' *British Journal of Educational Studies, 50*(4), 482–502.

Prizant, B.M., Wetherby, A.M., Rubin, E., Laurent, A.C. & Rydell, P.J. (2005) *The SCERTS™ Model: A Comprehensive Educational Approach for Children with Autism Spectrum Disorders*. Baltimore, MD: Brookes Publishing Company.

Reed, P., Osborne, L., Makrygianni, M., Waddington, E., Etherington, A. & Gainsborough, J. (2013) 'Evaluation of the Barnet Early Autism Model (BEAM) teaching intervention programme in a "real world" setting.' *Research in Autism Spectrum Disorders, 7*(6) 631-638.

Rees, K. (2017) 'Models of disability and the categorisation of children with severe and profound learning difficulties: Informing educational approaches based on an understanding of individual needs.' *Educational and Child Psychology, 34*(4), 30–39.

Robinson, L., Bond. C. & Oldfield, J. (2018) 'A UK and Ireland survey of educational psychologists' intervention practices for students with autism spectrum disorder.' *Educational Psychology in Practice, 34* (1), 58–72.

Royal College of Psychiatrists (2010) *Good Psychiatric Practice: Continuing Professional Development*. London: Royal College of Psychiatrists.

Shore, S. (Interviewee). Leading Perspectives on Disability: A Q&A with Dr Stephen Shore [Interview transcript]. Lime Connect website. Accessed 05/03/2021 at www.limeconnect.com/opportunities_news/detail/leading-perspectives-on-disability-a-qa-with-dr-stephen-shore.

Silberman, S. (2015) *Neurotribes: The Legacy of Autism and How to Think Smarter about People Who Think Differently*. Sydney: Allen and Unwin.

Singer, J. (1999) '"Why Can't You Be Normal for Once in Your Life?" From A "Problem With No Name" to the Emergence of a New Category of Difference.' In M. Corker and S. French (eds) *Disability Discourse*. London: McGraw-Hill Education.

Vygotsky, L.S. (1978) *Mind in Society: The Development of Higher Psychological Processes*. Cambridge, MA: Harvard University Press.

Wing, L. (1981) 'Asperger's Syndrome: a clinical account.' *Psychological Medicine, 11*(1), 115–129.

Wing, L. & Gould, J. (1979) 'Severe impairments of social interaction and associated abnormalities in children: Epidemiology and classification.' *Journal of Autism and Developmental Disorders, 9*, 11–29.

Wing, L. & Potter, D. (2002) 'The epidemiology of autism: Is the prevalence rising?' *Mental Retardation and Developmental Disabilities Research Reviews, 8*, 151–161.

World Health Organization (1995) *International Classification of Diseases – version 10 (ICD-10)*. Geneva: WHO.

CHAPTER 2

Current Autism Research: Implications for Educational Practice

Laura Crane and Elizabeth Pellicano

Editors: Judith Gainsborough and Jennifer Greene

Background and introduction

Although first described clinically by Kanner and Asperger in the 1940s, autism was not the focus of psychological study until decades later. The carefully designed and controlled experimental research of Hermelin and O'Connor in the 1970s, followed by Frith in the 1980s, lay the foundation for a vast, and ever-increasing, body of research on autistic children, young people and adults. From this pioneering work, we found out about some of the ways in which autistic people think and learn, the profiles of 'peaks and troughs' that characterize autistic cognition, and how autistic people fare when compared to non-autistic people (with and without disabilities). Hermelin and O'Connor, as well as Frith, have been widely lauded for the meticulous way in which they applied psychological theory and methods to an understudied group. Yet this research was followed by a long tradition of studies that focused on how autistic people compared against non-autistic standards, with 'deficit-focused' accounts of autistic cognition (e.g., poor theory of mind, executive dysfunction, weak central coherence) dominating psychological research and educational practice for decades after.

In recent years, we have begun to witness a shift in the way that autism is conceptualized. This shift is, in part, due to advances in our understanding of autism, particularly the broadening of the autism spectrum to include those without intellectual disability or language delays. It also results from advocacy led by autistic people, including a growing body of autistic researchers, who rightly demand that their voices are heard in research and practice. Autistic people and those who support them have long voiced their dissatisfaction with the landscape of autism research, and these groups have begun to challenge traditional ways of conducting research, that is, *with* autistic people, as opposed to *on*, *about*, or *for* them.

In this chapter, we examine six recent developments in autism research. These are not meant to be exhaustive, of course. But the developments summarized here have clear implications for those who support autistic people in a personal and/or professional context.

Research development 1: Making research matter – the importance of listening to autistic people and their allies

An ever-increasing amount of autism research is being funded and published. While just 100–200 autism research articles were published each year in the 1970s and 1980s, we have seen tremendous growth, with over 6400 articles featuring the word 'autism' being published in 2020 alone (see Figure 2.1).

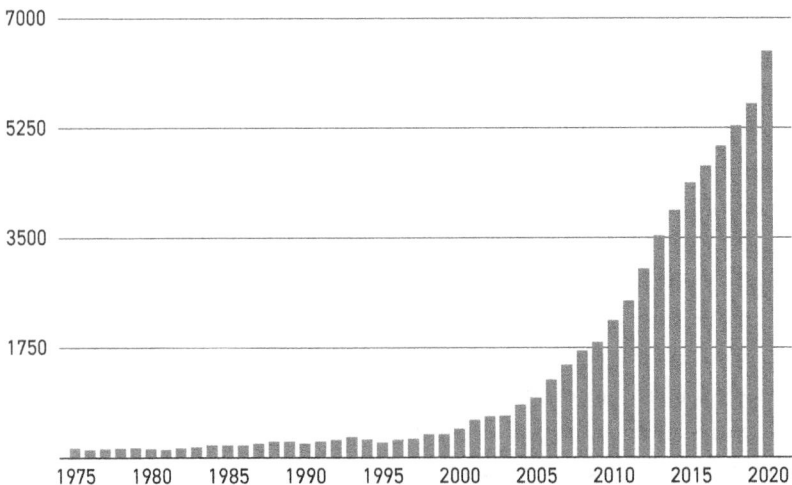

Figure 2.1: Number of autism-related journal articles published from 1975 to 2020 (data sourced from PubMed)

One would think that this growing knowledge about autism was simply a good thing. After all, the more information we have about autism, the better placed we should be to support autistic people, their family members and carers, and the educational, clinical, and allied-health professionals who support them. Yet there has been growing recognition of the 'translational gap' between autism research and practice. That is, if you ask autistic people and their allies about the impact that research has had on their day-to-day lives, the answer tends to be *not very much*.

How do we address this issue? Let's take an analogy: imagine we are buying a child a birthday present. We might have a fair guess about what kind of present to get them. We might, for example, look at popular gifts for children of that age, or we could ask their parents what they might like. Yet taking this approach is a bit risky. We might choose a present that they think is okay but isn't what *they* really want. Or they might really dislike the present that we chose for them! The ideal solution, and the one likely to lead to the best outcome, would be to just ask them directly.

There have been several attempts to do just this, directly eliciting the views of autistic people, family members and professionals about their priorities for autism research. For example, in the *A Future Made Together* project conducted in the UK, Pellicano, Dinsmore and Charman (2013, 2014) reviewed both autism research that had been funded (2007–2011) and autism research that had been published (in 2001 compared to 2011). This analysis revealed that over two-thirds of all autism research published and funded in the UK focused on understanding the underlying causes and biology of autism. Much less research focused on the areas of diagnosis, intervention, supports and services. Having surveyed the landscape of UK autism research, Pellicano and colleagues went on to present these findings to more than 1600 members of the UK autism community (autistic people, family members and professionals, including researchers). They found that two-thirds of their participants were dissatisfied with the way in which autism research was concentrated predominantly on so-called basic science. Instead, autistic people and their allies explained that they wanted autism researchers to prioritize areas that had more direct and practical relevance to their day-to-day lives. They wanted research to address questions such as: what are the best ways to improve the life skills of autistic people, and how can public services best meet the needs of autistic people? Essentially, autistic people and their allies wanted research that made a difference to their lives in the here and now.

Encouragingly, changes are starting to happen with regard to the way in which autism research is conducted and funded. For example, in 2016, the UK-based autism research charity Autistica conducted a Priority Setting Partnership to ensure that the autism research taking place in the UK aligns with the priorities of autistic people and their allies. The team at Autistica engaged with autistic people, their family members and the professionals working with them, on an equal footing. The aim was to identify 'evidence uncertainties', defined as areas that were important to these groups, but where more research was needed to confidently provide recommendations for practice. Once these evidence uncertainties were identified, they were prioritized with the goal of jointly agreeing a 'Top 10' set of research questions that needed to be addressed. The research areas identified through this exercise included gaining a better understanding of which interventions improve or reduce mental health problems in autistic people, determining the effectiveness of interventions to support the development of language and communication skills among autistic people, and identifying the most effective ways to provide social care support for autistic adults. Encouragingly, these priority areas are now being used to guide the research conducted in the UK, including determining where funding is allocated.

Fundamentally, the power balance in autism research is beginning to shift, albeit very gradually. While autism researchers had become accustomed to setting the agenda in terms of what they thought autism research could and should focus on, this is starting to change. Autistic people, their family members and the professionals who support them are now beginning to be invited to have a say in the research that shapes autistic people's lives – whether as a consultant during the research process, as part of an advisory group for the research, or as a research collaborator. Working *with* autistic children, young people and adults in this way – where they have greater power in the decision-making process – shouldn't just be limited to the research lab, however. It should also be extended to schools, clinics and communities.

Based on Research Development 1, readers should consider the following questions:

☞ Are autistic children, young people, and adults, and those who support them, able to have a say in the decisions that affect them (particularly with regards to education research and practice)?

☞ Are we putting children and young people at the centre of the decision-making, where possible, reflecting on what each young autistic person wants for their own lives?

Research development 2: Reframing cognitive *deficits* in autism – valuing cognitive *differences*

If you glance through a selection of the thousands of autism research papers published each year, it's likely that you'll learn about autistic people's *deficits, impairments, abnormalities*, and *weaknesses*. Ironically, this tendency is so deeply ingrained that even when autistic people perform *better* than non-autistic people in research studies, the results are still interpreted as autism-related deficits. As just one example, Hu and colleagues (2021) published a study assessing moral decision-making in autistic and non-autistic adults. The participants' task was to decide, either in public or private, whether to incur a personal cost for funding a 'good' cause or to receive a personal gain for funding a 'bad' cause. The authors found that autistic adults were more likely to reject the chance to benefit from supporting a bad cause, relative to their non-autistic peers. While this could (and perhaps should) be interpreted as autistic people having superior levels of moral reasoning relative to their non-autistic peers, the researchers interpreted this finding as due to autistic people being 'more inflexible' than non-autistic participants, related to 'reduced' theory of mind abilities.

The way in which Hu and colleagues interpreted their research findings is somewhat unsurprising given that *deficits* in theory of mind have long been associated with autism. In 1985, Baron-Cohen, Leslie and Frith published a seminal research paper posing the question 'Does the Autistic Child Have a Theory of Mind?' To assess theory of mind in this context, Baron-Cohen and colleagues used a test of false-belief called the Sally-Anne task. Here, young children are presented with two dolls: Sally (who has a basket) and Anne (who has a box). The children are shown Sally surreptitiously putting a marble in her basket before going for a walk. In Sally's absence, Anne then takes the marble out of the basket and puts it in her box. Sally returns and the children are asked where Sally will look for her marble. If children can reason about another person's mental state (i.e., they have developed theory of mind capabilities), they would correctly state that Sally would look for her marble where she left it – in her basket. However, if children have not yet developed this cognitive capability (i.e., if they cannot understand that another person's thoughts and beliefs can differ from both their own thoughts and beliefs, and also from reality), then they would erroneously say that Sally would look for the marble in the box (i.e., where it actually is).

Baron-Cohen and colleagues demonstrated that while 80 per cent of non-autistic children (both those who were typically developing and those with Down syndrome) successfully passed this false-belief test – that is, correctly identifying that Sally would look for the marble in her basket – only 20 per cent of autistic children did so. The authors therefore concluded that their results 'strongly support the hypothesis that autistic children as a group fail to employ a theory of mind... As a result of this, the autistic subjects are unable to impute beliefs to others and are thus at a grave disadvantage when having to predict the behaviour of other people' (1985, p.43). This 'absence' of spontaneous theory of mind in autistic individuals is thought to lead to a range of downstream effects on social learning (Happé 2015, p.199) and has been linked to 'deficits' in areas such as empathy (Lombardo *et al.* 2007) and social motivation (Chevallier *et al.* 2012).

Fundamentally, much of this work stems from the assumption that the way that autistic people experience and interact with the world is inherently *wrong*. While it is important not to overlook the challenges associated with being autistic, it is also essential that we reflect on how we frame *differing* performance between autistic and non-autistic people on cognitive tasks. Autistic scholar Damian Milton has emphasized the importance of viewing communication as a two-way endeavour, requiring effort from both parties. Milton (2012) reframes the notion of autistic people's *deficits* in theory of mind as a *double empathy problem*. The double empathy framework proposes that while autistic people may struggle to understand the inner workings of non-autistic people, the reverse is also true.

The double empathy problem has been supported by a range of empirical studies that have elegantly demonstrated how breakdowns in communication between autistic and non-autistic people are a result of *mutual* misunderstandings. As one example, Crompton and colleagues (2020a) tested a central assumption of the double empathy problem: that communication difficulties arise from a mismatch between neurotypes (i.e., whether a person is autistic or non-autistic). Crompton and colleagues (2020a) used an information transfer task, akin to the children's game 'telephone', where participants were divided into one of three groups (each comprising eight people). The first person in each group was told a story and they had to share it with the second person, who then had to share it with the third person, and so on. The researchers then assessed how many details of the story were shared at each stage. Crucially, these groups comprised people with a range of neurologies: there was an autistic group (comprising eight autistic people), a non-autistic group (comprising eight non-autistic people), and a mixed neurotype group (comprising four autistic and four non-autistic people). Crompton and colleagues found that the autistic group performed similarly to the non-autistic group in terms of how successful their information transfer had been. However, much less information was shared successfully in the mixed neurotype group. These findings therefore suggest a specific issue with information transfer between people of different neurologies.

As well as assessing how much information was shared between groups, Crompton and colleagues (2020b) asked participants about the level of rapport within the groups (i.e., how well different members of each group felt they got on with other group members). These results demonstrated that the mixed neurotype group experienced lower levels of rapport than the same neurotype groups. These findings align with qualitative research by the same team, who interviewed autistic adults about their interactions with both autistic and non-autistic people. In this work, Crompton *et al.* (2020b) found that autistic adults find spending time with other autistic people easier and more comfortable, leading to a sense of shared understanding. While autistic adults commonly reported feeling they had to conform to 'fit in' with the non-autistic majority, this was not so when they were with other autistic people: they felt as if they belonged and could be their authentic selves.

Crompton and colleagues' findings raise an interesting paradox: how do we strive for the meaningful inclusion of autistic young people (e.g., in educational settings), when autistic people appear to be more successful working with other autistic people, and feel more comfortable doing so? One step in this direction would be for education professionals to begin reframing autistic cognition – moving away from constantly comparing autistic people's performance against that of their non-autistic peers and appreciating the diversity of how different people view and experience the world. Another way would be to encourage non-autistic people to make their communicative style more inclusive, as opposed to forcing autistic people to adapt to non-autistic styles of communication.

Together, these lessons will go some way towards ensuring that both autistic and non-autistic people are able to thrive – in education and beyond.

Based on Research Development 2, readers should consider the following questions:

☞ How are non-autistic people interpreting – and describing – autistic cognition? Can there be a move away from taking a deficit-focused approach and comparing autistic performance against non-autistic standards?

☞ How can non-autistic readers change *their* communication to work more effectively with autistic young people?

Research development 3: Recognizing the benefits of shared autistic experiences

In the previous section, we touched on the long-standing goal of educational inclusion for autistic children and young people. In fact, this is more than just a goal – it is a *right* afforded to all disabled young people, without discrimination and based on equal opportunity. As stated in Article 24 of the UN Convention on the Rights of Persons with Disabilities, young people should not be excluded from the general education system based on their disability; they should be able to access an inclusive, quality, and free education in their community; and they should receive reasonable accommodations and supports to meet their educational needs. Fundamentally, inclusion means changing the environment to meet the needs of all learners. It is a way of respecting the diversity of learners and brings benefits to *all* children and young people. Yet while few would argue with autistic people's right to an inclusive education, some question whether this is an illusory concept (Pellicano, Bölte & Stahmer 2018).

In one research study, Humphrey and Lewis (2008) investigated autistic pupils' experiences of mainstream schooling. The title of the paper – 'Make Me Normal' – emphasized how pupils often perceived their autistic characteristics (e.g., in the areas of behaviour, cognition and learning preferences) in a negative way. For example, young people made references to 'not [being] normal', having a 'bad brain' and being 'odd' or a 'freak'. While there was a subset of pupils who had begun to accept, or even celebrate, their autistic differences, educational challenges were noted among the sample of pupils. For example, autistic pupils' social naivety was often felt to lead to them being the targets of bullying. Furthermore, several aspects of the school context (e.g., the school environment, the pressure of assessments) were perceived to cause high levels of stress and anxiety among pupils. Despite these challenges, autistic pupils reported that they wanted to fit in, and tried to assimilate themselves successfully within the mainstream school environment. Overall, these findings call into question precisely how pupils can be successfully included within the mainstream environment, given their autistic differences and often-challenging school surroundings.

Despite efforts to support autistic pupils in education, recent research has shown that autistic pupils *still* experience significant challenges in education, the consequences of which may include negative school experiences, school refusal and even school exclusion (Brede *et al.* 2017; Makin, Hill & Pellicano 2017; Totsika *et al.* 2020). These findings do not, however, suggest the notion that inclusion is an illusory concept. It may simply be the case that mainstream schools are fostering integration (encouraging autistic pupils to 'fit in' with the mainstream norm), as opposed to inclusion (changing educational provision so that it enables every child to reach their full potential). Indeed, if the underlying assumption of education professionals is that inclusive education will enable autistic young people to learn from their non-autistic peers (developing their social and communicative skills and enabling them to 'fit in' better), inclusion is destined to fail. There can be huge value in bringing together diverse minds, yielding benefits for autistic and non-autistic students alike.

That said, there may be value in providing opportunities for autistic young people to come together in a shared space, *without* non-autistic people. In a recent study, Crane and colleagues (2020) conducted an initial evaluation of a ten-week programme called Exploring Being Autistic, designed for adults diagnosed as autistic, as well as adults who thought they might be autistic. The overarching goal of the programme was to help participants learn more about autism within a supportive peer group context. In the interviews with participants about their experiences (immediately after the programme, and again six months later), autistic adults explained how they felt a strong sense of belonging in the group, a feeling that they did not always experience in predominantly non-autistic spaces. Furthermore, a unique feature of the Exploring Being Autistic programme was that it was autistic led – that is, the facilitator of the group was autistic herself. This feature contributed to participants feeling less judgement, which they reported to be in stark contrast to how they sometimes felt treated by non-autistic professionals. Taken together, participation in the group contributed to participants developing a positive, practical outlook on autism that they were able to apply to their day-to-day lives (e.g., the workplace).

Similarly, positive results have been reported when evaluating peer support groups designed for autistic young people. Gordon and colleagues (2015), for example, reported on the PEGASUS (Psychoeducation Group for Autism Spectrum Understanding and Support) programme: a psychoeducation group that aimed to enhance autistic young people's self-awareness by teaching them about their diagnosis in a supportive peer group context. Over the course of six sessions, the aim was to support young people in gaining greater insight into the strengths and challenges that were associated with their autism diagnosis. While the sessions were led by qualified clinical psychologists (who were not reported to be autistic), the programme had a strong neurodiversity principle at its core – that is, they presented autism as a different way of being, as opposed to a deficit that needed to be 'fixed'. Parallel parent sessions aimed to empower parents to reinforce such messages with their children and within their families. A promising initial evaluation demonstrated better knowledge and self-awareness among autistic children who had been part of the PEGASUS programme, suggesting it could be part of a more comprehensive package of clinical care for autistic young people.

Moving away from the community (Crane *et al.* 2020) and the clinic (Gordon *et al.* 2015), the benefits of autistic expertise and experiential knowledge have been considered with respect to education. Recent work by Wood and Happé (2021) has examined whether autistic children would benefit from having autistic educators. In this study, the researchers conducted a survey of 149 autistic school staff (in a range of educational settings and roles), questioning them on their experiences and lessons learned. From their results, Wood and Happé noted several barriers faced by autistic school staff and these, ironically, mirrored challenges encountered by autistic students (e.g., the inappropriate sensory environment of schools). Encouragingly, autistic education professionals also reported several opportunities, such as heightened understanding and empathy with their autistic pupils, which they felt could facilitate the inclusion of autistic pupils in schools. Participants additionally reported positive experiences of sharing their diagnoses with school communities, which was found to benefit pupils, parents and colleagues alike.

We should emphasize that autistic children and young people may not always have the benefit of working with autistic peers or with autistic professionals. Also, other characteristics, such as differences in age, gender and ethnic background, might also affect the extent of 'shared empathy' between autistic peers and professionals. On the flipside, collaborative working between autistic and non-autistic people can be positive. For example, in the evaluation of the Exploring Being Autistic programme (Crane *et al.* 2020), an academic who did not identify as autistic conducted interviews, and participants reported the experience to be positive. This outcome was likely, at least in part, due to the efforts made by the researcher to engage and develop a trusting relationship with participants prior to interviewing them, all on the advice of the autistic facilitator of the programme, as part of their co-produced research study (i.e., with the autistic facilitator and non-autistic researcher working together, as equal partners). Indeed, in a range of research studies and professional contexts it has been demonstrated that – irrespective of people's neurology – building trusting relationships between stakeholders, underpinned by mutual respect, is essential (see Cascio, Weiss & Racine 2020, for discussion).

Based on Research Development 3, readers should consider the following questions:

☞ What kind of whole-class, whole-school strategies might be useful to facilitate the inclusion – rather than just integration – of autistic pupils? Could autistic pupils (and their parents) be involved in the design and delivery of these strategies?

☞ Given the benefits arising from interactions between people with different neurologies, could there be benefits to peer support for autistic young people?

Research development 4: Developing effective methods to give marginalized groups a voice in autism research and practice

In the research we have discussed so far in this chapter, autistic self-advocacy has been vital: in addressing long-standing misconceptions around autism, in providing practical support to autistic people and in changing the landscape of autism research. Advocacy such as this is essential, as is the need to ensure that *all* autistic people have a voice in decisions that shape their lives. But the question that we need to ask is: how can we ensure that we elicit the voices of *all* autistic people, especially those who are marginalized from research and practice?

Within education, pupil voice is seen as a central aspect of good practice. Article 12 of the UN Convention on the Rights of the Child (1989) emphasizes that children and young people have a right to express their views, to have these views taken seriously and to be involved in the decisions that affect them. National guidance in England very much aligns with this. For example, in 2014, Education, Health and Care (EHC) plans for vulnerable children and young people were implemented. These plans were designed to identify children and young people's education, health and social care needs and set out the additional support required to meet those needs. As part of this policy initiative, EHC plans include a dedicated section that *must* include the child's own perspective, and parents' views must not be used as a proxy for the young person's view. Overall, there is certainly a commitment – at least on paper – to giving autistic children and young people a voice.

Yet attempts at eliciting the voices of autistic children and young people can raise a host of ethical implications. Challenges can arise, for example, when the views of autistic children and young people conflict with those of significant others. One illustration of this conflict comes from a research study investigating the friendships and social networks of autistic children in mainstream schools. In this work, Calder, Hill and Pellicano (2013) sought the views of parents, teachers and, importantly, pupils themselves. While Calder and colleagues found much convergence between the views of these different participant groups, the areas of divergence were perhaps the most interesting. Some children spoke of how challenging and overwhelming the social aspects of school could be, leading to one child commenting: 'Sometimes I just want to play by myself'. Yet while parents and teachers acknowledged children's preferences for being alone, they also expressed unease with this prospect, detailing often unsuccessful strategies to encourage the children to engage in the games and activities of other children. These findings raise complex ethical issues about how best to support the social development of autistic children and young people, balancing how to respect their personal preferences while simultaneously ensuring that they are not socially isolated.

Notably, the young people in the research by Calder *et al.* (2013) were all educated in mainstream classrooms and were able to participate in interviews, verbalizing their views to an interviewer. A further ethical question arises around how we can give a 'voice' to autistic young people who cannot convey their views in such a way because they do not use traditional forms of communication. Recently, there has been innovative work directly tackling this issue. Richards and Crane (2020), for example, conducted a case study within a residential special school in England. This school catered for autistic young people with a range of complex needs such as additional communication, social, sensory, cognitive, emotional and physical needs.

Meaningfully eliciting the voices of pupils had been identified as a key target for development within the school, so Richards and Crane designed a small-scale piece of action research to identify how best to address this issue. The researchers began by conducting a review of existing literature on eliciting voice from children and young people. These findings were then presented to staff at the school, who reflected on the approaches most suitable for their pupils and in their specific school context. Based on these findings, they developed shared wall spaces called 'Talking Walls', on which pupils were supported to record positive, negative and neutral/indifferent experiences. The goal was to give the young people a voice – to support them in sharing their feelings, making their wishes known and, ultimately, to develop their independence. Talking Walls were then trialled over a six-month period, using interviews with staff and observations with pupils to evaluate how well they worked. The findings of this evaluation were encouraging. Despite no pupils showing spontaneous, independent use of the Walls, the young people did engage with the Walls through gestures and other methods of communication such as proximity and eye gaze. Further, the evaluation identified areas of further development, such as the need to support the young people in identifying and expressing a range of emotions (as use of the Walls tended to centre on positive experiences). Taken together, the Talking Walls appeared to be a promising method of eliciting the voices of young people who are seldom heard in autism research or practice.

Similar challenges around eliciting pupil voice have been reported in very young autistic children. For example, Parsons and colleagues (2020) provided an example of an EHC plan given to a four-year-old autistic boy, Oscar. In the section of Oscar's EHC plan devoted to presenting his own views and experiences was the following statement: 'Oscar is not able to give his own views'. To address this issue, the research team, comprising academic researchers and early years practitioners, used an innovative digital storytelling methodology. Specifically, digital cameras were placed throughout the nursery and the children wore wearable cameras during everyday activities. Using an iterative process of coding, concept mapping and eliciting feedback, Digital Stories were finalized for each of the four children involved in the study. These stories gave detailed insights into the children's likes and dislikes, their actions and perspectives, and effective ways to support the children. Taken together, the research team stated that these stories clearly demonstrate how young autistic children *can* share their own views. Further, the Digital Stories provided a holistic view of the children, as opposed to the often deficit-focused accounts that dominate education planning for autistic children.

By eliciting the voices of autistic children and young people who are often excluded from research, we are taking small, but critically important, steps towards making autism research and practice more inclusive. Yet, the exclusion of other groups from autism research can sometimes be even more subtle. As one example, Crane and colleagues (2016) conducted an online survey of over 1000 parents of autistic children in the UK about their experiences of accessing an autism diagnosis. The results of this work highlighted the lengthy delays that parents faced to access an autism diagnosis for their children (on average, three and a half years), as well as the lack of satisfaction with the support offered to autistic children and their families following the diagnosis. While this was certainly a large sample of parents to take part in a research study in the UK, inspection of the characteristics of the sample revealed that 95 per cent described themselves as being from a white ethnic background. It is difficult to determine how common this bias is, given that many studies fail to report data on ethnicity in their research (Pierce *et al.* 2014; West *et al.* 2016). It is also an issue that is not unique to autism research (Rad, Martingano & Ginges 2018). Nevertheless, it raises serious challenges for autism research and practice. Under the UN Convention on the Rights of the Child (1989), children have a right to a cultural identity, including being connected to culture, community and language in school. Yet if most autism research is based on the experiences and realities of predominantly white autistic people and their families, this means that practitioners and policy makers are designing services and supports around the needs of white parents. The question then arises of what happens if the experiences and perspectives of autistic people and families from minority ethnic backgrounds are markedly different from those of the parents whose experiences and perspectives are being reported in the autism research literature? This issue is considered further in Chapter 9.

Overall, it is essential that researchers set out to understand the experiences of *all* autistic people and their families. It may not be possible to make autism research inclusive to everyone, all of the time. Yet we must be clear about who our research findings do and don't apply to. And if our research findings do not apply to certain groups, we must reflect on why, considering whether bespoke ways of eliciting their views and experiences could be useful. These efforts will ensure that services are designed and developed with the needs of all autistic people and their families in mind – and, ideally, with their involvement throughout.

Based on Research Development 4, readers should consider the following:

☞ The most effective – and non-tokenistic – ways of eliciting the views and experiences of autistic children and young people, especially those who are often left out of autism research and practice, including autistic children with complex needs and young autistic children.

☞ The need to ensure we understand the unique cultural and linguistic context of children and young people, as well as their families, and to ensure that no groups are left behind in research or practice.

Research development 5: The need to take a lifespan approach to autism research and practice

In most research presented in this chapter, researchers have attempted to understand the lives of autistic people and their families by taking a snapshot of their experiences at a specific moment in time. Indeed, during an autism diagnostic assessment, or any assessment that precedes or follows it, we observe an autistic person's characteristics in the here and now: both the challenges that they are experiencing, as well as the strengths. While some research has involved asking autistic people or their allies to reflect on their experiences over time – for example by asking either autistic adults to reflect on their school days (e.g., Parsons 2015), or parents to reflect on their children's early development (e.g., Whitaker 2002) – these findings will inevitably be contextualized in a person's current circumstances.

There have been few longitudinal studies tracking autistic children's development over time, at either a group level (i.e., do all autistic children show the same cognitive and behavioural profile?) or an individual level (i.e., do autistic children maintain a consistent cognitive and behavioural profile over time?). In one of the few attempts to address these questions, Pellicano and colleagues examined autistic children's cognitive and behavioural profiles at three different time points over a 12-year period, from early childhood to emerging adulthood. Initially, Pellicano (2010) recruited 45 autistic children, between four and seven years of age, all described as cognitively able (i.e., with no diagnosed intellectual disability, and verbal and non-verbal IQ scores within the average or above-average range). The children completed tasks assessing theory of mind (false-belief understanding), executive function (planning, inhibition and cognitive flexibility) and central coherence (identifying local elements from global images or constructing segmented patterns). Thirty-seven of these autistic children were followed up again three years later and, at both time points, autistic children were compared against non-autistic children of a similar age and ability level.

As a group, Pellicano found that autistic children showed a clear cognitive profile at both time points. Specifically, autistic cognition was characterized by difficulties on theory of mind tasks and challenges with aspects of executive function, as well as by a detail-focused cognitive style/advantage. Yet examining this profile within the 37 children on an individual basis, Pellicano found that this profile was not consistent across the sample at either time point. As can be seen in Figure 2.2, at intake, only 22 of the 37 participants showed the expected cognitive profile of autistic children (i.e., the cognitive profile observed at a group level: poor theory of mind, poor executive function, enhanced local processing). Some children showed a combination of characteristically autistic cognitive features but not others (e.g., six children showed difficulties on theory of mind tasks and enhanced local processing, but no executive function difficulties; seven children showed enhanced local processing, but no difficulties with theory of mind or executive function) and one child did not show any of these cognitive features. At follow-up, the pattern was even more variable – only seven autistic children showed the expected cognitive profile, with many more showing either isolated cognitive characteristics, combinations of cognitive characteristics or no cognitive characteristics that are typically seen among autistic children.

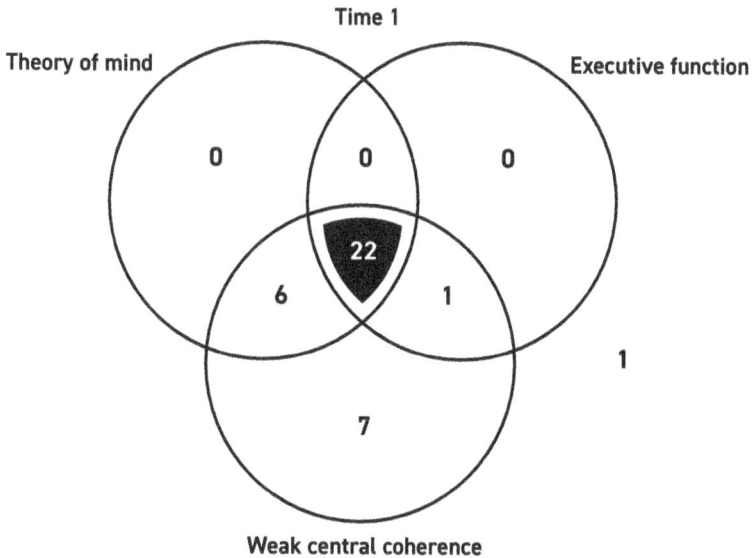

Figure 2.2: Autistic children's individual cognitive profiles at Time 1 (baseline; n = 37) and at Time 2 (three years later; n = 37), as reported in Pellicano (2010).

What happened to these children later in life? Pellicano and colleagues followed up 28 of these young people 12 years later, when they were, on average, 18 years of age. As reported in Kenny, Cribb & Pellicano (2018), the team measured participants' autistic features (focusing on socialization, communication and repetitive behaviours) as well as their adaptive behaviour (focusing on socialization, communication and daily living skills). The focus of this research was to assess the predictive power of early cognitive features (theory of mind and executive function difficulties, enhanced local processing) on later outcomes. The researchers' results demonstrated that early executive function skills were especially important for autistic people's later outcomes: not only did executive function performance in early childhood predict adolescents' autistic features (over and above age, intellectual ability and theory of mind); it also predicted autistic young people's adaptive skills 12 years later.

In sum, Pellicano's work emphasizes two key considerations for autism research and practice. First, it highlights the need to examine autistic characteristics at both a group and an individual level – recognizing the considerable variability across different individuals who fall under the broad autistic spectrum. Second, the work draws attention to the need to track autistic characteristics over time – recognizing that an autistic person's strengths or challenges at any one time can change with development.

Pellicano's work also emphasizes how autistic children will develop into autistic adults, and yet little is known about how we support this group during this transition, nor the areas in which autistic young people might need targeted support. When Pellicano, Cribb and Kenny (2020) followed up their sample of autistic young people in early adulthood, they also interviewed the autistic young people and their parents. This work was felt to be crucially important for three key reasons. First, researchers and practitioners have traditionally tried to apply 'objective' criteria when assessing autistic young people's long-term outcomes – that is, evaluating them against markers for standard non-autistic young people, such as whether they are in paid employment, are living independently or are in a long-term relationship. Yet early adulthood now tends to be characterized by experimentation and uncertainty, such as travelling to different places in the world, exploring different potential career options and so on. As such, traditional, objective outcomes are now unlikely to be a good marker of success for any young person, yet alone autistic young people. Second, these objective markers of 'successes' tend to be based on normative assumptions of a successful outcome, largely derived from what non-autistic researchers and practitioners think is a good outcome, rather than autistic people themselves. It may be that more subjective factors (e.g., a person's quality of life) are of crucial importance; and these may not correspond with successes as evaluated by more traditional, objective criteria. Finally, evaluating outcomes by focusing on normative markers of success tends to concentrate on the outcome itself (e.g., having paid employment) as opposed to the journey to that outcome and how it has been achieved. After all, a young person may 'tick a box' by being in paid employment but they could experience significant challenges in obtaining and maintaining that job, could be in a job that is not commensurate with their skills, or could be in a job that they find deeply unsatisfying.

Eliciting subjective accounts from autistic young people and parents about this transitional stage of their lives, as well as their aspirations for the future, Pellicano and colleagues found that participants typically wanted the same kinds of outcomes as non-autistic young people and their parents (see Cribb Kenny & Pellicano 2019). These outcomes included autonomy in decision-making, having quality connections (with friends and family), and having good mental health. Pellicano and colleagues also found that the young people were optimistic about their outcomes (at least more optimistic than one might suspect based on traditional studies of autistic people's outcomes in adulthood), and embraced this time in their lives: exploring, trying new things out and broadening their horizons. Parents tended to agree with their children's goals and aspirations but did express concerns about the nature and extent of the support their children might need in the future. Parents were therefore very keen to support their children in developing auton-omy, especially given concerns about who might look after their children when they were no longer around.

Based on Research Development 5, readers should consider the following:

☞ The need to understand how the strengths and skills of autistic children and young people might wax and wane with time, and what specific supports are needed to foster such strengths and skills at different points in time.

☞ What a good life means to the autistic children and young people they support, and how they can be supported to live a flourishing life.

☞ How best to promote self-advocacy and autonomy among autistic children and young people.

Research development 6: Recognition of the need to take a collaborative approach to autism research

So far in this chapter, we have discussed several challenges to the traditional focus and framing of autism research. However, the issues that have plagued autism research over the years go much deeper than this. There is now growing recognition of the need to address the way in which autism research is conducted. Earlier in this chapter, we considered the report *A Future Made Together* (Pellicano *et al.* 2013, 2014), in which a team of researchers examined the landscape of autism research in the UK, as well as the research priorities of autistic people and their allies. In this project, the team also examined different levels of engagement with the research process. Engagement with autism research can take several forms, and these are often linked to the degree of power that each person has within the research process. Pellicano and colleagues delineated three different levels of engagement in autism research, each associated with increasing power of autistic people.

At the first level was *dissemination*, or being informed about research. At this level, all of the power is with the researcher: they decide what the research should focus on, how it should be carried out, how it gets interpreted and how it gets shared. In contrast, autistic people are involved as participants, who take part in the work and then get to hear about the final outcomes of the research (i.e., what the researcher found). The next level of engagement was *dialogue*, where there is some degree of communication or consultation between researchers and research participants. This could comprise checking in with autistic people about some element of the research process, getting some advice about how to recruit participants, or getting input on sharing the research findings. While there is some degree of involvement from community members, the power (and decision-making) still firmly lies with the researcher. The final level of engagement identified was *partnership*, involving joint working between researchers and community members. At this level, researchers (who may or may not be autistic) and community members collaboratively set the goals for research and decide how the research gets designed, analysed, interpreted, and shared. Power is shared equally, as is decision-making, across the entire research process.

As part of the *Future Made Together* project, stakeholders were asked their views on these different levels of engagement in research, based on their own experiences. Pellicano and colleagues found that autism researchers thought they were doing quite well in terms of engaging in dissemination and dialogue with the autistic and broader autism communities. However, this view tended not to be shared by autistic people and their allies. Instead, several negative examples of research involvement were noted. For example, autistic people reported instances of taking part in research and never finding out the outcomes or trying to convey their views on the research but feeling as if these views were not being taken seriously. One thing that all groups did tend to agree on, however, was that active research partnerships – where researchers and members of the autism communities work together, sharing decision-making from the very start to the very end of the project – were a rare occurrence.

Encouragingly, there is a growing shift towards more collaborative ways of working. One example is the Pan London Autism Schools Network (PLASN, see Parsons *et al.* 2013), a collective of autism special schools and academic researchers who meet regularly in a mutually beneficial partnership, where school staff share their experiences of 'what works' in terms of supporting autistic young people in education, and researchers provide their insights on conducting rigorous scientific research to address research questions of direct relevance to the schools. Likewise, there have been a range of innovative research partnerships where autistic and non-autistic collaborators have worked together to answer research questions set by autistic people themselves (e.g., Crane *et al.* 2019; Nicolaidis *et al.* 2011; Pellicano *et al.* 2020) – even with 'seldom heard' autistic children and young people with intellectual disability (Pellicano 2017). Such partnerships have the potential of doing research – and educational practice – that is more relevant to people's everyday lives, more tailored to their strengths, preferences and needs and consistent with their values. It is now essential that we take this model and apply it to educational practice.

Based on Research Development 6, readers should consider:

☞ Working in collaboration with young people and their families, plus their teachers, to set the agenda for their own supports and services.

Chapter conclusion

Autism research and practice have grown enormously over the past few decades. There has also been a rise in autistic advocacy, with many autistic people rightly demanding to be more directly involved in the key decisions that affect their lives. In this chapter, we have described some slowly emerging shifts in the field that respond, at least in part, to these demands. We have also highlighted how allies of autistic people can begin to respond in their own practice, largely by working with autistic children and young people in a different way, by being attentive to their everyday experiences and open to their views and perspectives. Ultimately, we need to do better to learn from these experiences and about these experiences, if we are to have any chance of doing what we can to help autistic children and young people lead flourishing lives.

References

Autistica (2016) *Your research priorities*. Accessed 09/12/2021 at https://www.autistica.org.uk/our-research/our-research/your-research-priorities.

Baron-Cohen, S., Leslie, A.M. & Frith, U. (1985) 'Does the autistic child have a "theory of mind"?' *Cognition, 21*(1), 37–46. doi: 10.1016/0010-0277(85)90022-8.

Brede, J., Remington, A., Kenny, L., Warren, K. & Pellicano, E. (2017) 'Excluded from school: Autistic students' experiences of school exclusion and subsequent reintegration into school.' *Autism & Developmental Language Impairments.* https://doi.org/10.1177/2396941517737511.

Calder, L., Hill, V. & Pellicano, E. (2013) '"Sometimes I want to play by myself": Understanding what friendship means to children with autism in mainstream primary schools.' *Autism, 17*(3), 296–316. https://doi.org/10.1177/1362361312467866.

Cascio, M.A., Weiss, J.A. & Racine, E. (2020) 'Person-oriented ethics for autism research: Creating best practices through engagement with autism and autistic communities.' *Autism, 24*(7), 1676–1690. https://doi.org/10.1177/1362361320918763.

Chevallier, C., Kohls, G., Troiani, V., Brodkin, E.S. & Schultz, R.T. (2012) 'The social motivation theory of autism.' *Trends in Cognitive Sciences, 16*(4), 231–239. https://doi.org/10.1016/j.tics.2012.02.007.

Crane, L., Chester, J.W., Goddard, L., Henry, L.A. & Hill, E. (2016) 'Experiences of autism diagnosis: A survey of over 1000 parents in the United Kingdom.' *Autism, 20*(2), 153–162. https://doi.org/10.1177/1362361315573636.

Crane, L., Adams, F., Harper, G., Welch, J. & Pellicano, E. (2019) '"Something needs to change": Mental health experiences of young autistic adults in England.' *Autism, 23*(2), 477–493. https://doi.org/10.1177/1362361318757048.

Crane, L., Hearst, C., Ashworth, M., Davies, J. & Hill, E.L. (2020) 'Supporting newly identified or diagnosed autistic adults: An initial evaluation of an autistic-led programme.' *Journal of Autism and Developmental Disorders.* https://doi.org/10.1007/s10803-020-04486-4.

Crompton, C.J., Hallett, S., Ropar, D., Flynn, E. & Fletcher-Watson, S. (2020a) '"I never realised everybody felt as happy as I do when I am around autistic people": A thematic analysis of autistic adults' relationships with autistic and neurotypical friends and family.' *Autism, 24*(6), 1438–1448. https://doi.org/10.1177/1362361320908976.

Crompton, C.J., Ropar, D., Evans-Williams, C.V., Flynn, E.G. & Fletcher-Watson, S. (2020b) 'Autistic peer-to-peer information transfer is highly effective.' *Autism, 24*(7), 1704–1712. https://doi.org/10.1177/1362361320919286.

Cribb, S., Kenny, L. & Pellicano, E. (2019) '"I definitely feel more in control of my life": The perspectives of young autistic people and their parents on emerging adulthood.' *Autism, 23*(7), 1765–1781. https://doi.org/10.1177/1362361319830029.

Gordon, K., Murin, M., Baykaner, O., Roughan, L. *et al.* (2015) 'A randomised controlled trial of PEGASUS, a psychoeducational programme for young people with high-functioning autism spectrum disorder.' *Journal of Child Psychology and Psychiatry, 56*(4), 468–476. https://doi.org/10.1111/jcpp.12304.

Happé, F. (2015) 'Autism as a neurodevelopmental disorder of mind-reading.' *Journal of the British Academy, 3,* 197–209. doi: 10.5871/jba/003.197.

Hu, Y., Pereira, A.M., Gao, X., Campos, B.M. *et al.* (2021) 'Right temporoparietal junction underlies avoidance of moral transgression in autism spectrum disorder.' *Journal of Neuroscience, 41*(8), 1699–1715. https://doi.org/10.1523/JNEUROSCI.1237-20.2020.

Humphrey, N. & Lewis, S. (2008) '"Make me normal": The views and experiences of pupils on the autistic spectrum in mainstream secondary schools.' *Autism, 12*(1), 23–46. https://doi.org/10.1177/1362361307085267.

Kenny, L., Cribb, S.J. & Pellicano, E. (2018) 'Childhood executive function predicts later autistic features and adaptive behaviour in young autistic people: A 12-year prospective study.' *Journal of Abnormal Child Psychology, 47*(6), 1089–1099. https://doi.org/10.1007/s10802-018-0493-8.

Lombardo, M.V., Barnes, J.L., Wheelwright, S.J. & Baron-Cohen, S. (2007) 'Self-referential cognition and empathy in autism.' *PLoS ONE, 2*(9), e883. https://doi.org/10.1371/journal.pone.0000883.

Makin, C., Hill, V. & Pellicano, E. (2017) 'The primary-to-secondary school transition for children on the autism spectrum: A multi-informant mixed-methods study.' *Autism & Developmental Language Impairments.* https://doi.org/10.1177/2396941516684834.

Milton, D.E.M. (2012) 'On the ontological status of autism: The "double empathy problem".' *Disability & Society, 27*(6), 883–887. doi: 10.1080/09687599.2012.710008.

Nicolaidis, C., Raymaker, D., McDonald, K., Dem, S. *et al.* (2011) 'Collaboration strategies in non-traditional CBPR partnerships: Lessons from an academic-community partnership with autistic self-advocates.' *Progress in Community Health Partnerships: Research, Education, and Action, 5*(2), 143–150.

Parsons, S. (2015) '"Why are we an ignored group?" Mainstream educational experiences and current life satisfaction of adults on the autism spectrum from an online survey.' *International Journal of Inclusive Education, 19*(4), 397–421. doi: 10.1080/136031 16.2014.935814.

Parsons, S., Charman, T., Faulkner, R., Ragan, J., Wallace, S. & Wittemeyer, K. (2013) 'Commentary – bridging the research and practice gap in autism: The importance of creating research partnerships with schools.' *Autism, 17*(3), 268–280. https://doi.org/10.1177/1362361312472068.

Parsons, S., Ivil, K., Kovshoff, H. & Karakosta, E. (2020) '"Seeing is believing": Exploring the perspectives of young autistic children through digital stories.' *Journal of Early Childhood Research.* https://doi.org/10.1177/1476718X20951235.

Pellicano, E. (2010) 'The development of core cognitive skills in autism: A 3-year prospective study.' *Child Development, 81*(5), 1400–1416. https://doi.org/10.1111/j.1467-8624.2010.01481.x.

Pellicano, E. (2017) 'Engaging "Seldom Heard" Individuals in Participatory Autism Research.' In D. Milton & N. Martin (eds) *Autism and Intellectual Disability in Adults* (Vol. 2, pp.29–34). (Learning from success series). Hove: Pavilion.

Pellicano, E., Cribb, S. & Kenny, L. (2020) 'Patterns of Continuity and Change in the Psychosocial Outcomes of Young Autistic People: a Mixed-Methods Study.' *Journal of Abnormal Child Psychology, 48*(2), 301–313.

Pellicano, E., Dinsmore, A. & Charman, T. (2013) *A Future Made Together: Shaping Autism Research in the UK.* London: Institute of Education.

Pellicano, E., Dinsmore, A. & Charman, T. (2014) 'What should autism research focus upon? Community views and priorities from the United Kingdom.' *Autism, 18*(7), 756–770. https://doi.org/10.1177/1362361314529627.

Pellicano, L., Bölte, S. & Stahmer, A. (2018) 'The current illusion of educational inclusion.' *Autism, 22*(4), 386–387. https://doi.org/10.1177/1362361318766166.

Pierce, N.P., O'Reilly, M.F., Sorrells, A.M., Fragale, C.L. *et al.* (2014) 'Ethnicity reporting practices for empirical research in three autism-related journals.' *Journal of Autism and Developmental Disorders, 44*(7), 1507–1519. https://doi.org/10.1007/s10803-014-2041-x.

Rad, M.S., Martingano, A.J. & Ginges, J. (2018) 'Toward a psychology of *Homo sapiens*: Making psychological science more representative of the human population.' *Proceedings of the National Academy of Sciences of the United States of America, 115*(45), 11401–11405. https://doi.org/10.1073/pnas.1721165115.

Richards, N. & Crane, L. (2020) 'The development and feasibility study of a multimodal "Talking Wall" to facilitate the voice of young people with autism and complex needs: A case study in a specialist residential school.' *Journal of Autism and Developmental Disorders, 50*(12), 4267–4279. https://doi.org/10.1007/s10803-020-04476-6.

Totsika, V., Hastings, R.P., Dutton, Y., Worsley, A. *et al.* (2020) 'Types and correlates of school non-attendance in students with autism spectrum disorders.' *Autism, 24*(7), 1639–1649. https://doi.org/10.1177/1362361320916967.

United Nations (1989) *Convention on the Rights of the Child.* www.unicef.org.uk/wp-content/uploads/2010/05/UNCRC_united_nations_convention_on_the_rights_of_the_child.pdf.

West, E.A., Travers, J.C., Kemper, T.D., Liberty, L.M. *et al.* (2016) 'Racial and ethnic diversity of participants in research supporting evidence-based practices for learners with autism spectrum disorder.' *Journal of Special Education, 50*(3), 151–163. https://doi.org/10.1177/0022466916632495.

Whitaker, P. (2002) 'Supporting families of preschool children with autism: What parents want and what helps.' *Autism, 6*(4), 411–426. https://doi.org/10.1177/1362361302006004007.

Wood, R. & Happé, F. (2021) 'What are the views and experiences of autistic teachers? Findings from an online survey in the UK.' *Disability and Society.* https://doi.org/10.1080/09687599.2021.191688

Understanding Parenting and Developing Relationships with Autistic Children and Young People

Editors: Laura Cockburn and Lindsay Panton

Introduction

This chapter focuses on furthering our understanding of autistic children and young people particularly regarding some of the challenges for parents in developing communication and relationships with their children.

Chapter 1 highlighted how our understanding of the autism spectrum has developed over time and also the rise in diagnostic rates. Increasingly, as autism has become one of the key issues in schools, a number of different professionals including teachers and educational psychologists often become involved in working together with parents who have autistic children (diagnosed and undiagnosed).

Making sense of behaviour and communication

Before any diagnostic assessment has even been suggested, children may present with behaviour that is perceived to be complex and challenging, behaviour that professionals and parents struggle to understand. This can prove difficult as there are often many possible reasons to explain children's and young people's behaviour and communication. Assessment and interventions may help to make more sense of the child; it is important that the child is understood.

Even before any assessment, parents may experience significant pressure when asked to explain their child's behaviour. Often parents have already tried to cope with the considerable challenges in managing their child and trying to form a relationship with them; they may be blaming themselves for poor parenting. Indeed parents, particularly mothers, have often been criticised for their children's challenging or atypical behaviour.

When reviewing the history of autism, it is interesting to note that in in his early observations of children's behaviour, Kanner (1949) remarked that there appeared to be a lack of warmth among the parents of autistic children. Kanner went on to use the term 'refrigerator mother' to describe such mothers and hypothesized that the mother's apparent cold and uncaring style had traumatized the child, who subsequently became autistic. This term was adopted by some professionals and continued to be used for many years. Thankfully, it is now discredited among the majority of professionals and it is understood that parenting styles do not cause autism.

There is now good awareness in many countries that autism is a neurodevelopmental condition. While we still do not have conclusive research about the causes of autism, there is strong evidence to suggest that autism can be caused by a variety of factors, most of which affect brain development, and there is some evidence that autism may be genetic. Fletcher-Watson and Happé (2019) provide useful evidence and insights into current thinking and research.

There is no evidence that autism is due to emotional deprivation or the way a person has been brought up. In our experience, parents in particular continue to want to understand their child as they spend a lot of time with them, trying to make sense of their behaviour. However, understanding autism and making sense of a child's behaviour continue to be complex and not necessarily the same around the world and in different communities. Grinker (2008), a parent of an autistic child and an anthropologist, completed research across several different countries when researching autism. He explored how cultural differences may result in varying attitudes and diagnostic processes with regards to autism. This helps to understand some of the experiences of parents, including those in the UK. Culture and diversity may impact the approach to understanding children and the parenting relationship.

In Chapter 9, Venessa Bobb, a parent of two autistic children, highlights how she was misunderstood by different professionals and sent on unhelpful parenting courses. She also talks about how professionals may listen to what is said about the child's behaviour in school rather than investigating the challenges being experienced in the home context.

Autistic people may present with differences in their behaviour and ability to relate to and communicate with others; these issues often prove to be their most significant challenges, though each autistic person is different. Understanding how children develop relationships, particularly with their parents and other family members, can be key in developing our understanding of them. The following contributions will explore these issues further from three different perspectives.

Insights from a professional

The following contribution is the outcome of an interview with Heather Moran by Laura Cockburn to discuss Heather's work on diagnostic assessment and the differentiation between autism spectrum disorders (ASD) and attachment disorders. This interview explores her research and reflections in developing more understanding of autism and attachment.

UNDERSTANDING AUTISM AND ATTACHMENT

Heather Moran

The interview with Heather was designed to assist in developing more understanding of the nuances and challenges of being a parent of children and young people exhibiting a range of challenging behaviour. This particularly focused on making sense of the concept of attachment and how it might relate to autistic children and young people and their parents. Ongoing efforts in developing more understanding of complex children have led to discussions among clinicians and researchers about the similarities or overlap between autism and attachment disorders. Observed behaviour in both these conditions had appeared to be similar. These were seen to be two distinct diagnoses leading to the conclusion that autistic children did not present with 'attachment' in their relationships.

Attachment disorders were understood to link to the individual struggling to attach within their early relationships, which were sometimes associated with abuse or a lack of care. Over time, Heather's work has helped to develop more understanding of this complex issue.

Heather's reflections and learning from being a parent and a professional

Heather qualified as both a clinical psychologist and an educational psychologist; she acknowledged that these roles, together with being a foster and adoptive parent, had impacted her thinking and actions in understanding neurodevelopmental assessment as well as being a parent. She commented that being qualified in these two professions had been helpful in providing more insights between different professions and within the school context.

Heather commented that both professionals and parents are often presented with a child who is confounding them and impacting the family and relationships. She reflected that 20 years ago, discussions about complex children and young people were taking place across professional groups. Professionals from the medical world might be considering neurodevelopmental issues within a more categorical and medicalized perspective. This could be compared to the practice of social workers who would likely be more focused on parenting and attachment issues. It might be the parents, psychologists and school staff who were trying to make sense of this.

On the EP-ASIG study days, Heather talked about being a parent, working with social care and within diagnostic assessment where ASD was being considered. She fostered children with known relationship and behavioural difficulties, and later went on to adopt four children together with her partner. As a result, she had needed to think more about parenting children with potential neurodevelopmental differences. Heather commented, 'We didn't intend to adopt children who would be clinically helpful, but they have been. I've got one child with ADHD and dyslexia. One of the problems with diagnostic processes is that they try and put you in one place at a time.' We discussed how difficult it can be to carry out 'neat' assessments where children are expected to fit into one category.

Heather provided feedback about her experiences of dealing with adolescents who present with challenging behaviour, commenting that at this stage their presentation is often reliant on a secure attachment base. She talked about how one of her children appeared fine during their early years but as a teenager had become much more challenging. She would not have expected the number of difficulties to the degree they had. Heather reflected, 'Adolescents are not very good anyway at accommodating other people's views and adjusting their behaviour unless they feel like it.'

Reviewing the developmental profile as children and young people grow up is important; this can help to reveal differences between autistic children and those with attachment difficulties.

Heather highlighted the fact that parents may be criticized for their child's behaviour even though the parent has usually acknowledged their difficulties in making sense of their child. Providing more understanding of the child or young person is what parents need and can be extremely helpful and empowering to them. Some parents may not know enough about managing complex children because they did not expect this level of knowledge and skill to be needed. Parents do not necessarily understand how children may develop differently from what they expected. She commented that as parents, she and her partner were helped by having been foster carers and working in schools with difficult children. Heather felt that they had developed quite a 'gut instinct' about what might be happening. She commented, 'This can be difficult if you have little understanding of this alternate world. Emotionally, it is a great strain and it's very upsetting.'

Of all experiences, Heather felt that it is most important for parents to look for those ways that they can improve their communication with their child. As parents she and her partner found simple activities, such as going on a long hike, were helpful with one of their children and stressed the importance of having an open mind about how you are going to address some of the problems. She recognized how parents benefit from being supported to understand and develop their communication skills with their children.

Heather commented that research is now showing that autistic children can make attachments and that this often depends on how able the family is to form a relationship with the child. However, as McKenzie and Dallos (2017) highlight, the research in this area is 'complex and contradictory' (p.7). The meta-analysis revealed that while autistic children are less likely to be securely attached to their caregiver, some do develop secure attachments.

Heather stated that this may also depend on the range of challenges that the child has, such as additional medical or learning disabilities. The parent who has previous experience or knowledge of autism may have an easier time than others. She said that she had met some fantastic parents whom, given the level of their child's difficulties, she would have expected to have experienced more obstacles and problems. These experiences, together with a range of work within neurodevelopmental diagnostic assessment as a professional, resulted in Heather and her colleagues engaging in several different conversations and developmental work to assist in deepening our understanding of children and young people.

The development of the Coventry Grid

Heather worked with several other professionals in order to develop the Coventry Grid (Moran 2010), which was further adapted over time. She highlighted that this came from a lot of collaboration with colleagues in her professional setting. They met to discuss the similarities and differences between children on the autism spectrum and children with attachment problems, together with their responses to interventions. The Grid was developed to try to identify differences between the two groups. It was also noted that there would likely be a number of children who might have both autism and attachment difficulties.

Heather described the Coventry Grid as an attempt to differentiate between autism and attachment problems based on clinical work with children rather than research. She focused on a number of children and young people where it was difficult to assess whether or not they were autistic or if they had an attachment disorder, recognizing that at times the behaviour presented as remarkably similar, and this was confusing. The Grid has proved useful to clinicians and professionals working with children and adolescents. Heather emphasized that the Grid was always meant to be 'work in progress' and was never meant to be conclusive. She commented that she and her colleagues wanted to encourage both practitioners and researchers to investigate this diagnostic issue. Since the original paper was written, a number of adaptations have been published which have helped to further develop what Heather had been hoping for.

In 2017, the Coventry Grid was updated and 'modified' (Flackhill *et al.* 2017) and named 'Version 2' (Moran 2015). A group of speech and language therapists who worked in youth justice provided updates, and additional descriptors were added to some sections, together with some small changes. The Grid was developed too into an interview format to support clinicians to be able to use it during the assessment process. Eaton, Duncan and Hesketh (2017) further modified the Coventry Grid interview by including information on the pathological demand avoidant (PDA) profile. An adult version (Cox *et al.* 2019) was developed too through collaboration of interested clinicians. This may be useful to review when working with older young people as well as adults.

Heather wanted to create interest and discussion in this complex area to support more understanding of children and young people. Heather's work has always been influenced by her efforts to collaborate with both parents and professionals. She wanted to use their observations and reflections to assist in further understanding children and young people presenting with a range of complex needs. Heather continues to encourage feedback from different people around the world by leaving her contact on her website (see References). She still receives emails from parents and professionals that provide interesting feedback.

Learning from the Coventry Grid

On the study day, Heather's presentation supported the audience in helping them to reflect on some of the similarities and differences between attachment and autism. She highlighted that discriminating between autism and attachment disorder is not always easy or possible and that focused observations, based on certain questions, seems to be one of the best ways to help to discriminate within complex casework. For example, she highlighted that in the area of attachment there is often a need to address the child's 'distance and dependence', and also that there is usually more of a need to address environmental stressors when working with autistic children.

Heather advised caution when carrying out neurodevelopmental diagnostic work with both adopted and foster children: 'We should use terms wisely, with evidence to back up a diagnosis.' She provided some useful questions to help to think more about the potential differences between the two groups of children being discussed. These may also be interesting to school staff, other professionals and parents:

- *Flexibility:* what are the children flexible about?

- *Play:* what is their choice of toys and what do they do with them?

- *Social interaction:* what is their intention underlying interaction?

- *Theory of mind:* does the child seem to be trying to work people out?

- *Communication:* are they aware of their audience?

- *Emotional regulation:* what triggers a stress reaction?

- *Executive function:* do emotions affect skills and recall?

Heather also highlighted that both autistic children and children with attachment challenges could be supported by using some similar interventions such as sensitive care, predictability and direct teaching in social skills, relationships and emotional regulation.

Heather suggested that more detailed analysis of the key factors involved in parenting and developing relationships might be helpful. These could include factors such as parent and child temperament, the context of the family, and the child's previous background. Context and sociocultural issues such as being homeless or living in a hostel would undoubtedly impact the behaviour and emotions of all children and other family members. This highlights the importance of understanding the child's background and social context.

Heather commented that if she could go back and change one thing, she would make it clearer that her original paper about the Coventry Grid was about raising the issue rather than people thinking that she and her team had all the answers. She tried to be as open as possible, and the idea was to make the discussion more public (for both parents and professionals). She wanted to ensure that there was discussion about whether autism or attachment, or both, were likely to be impacting a child's development. Heather shared her learning from her experience:

- We should expect that problems overlap across mental health and neurodevelopmental conditions.

- We should use interventions across diagnoses, if helpful.

- We should assess children's challenges rather than focusing on them meeting diagnostic criteria.

- If we are not careful, we will spend all our resources assessing rather than helping children and young people.

Heather's knowledge of the educational context helped to provide further reflections on how adults in school can also assist in understanding children who may be perceived as challenging. Teachers may build on a framework using 'plan, do and review' which can help in understanding the impact of different interventions. Children who present primarily with attachment difficulties may benefit from lots of nurture and understanding. In comparison, autistic children are more likely to need more specific autism-friendly interventions such as Social Stories and visual supports (see Chapter 1). Across the two groups of children, it will be important to recognize how each child expresses their anxiety, as this can be manifested in many different ways.

Summary and suggestions for moving forward

During the interview, Heather emphasized the timeline linked to our understanding of autism and reflected that we have come a long way in terms of making sense of neurodevelopmental conditions. She reflected that it is important to remember that since 2010 there has been a great deal of development in further understanding autism and the different profiles (see Chapter 1). In addition, there have been further developments in understanding attachment and any related difficulties. We discussed how different the work with older children compared to younger children could be. More is now known about attachment disorder, and the interventions being developed focus on developing and strengthening emotional relationships for both autistic children and others.

Heather summarized how research has shown that autistic children can form good attachments to people and transfer those attachments to others. Difficulties in relationships might link to the parents' experiences of managing and parenting children and whether the child had additional difficulties. More recent research highlights the importance of understanding the overall profile of needs of children and young people rather than the focus being only on the diagnostic label. Heather commented how helpful it can be to develop more understanding of the child's developmental profile. This can potentially help to bring more insight into what presents as challenging behaviour and we can then work on appropriate interventions leading to more supportive and collaborative relationships.

Heather has tried to bring more of a formulation-based approach (Johnstone & Dallos 2014) to understanding autistic people rather than categorizing them into a specific diagnosis. As discussed in Chapter 1, developing a formulation can be useful in explaining more about the reasons for children's differences. McKenzie and Dallos (2017) reviewed the research linking to understanding autism and attachment. They also concluded that assessments based on formulation may be helpful in these cases. They highlighted that consideration of a number of issues, including developmental and relational factors, is needed.

Heather's recent work has been focused on 'Dimensions of Health and Well-being'.[1] The Dimensions Tool is a free online tool providing personalized information to help support a person's well-being and mental health and understand their overall needs.

Insights from researchers

In the current chapter, we have discussed how parent–child interaction and management can be significantly impacted where a child presents with challenging behaviour and communication difficulties. Over time, there have been a number of different approaches developed to support parents and other adults, to help improve interaction and communication with autistic children.

Video Interactive Guidance (VIG) has been one approach which has been used by a number of different professionals. Vicky Slonims has worked closely together with other researchers to investigate the use of parent–child interaction (PCI) approaches, incorporating the use of video feedback specifically with autistic children.

CAN PARENT-CHILD INTERACTION (PCI) TREATMENT HELP YOUNG CHILDREN WITH AUTISM?

Vicky Slonims and Jennifer Baulcomb

Intervention approaches

Intervention approaches to support autistic children, particularly in the early years, often seek to address core difficulties such as impairment in the development of social communication which spontaneously occurs in most infants. The National Institute for Health and Care Excellence (NICE 2017) guideline for support and management of autism in under-19s recommends the consideration of interventions for the core features of autism. These include play-based strategies with parents, carers and teachers to increase joint attention, engagement and reciprocal communication in the child or young person. A recent systematic review and meta-analysis of early interventions for Autism noted that they

---

1   https://dimensions.covwarkpt.nhs.uk

are informed by frameworks that include behavioural, developmental, naturalistic, environmental, and sensory or technological approaches (Sandbank *et al.* 2020).

PCI approaches and video feedback

An area of increasing interest in the field of autism intervention is the use of PCI approaches, incorporating the use of video feedback. The expectation is that PCI interventions can address difficulties in social interaction and communication and might enhance the quality of the relationship between parent and child.

Research on typical parent–infant interaction over many years established the basis of our understanding of this important early relationship and introduced the term *primary intersubjectivity,* defined as a basic shared understanding between two individuals, usually the infant and caregiver (see Trevarthen & Aitken 2001 for a review). Researchers in the Netherlands developed Video Interaction Guidance (VIG) in the context of attachment-based therapy (Juffer, Bakermans-Kranenburg & van IJzendoorn 2012, 2017), and subsequently the strategy has been adopted in many 'contexts', for example in education, maternity, child development and social care settings where parent–child interaction is at risk or difficult to establish. Parents are filmed interacting with their child and they then watch themselves while being supported by a trained practitioner. Together they observe and comment on positive aspects of the parent's behaviour or language that facilitate interaction, and by this means, positive reflections help to shape and develop the parent's skills in interacting with their child (Kennedy, Landor & Todd 2010). There is growing evidence that VIG supports the development of the relationship between a parent and their child, in terms of increasing parent sensitivity (Barlow & Schrader McMillan 2010) and positive parenting skills (Fukkink 2008).

Research into parent–child interaction indicates that when an infant provides weak or ambiguous communication signals there may be difficulty establishing a good 'communicative fit' (Spiker, Boyce & Boyce 2002). This can result in reduced meshing (asynchrony) and parental perplexity since parent–child interaction is usually intuitive and automatically follows from dyadic interaction. In the absence of opportunities to respond to their infant, parents may 'fill the gaps' and resort to a more didactic style or perhaps become despondent and less communicative. If parents increase their initiations, infants may have fewer opportunities to initiate and practise their expressive skills. Interactions may, thus, unintentionally become less reciprocal. Additional support may be required to assist parents to identify and respond to weak or ambiguous behaviours, for example to recognize communication signals in a child who has sensory impairment (deaf, blind) or has a physical impairment or neurodevelopmental disorder affecting communication.

Some researchers interested in enhancing social communication in autistic children have developed interventions with the aim of helping to create the typical exchanges that occur in parent–infant interactions with parents whose children who do not develop these behaviours spontaneously.

The Preschool Autism Communication Trial (PACT) (Green *et al.* 2010) was a randomized controlled trial of a parent-mediated social communication intervention for preschool autistic children. The parent or carer in the intervention group received 18 one-to-one clinic or home-based sessions with a therapist and their child over a period of 12 months. The aim of the intervention was to increase parental sensitivity and responsiveness to child communication. The hypothesis was that this might reduce autism symptoms assessed using the Autism Diagnostic Observation Schedule (ADOS) (Lord *et al.* 2000).

The manualized treatment was delivered consistently across three sites in the UK (North West location, North East location, and a South East location). Each session consisted of a short discussion of progress during the intervening period using a video of the parent and child playing. This provided an opportunity for the parent to watch the video alongside the therapist without comment, and then there was a period of feedback and discussion prior to writing the programme for the following period. PACT has six stages: the first three are focused on the foundations of interaction and parent-sensitive responding (1. Establishing shared attention; 2. Developing parental synchronicity and sensitivity; and 3. Focusing on the parent's language to the child). The final three stages focus on enhancing emerging communication (4. Establishing routines and anticipation; 5. Increasing the child's communication functions; and 6. Helping the parent to expand the child's language and develop conversations). Video feedback methods were used to modify parent–child interaction.

PACT is a manualized intervention with hierarchical stages, but it differs from many programmes in that there is no curriculum or prescribed content for teaching. The therapist evaluates the interaction between each parent and child and provides a uniquely tailored intervention that focuses on their specific abilities or difficulties. There are specified competencies for child and parent before the next stage is introduced but parents and children move at their own pace and there is no requirement to progress through stages. Some families will move through all stages, but others may remain at the very earliest levels throughout. Parents are not aware of the entire programme and are only introduced to new goals as they become appropriate. This avoids any pressure or risk of a sense of failure in dyads where there are significant barriers to progress.

Study results indicated that the intervention strongly influenced behaviour in the majority of parent–child dyads. There were modest but non-significant reductions of autism symptoms with non-treated children. There was a significant increase in both parent synchrony and child initiations – the behaviours of interest in terms of the foundations of interaction and potentially in the parent–child relationship. A mediation analysis (Pickles *et al.* 2015) demonstrated that change in parent synchrony led to an increase in child initiation, thus supporting this theoretical approach (see Figure 3.1). A follow-up study of the same cohort by Pickles *et al.* (2016) found sustained reduction in child autism symptoms and improved social communication with parents, which remained at nearly six years after the end of treatment. These findings support the potentially long-term effects and value of early parent-mediated interventions for autism. Figure 3.1 provides a visual overview of the theoretical mechanism to support improvements in child–parent interaction.

Research with very young infants and parents has revealed several infant behavioural and neural atypicalities, such as attention to social information (Chawarska, Macari & Shic 2013) and level of attention to eyes (Jones & Klin 2013), that co-occur with alterations in parent–infant interactions from at least eight months of age (Wan *et al.* 2012), and by 14 months are associated with a diagnosis of ASD at 3 years (Wan *et al.* 2013). These findings and those with children with other neurodevelopmental disorders (Slonims, Cox & McConachie 2006) suggest that aspects of behaviour in infants diverging from typical development can affect the parent–child interaction on which social, intellectual and communication development depends.

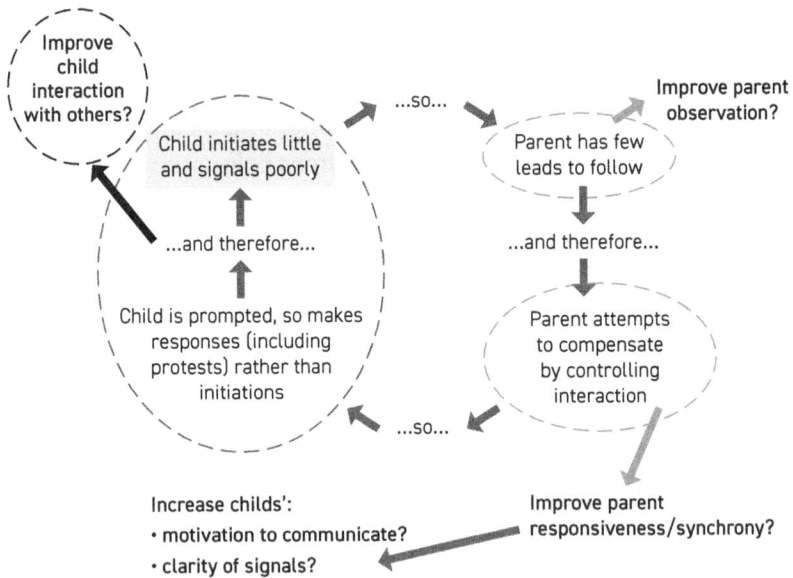

Figure 3.1: Parent-mediated, communication-focused intervention

A small randomized control trial (RCT) with 54 families of infants at familial risk of autism aged seven to ten months delivered an amalgamation of the PACT treatment modified for infants and the Video Interaction for Promoting Positive Parenting (VIPP PCI) treatment (Green *et al.* 2015). Twenty-eight families receiving the intervention had six home-based sessions with an additional six booster sessions to allow for any modifications needed for infants with possible neurodisability. The sessions focused on helping parents to interpret the infants' behaviour and recognize their intentions, develop sequences of sensitive responding during everyday activities, support emotional attunement and enhance patterns of verbal and non-verbal interaction. The study found a pattern of moderate but not significantly decreased early autism symptoms and improved child dyadic attentiveness, communication, initiation and parent non-directiveness. However, this study was not sufficiently large to provide strong evidence.

Recent work exploring the value to parents of the PACT intervention reported positive changes in their interaction and relationship with their child and improvements to their child's communication and interaction. Some also highlighted poignant realizations and emotional challenges associated with taking part in the therapy, but some practical difficulties were also emphasized (Leadbitter *et al.* 2020).

The sum of these findings supports the purported mechanism of increased parent synchrony leading to increased child initiations for children with autism. Parents appear to recognize and value these improvements in their children.

Insights from parents

In the next section, Carrie Grant provides reflections and experiences of being a parent of four children and encourages the reader to reflect on the joys and challenges of parenthood and the process of developing relationships with neurodivergent children and young people. She also includes insights from David Grant, her husband and father of the children.

ENTERING YOUR CHILD'S WORLD

Carrie Grant

If you talk to most parents/carers before they have children, they will tell you they have very definite expectations about how they will raise their child – a style that is loosely based on what did or didn't work in their own childhood, and if they are in a parenting partnership, then a combination of the two partners' experiences.

Parenting neurodiverse children calls for a different approach. We need to discover a highly individualized and micro-adaptable way of doing things. One-size-fits-all won't work. The uniqueness is magnified in these amazing children, creating mums, dads and carers who become shapeshifting parents. The evolution in us becoming the best parents for our children has been very challenging but we don't have the option to give up, because these are our precious children, and we love them, no matter how challenged we are.

Our four children have a variety of needs; two are autistic. We have had to find out who each child is and what they need for their own individual growth, enabling them to discover their best selves. Society dictates a standard set of parental behaviours. You put the right ingredients in, you work to the recipe and hey presto, you get cookie-cutter, perfect kids. Our children are not like this: they don't work to the normal recipe, they are different. If we constantly demand that our children conform to a neurotypical stereotype, very soon they will begin to break. The sooner we let go of the stringent narrow demands of societal pressure the better. Our children need an open field not a tightrope.

As we walk the new path towards becoming shapeshifting parents, our concepts of parenting are expanded. If there is any grief in having neurodiverse children, it is knowing that as parents and carers we will walk a lonely path that most people will not understand and will judge us for. We have the added pressure of having to educate society, our family and friends on why we are doing things the way we are. Society, culture, faith and our own individual belief systems often bring an expectation of a certain type of parenting and sadly often a rule-bound rigidity that goes along with the thinking. It's important that we remain resolute in our commitment to help our child and understanding what is best for them. This becomes even more important once our children are in school, especially if it's mainstream school. Sadly, it is at this point that many of us find our greatest battle is not within the home but in the outside world. Sometimes it is only in the special needs community that you will find other parents/carers who really get it. A new type of family support system rises up.

Also, to add at this point, I spend a lot of time questioning why and how and what I'm doing. I often get things wrong. I listen a lot to other special needs parents and professionals to glean as much information as I can, and I still have a huge amount to learn. Doubt leads to discovery.

Quality of relationships

Part of our growth as parents has been in our understanding of how people love. Not all people love in the same way, and no one's way of loving should be diminished or overlooked. One of my children receives love in very practical ways, another with affection, one needs to chat incessantly, and another just wants to share the silence. If I decide I will only share the silence with the chatty child, they are going to find the relationship very unfulfilling. If I demand that my child is only able to reciprocate love the way I love, we will both miss out.

It really is about trusting the attachment, trusting that it is enough, that as parents we are enough. The way our children love is the doorway to connection. Sometimes our children have very hidden doorways and it's here that we begin the adventure of discovering a route in. When we find the place of mutual connection, it's magical and a deep intimacy is achieved.

Finding the baseline

We look for our child's personal usual baseline for mood, communication, interaction and behaviour and then work from that place. Our children may have a consistent low mood, anxiety or be constantly fidgety brained, so knowing their general landscape and understanding them from this position is really helpful. One of our autistic children hates to be asked to do something because they hate to be demanded of in any way. Our adopted child, however, may have the same response to being asked to do something but for totally different reasons. Perhaps he fears he may fail at the request and that could lead to catastrophic results. With the first child, we learn to negotiate, with the second child, we work at building the trust relationship.

The long game

One thing we have realized is that we are playing the long game. Quick results are rare with our children, which has a direct impact on how we strategize. We've observed that our children are about five years younger in terms of maturity than their actual age. This means their bodies are on a par with their peers but their inner world is younger. Consistency in parenting is paramount, and we must repetitively reinforce until something clicks. This repetition could be challenging their beliefs about themselves, specific behaviours or practical learning, from tying shoelaces to believing they are 'enough' – and all points in between.

Parental unity

Obviously, there are many different family set-ups for parent/carers and many different environments: singles, partners, separated with or without other children, living in poverty or with disability and so on. Unity may need to be achieved across a number of relationships depending on your own personal situation. One of the hardest challenges David and I have faced is attempting to get on the same page with our parenting styles. We both came from strict upbringings and we were determined that our children would have the same style of upbringing as us. I realized in about 2009 things needed to change. David fully caught up in about 2012. Those three years were hell! Both of us were able to make completely logical arguments for our contrasting positions but it took time for us both to let go of our conditioning and to put each child into the middle and ask, 'What is best for this child?' and 'What does this child need?'

To begin with it felt like a loss of parental control: our leadership felt undermined. We wanted to rid ourselves of being the passive or aggressive parent and find the middle ground. Eventually we found it and to this day it's continually updated and in process. We are always up for learning and mindset changes. We remain curious about what it means to parent each child through every season of their lives. We welcome new ideas and are keen to try things out to see if something different works better for our child. Often we are wrong, but we keep trying.

Prioritizing behaviours

We have three steps we look at in our children's behaviours and responses:

1. We try not to sweat the small stuff, and we let go of the rules and write some new, highly flexible ones. If my child does not do homework, their bedroom is a mess or they only ate three out of their five-a-day fruit and veg, do I need to take them to task about this? On one level, everything in me wants to say, 'Yes you must push for all of this,' but when we are perhaps trying to keep a child off suicide watch or from self-harming, these things become less important. Something we have noticed with our two autistic children is that the more they are weighed down by demands the worse their mental health becomes; they really do crumble under the weight.

2. We identify the behaviours we really need to work on. There are often a lot of things in this second area but as parents we decide the order of priority.

3. We identify the top priority for change. With neurodiverse children we must be exceedingly careful that we are not trying to change something that is an autistic trait. We want our autistic children to be their autistic selves. If a child hits out, swears, slams doors and stomps off, we may need to break all of those behaviours down. If you visit our home and you see a child has sworn and stomped off, you may be shocked. In our world, we

are celebrating the result. They didn't hit out or throw anything. They are learning self-control, self-regulating and how to communicate better. Our visitors may think we are terrible parents, but we are leading well and between us and our children we are working to plan! Together with our children, we strategize and find ways through. This collaborative approach takes the shame and judgement out of challenging behaviours. We all have stuff we need to work on.

No punishments or rewards

David and I have taken out all punishments and rewards. To begin with this felt like our entire armoury had been removed! Punishments bring shame, and shame is the 'appendix of the mind' – totally unnecessary. Rewards can perpetuate anxiety, fear of loss or not being enough. Understanding we have behaved wrongly is not the same as the overwhelming unravelling that so often accompanies shame. We have noticed that shame often leads to impulsive and compulsive behaviour, neither of which is helpful; in fact it can lead to addictive behaviour. When we removed punishments and rewards from our children, very quickly we saw a different pattern emerging which included apology, discussion around how to lessen the behaviours and why they might be occurring in the first place. Our children began to problem-solve because it was logical to do so. A safe, judgement-free environment had been set. In place of rewards, our children are regularly given little gifts that mark our love for them, letting them know we are always thinking about them.

They may ask, 'Why did you give me this?'

We answer, 'Because we love you.'

Our love is shown to be unconditional.

Holding the space?

But what happens when you have a very demand-avoidant child? When it feels as if nothing works? A demand-avoidant child may need to control things but underneath the refusal to cooperate there is an intense desire to know they are 'held' in their space, that they are safe and that there are boundaries. It's painful to watch our children refuse even their own demands, mitigating against their own desires even when they know they desperately want to do something. There is a direct co-relation between anxiety, demand and toleration. If the anxiety can be lowered, the toleration goes up and the demands can be greater. In our children, we make minute-by-minute judgements on what they can manage. With our autistic child who has been out of school for three years, the demand to interact with the teaching assistant who comes to the house is always a priority because we know it makes that child feel so much better when they do. However, some days we have to accept they won't leave their bedroom and they just cannot manage to come downstairs. This child has been so traumatized by school, we understand the landscape but we also have to try to draw them back out into the world very, very slowly. More often than not it's two steps forward and one step back.

The pause

In every interaction we have with our children, we have learned to pause before we respond. This has become a way of life. Questions we put to ourselves as we interact include:

- Am I reading my child?
- Am I listening to their words, noises, sighs or groans?
- What am I observing in their body language?
- Is this early morning? How do they feel about mornings?
- Is this school anxiety?
- Is it late at night? Are they tired?
- Are they hungry?
- Are they too hot/cold?
- What outside stressors are happening? Relationships and so on?
- We also read our own gut instincts too. What is this child 'giving off' that I cannot see or hear but I feel? What are they trying to tell me? Like many neurotypical people, autistic people may not always be able to find the words to express their inner thoughts, so we have to read and pick up on other cues.

In times of conflict, we encourage everyone to slow the pace of conversation as it helps us all process our thinking a bit better – the pauses help.

Increasing presence

One of the things we have found really difficult is knowing how to meet the needs of a suicidal teenager, and we have had two so far. Sometimes we have to accept we cannot shift or change someone; sometimes we cannot influence their thinking, and we feel powerless; sometimes we just have to sit with them in their space. There is certainly a time to leave them alone, but we have also found increasing our presence without any demands or even words helps. I remember when I first went into my child's bedroom and sat myself down silently. At first, they told me to go away and I said I would leave in one minute, then over time, I increased this to two or three minutes. After a while they got used to me coming into their space and just sitting for a few minutes and still later began to ask me to come in and sit with them.

They would say something like, 'I feel bad.'

I would say, 'I know, it's hard, you feel bad.'

Sometimes just being heard is enough to get them through that moment. None of us are heard enough but on a societal and educational level these particular children are some of the most unheard.

Mirroring

Sometimes I wish I could climb into the skin of my child and lead them out of their crisis moments. When words fail, gestures fail, adjustments fail, the weight on everyone is immense. My child may crawl into a ball on the floor and scream. I know at this moment nothing I do or say will be right so sometimes I just crawl into a ball right next to them on the floor. After a time, I might make calming sounds, reaching out with groans when words aren't enough. Occasionally, when the mood is lighter, my child and I will sit face to face, our foreheads and noses touching, just gently breathing in unison. These moments are precious and no words are necessary.

Remembering who we are

Climbing into my child's world is so important but, equally, I regularly look in the mirror and tell myself: I am not my child, I am not anxious, I am well, I am leading. It's important that our empathetic heart doesn't overtake us, leaving us identity-less. We must remember who we are, apart from our children – our desires, our innate gifts, our passions and drivers. When we are full-time carers, it's hard to find time but if we are living in a period of crisis it is important that we recover our own mental health. In the midst of uncertainty, chatting to other parents has been a lifeline for us. A number of years ago David and I started a support group for families with autistic girls (including non-binary and transgender) and this group has sustained us through some of our darkest times. The group has also birthed a separate space for our children to meet other autistic children like them. With many of the group's children attending mainstream school, this has often been their first encounter with other autistic children.

Identity

Helping our child to fully embrace their autistic self is often a long journey. It is rare for any of us to just be one thing. The intersections of life are fascinating and allow for a rich culture to emerge. Children may be autistic or have ADHD but they may also be adopted; they may be non-binary or transgender, Afro-Caribbean, Asian or mixed race; they may be gay or queer or pansexual; they may have faith or none. Our children are discovering their identity in many ways. They know they are different. As parents, we encourage them to explore their identity without fear or judgement. With autism, sadly, society has such a poor, distorted and uninformed view of autistic people that it's unsurprising our children shy away from the diagnosis. Our autistic children have so much to offer the world, and their worldview should be valued; they should be cherished and understood. When our children grow in their understanding of who they are and learn to stand, self-advocate and take their place confidently in society, they enrich the world. This is what we as parents pledge to lead them towards.

Chapter conclusion

This chapter has explored ways in which we can develop a deeper understanding and provide effective support to autistic children, particularly in relation to their communication and interaction. The focus has been on recognizing the importance of relationships and how complex these can be.

If practitioners have a greater understanding of the challenges involved in being a parent of an autistic child, they may be encouraged to question how parents are supported. Just as other parent contributors to this book have done, Carrie Grant discussed her journey as a parent and the importance of valuing her own skills, insights and learning.

Fortunately, research and developments in clinical practice have begun to help parents feel less blamed and responsible for their children's challenging behaviour. New developments in research and the use of technology have helped us to recognize different ways of improving relationships with autistic children. Vicky Slonims and Jennifer Baulcomb have provided a helpful overview of an increasing interest area in the field of autism intervention and technology using Parent Child Interaction (PCI) approaches, incorporating the use of video feedback. The expectation is that PCI interventions can address difficulties in social interaction and communication and might enhance the quality of the relationship between parent and child. The positive findings support the potentially long-term effects and value of early parent-mediated interventions for autism. In addition, parents appear to recognize and value these improvements in their children. EPs (e.g., Kennedy *et al.* 2010) have already been using VIG in several different contexts and this has proved useful in supporting their work with autistic children and young people, including 'attuned interaction'. Such interventions might be helpful with more children in schools if professionals and parents develop greater understanding of this way of observing and understanding children's behaviour and communication.

We hope that this chapter will encourage parents and professionals to recognize that parenting neurodiverse children needs to include thinking 'out of the box'. Professionals need to be aware of the importance of developing support and collaboration together with parents and recognize the complex process of being a parent. There are many factors that can affect autistic children and young people. These may impact on their relationship with parents as well as with other professionals, including in the school environment. Heather Moran highlighted how the use of formulation within assessments helps to improve professional practice as this needs to include the 'bigger picture', that is, consideration of social context and culture together with developmental and relational factors that may contribute to how the child presents and interacts with others.

POINTS FOR REFLECTION

☞ Assessments may be most helpful and informative when they are based on formulation, and provide a contextual view in terms of family culture and relationships in and out of the home (i.e., the 'bigger picture').

☞ The need to take account of the parents/carers' experiences and developmental history is central in any understanding of behaviour and communication.

☞ Practitioners and, perhaps, particularly EPs have a key role in challenging barriers, prejudices and misconceptions. (See Chapter 9 for a further exploration of these issues.)

Resources

Some references can be found on Heather Moran's website. Accessed 22/04/2021 at www.drawingtheidealself.co.uk/index.php?p=1_7.

Dimensions. Accessed 22/04/2021 at https://dimensions.covwarkpt.nhs.uk.

National Autistic Society. Accessed 20/02/2021 at www.autism.org.uk/advice-and-guidance/what-is-autism/the-causes-of-autism.

References

Barlow, J. & Schrader McMillan, A. (2010) *Safeguarding Children from Emotional Maltreatment: What Works*. London: Jessica Kingsley Publishers.

Chawarska, K., Macari, S. & Shic, F. (2013) 'Decreased spontaneous attention to social scenes in 6-month-old infants later diagnosed with autism spectrum disorders.' *Biological Psychiatry, 74*(3), 195–203.

Cox, C., Bulluss, E., Chapman, F., Cookson, A. & Sharp, A. (2019) 'The Coventry Grid for Adults: A tool to guide clinicians in differentiating complex trauma and autism.' *Good Autism Practice, 20*(1), 76–87.

Eaton, J., Duncan, K. & Hesketh, N. (2017) 'Modification of the Coventry Grid Interview (Flackhill *et al.* 2017) to include the pathological demand avoidant profile.' *Good Autism Practice, 19*(2), 12–24.

Flackhill, C., James, S., Milton, K. & Soppitt, R. (2017) 'The Coventry Grid Interview (CGI): Exploring autism and attachment difficulties.' *Good Autism Practice, 18*(1), 62–80.

Fletcher-Watson, S. & Happé, F. (2019) *Autism: A New Introduction to Psychological Theory and Current Debate*. London: Routledge.

Fukkink, R.G. (2008) 'Video feedback in the widescreen: A meta-analysis of family programs.' *Clinical Psychology Review, 28*(6), 904–916.

Green, J., Charman, T., McConachie, H., Aldred, C. *et al.* (2010) 'Parent-mediated communication-focused treatment in children with autism (PACT): A randomised controlled trial.' *The Lancet, 375*(9732), 2152–2160.

Green, J., Charman, T., Pickles, A., Wan, M.W. *et al.* (2015) 'Parent-mediated intervention versus no intervention for infants at high risk of autism: A parallel, single-blind, randomised trial.' *The Lancet Psychiatry, 2*(2), 133–140.

Grinker, R. (2008) *Unstrange Minds: A Father Remaps the World of Autism.* London: Icon Books.

Johnstone, L. & Dallos, R. (2014, first edition 2006) (eds) *Formulation in Psychology and Psychotherapy.* London: Routledge.

Jones, W. & Klin, A. (2013) 'Attention to eyes is present but in decline in 2–6-month-old infants later diagnosed with autism.' *Nature, 504*(7480), 427–431.

Juffer, F., Bakermans-Kranenburg, M.J. & van IJzendoorn, M.H. (eds.) (2012) *Promoting Positive Parenting: An Attachment-Based Intervention.* New York, NY: Taylor and Francis.

Juffer, F., Bakermans-Kranenburg, M.J. & van IJzendoorn, M.H. (2017) 'Pairing attachment theory and social learning theory in video-feedback intervention to promote positive parenting.' *Current Opinion in Psychology, 15,* 189–194.

Kanner, L. (1949) 'Problems of nosology and psychodynamics in early childhood autism.' *American Journal of Orthopsychiatry, 19*(3), 416–426.

Kennedy, H., Landor, M. & Todd. L. (2010) 'Video Interaction Guidance as a method to promote secure attachment.' *Educational and Child Psychology, 27*(3), 59–72.

Leadbitter, K., Macdonald, W., Taylor, C. & Buckle, K.L. (2020) 'Parent perceptions of participation in a parent-mediated communication-focussed intervention with their young child with autism spectrum disorder.' *Autism, 24*(8), 2129–2141.

Lord, C., Risi, S., Lambrecht, L., Cook, E.H., Jr. *et al.* (2000) 'The Autism Diagnostic Observation Schedule-Generic: A standard measure of social and communication deficits associated with the spectrum of autism.' *Journal of Autism and Developmental Disorders, 30*(3), 205–223.

McKenzie, R. & Dallos, R. (2017) 'Autism and attachment difficulties: Overlap of symptoms, implications and innovative solutions.' *Clinical Child Psychology and Psychiatry, 22*(4), 632–648.

Moran, H.J. (2010) 'Clinical observations of the differences between children in the autism spectrum and those with attachment problems: The Coventry Grid.' *Good Autism Practice, 11*(2), 46–59.

Moran, H.J. (2015) *The Coventry Grid Version 2* (modified version). Accessed 22/04/2021 at www2.oxfordshire.gov.uk/cms/sites/default/files/folders/documents/virtualschool/processesandforms/resourcesandpublications/CoventryGrid.pdf.

National Institute for Health and Care Excellence (UK) (2017) *Autism Spectrum Disorder in Under-19s: Recognition, Referral and Diagnosis.* Accessed 22/04/2021 at www.nice.org.uk/guidance/cg128.

Pickles, A., Harris, V., Green, J., Aldred, C. *et al.* (2015) 'Treatment mechanism in the MRC Preschool Autism Communication Trial: Implications for study design and parent-focussed therapy for children.' *Journal of Child Psychology and Psychiatry, and Allied Disciplines, 56*(2), 162–170.

Pickles, A., Le Couteur, A., Leadbitter, K., Salomone, E. *et al.* (2016) 'Parent-mediated social communication therapy for young children with autism (PACT): Long-term follow-up of a randomised controlled trial.' *The Lancet, 388*(10059), 2501–2509.

Sandbank, M., Bottema-Beutel, K., Crowley, S., Cassidy, M. *et al.* (2020) 'Project AIM: Autism intervention meta-analysis for studies of young children.' *Psychological Bulletin, 146*(1), 1–29.

Slonims, V., Cox, A. & McConachie, H. (2006) 'Analysis of mother-infant interaction in infants with Down syndrome and typically developing infants.' *American Journal on Mental Retardation, 3*(4), 273–289.

Spiker, D., Boyce, G.C. & Boyce, L.K. (2002) 'Parent-child interactions when young children have disabilities.' *International Review of Research in Mental Retardation, 25,* 35–70.

Trevarthen, C. & Aitken, K.J. (2001) 'Infant intersubjectivity: Research, theory, and clinical applications.' *Journal of Child Psychology and Psychiatry, and Allied Disciplines, 42*(1), 3–48.

Wan, M.W., Green, J., Elsabbagh, M., Johnson, M., Charman, T. & Plummer, F. (2012) 'Parent-infant interaction in infant siblings at risk of autism.' *Research in Developmental Disabilities, 33*(3), 924–932.

Wan, M.W., Green, J., Elsabbagh, M., Johnson, M., Charman, T., Plummer, F. & the BASIS Team (2013) 'Quality of interaction between at-risk infants and caregiver at 12–15 months is associated with three-year autism outcome.' *Journal of Child Psychology and Psychiatry, 54*, 763–771.

CHAPTER 4

Challenging Behaviour or Behaviour that Challenges Us?

Editor: Judith Gainsborough

Introduction

The subject of behaviour that is perceived to be challenging is a vast and diverse one. Indeed, many volumes have been written on the subject. This one chapter cannot provide an all-encompassing overview, but it can explore some very different perspectives. All three perspectives have, at their core, systematic planning to develop a profile of a child in order to understand better a child's needs and how to help. They also represent the notable shift in emphasis away from labelling a child's behaviour as 'challenging' and towards a much more positive and constructive explanation based on concepts such as emotional regulation and engagement.

All contributors discuss the importance of improving engagement for autistic learners, and the statistics on school exclusions are mentioned by Scot Greathead and Rhiannon Yates. Chapter 7's exploration of autism and the criminal justice system also explores these statistics and the unfortunate links between exclusion and later involvement with the CJS. This ably demonstrates the importance of early identification and systematic frameworks for intervention as well as effective involvement and support of families and multidisciplinary working.

In this chapter, Scot and Rhiannon present a bio-ecological model, plotting both personal characteristics and factors in the environment in order to develop a greater understanding of a child's profile and also to provide detailed information about the reasons for the child's behaviour. This can then inform interventions to increase the child's level of engagement.

Next, Phil Christie provides an overview and insights into pathological demand avoidance (PDA). Phil's work in developing the understanding of PDA and supporting it has been tireless and he describes an immensely useful account of the history of PDA together with many of the interventions that are key to working with children and young people described as having a PDA profile. It should be noted that the lack of research on PDA presents challenges for many in the medical community and other professionals. As Phil has highlighted, there continues to be some controversy about the place of PDA within classification systems. There are no agreed diagnostic algorithms to help to determine diagnostic criteria. Some parents and professionals have been a driving force behind promoting the diagnostic term 'PDA' in clinical practice as a result of their recognizing how the profile and suggested interventions have had a significant impact. Phil stresses the importance of improving our understanding of an individual's profile and making the adaptations needed to enhance the educational experience and outcomes for all autistic learners.

The chapter ends with a personal account by Bola Abimbola of her experiences as the mother of a young boy who exhibits behaviour that could be perceived as extremely challenging. She describes her long journey, and how she was instinctively driven to seek an understanding of her son and his needs. This echoes Carrie Grant's account of her quest to find ways to understand the diverse needs of her children in Chapter 3. Bola's story describes her developing knowledge and self-confidence in her skills as a parent, which led ultimately to significant improvements in her son's capacity to engage with her and others and begin to make progress. Bola's story and those of other parents featured in this book demonstrate the huge role that a family's 'culture' and instinctive parenting/caring skills can play in finding ways to understand a child's needs and ameliorate their difficulties. It is vital, therefore, that all professionals and educators work in equal partnership with families in order to find the most appropriate and effective solutions for meeting the needs not only of the child but also of the family around the child.

PROMOTING INCLUSION THROUGH INCREASING LEARNER ENGAGEMENT: USING THE SCERTS MODEL WITHIN A BIO-ECOLOGICAL APPROACH

Scot Greathead and Rhiannon Yates

Broadly defined, engagement is a dynamic construct that describes the way that learners respond to opportunities and challenges within their classroom (Sparapini *et al.* 2016). In September 2021, schools in the UK will be required to use the 'Engagement Model' to assess and track progress of children working below national curriculum levels (Standards and Testing Agency 2020). Yet it is equally important that teachers know how to increase learner engagement across *all* developmental stages: engagement is a predictor of positive educational outcomes and emotional well-being (Wang & Degol 2014).

Why is engagement important for autistic learners?

Autistic learners are at increased risk of exclusion and so it is vital that we develop our understanding of how they engage in schools. A survey of parents of autistic children found that nearly one in five had received at least one fixed-term school exclusion, and one in 20 had been permanently excluded (Moore 2016). Autistic children who had been excluded from school, and their parents, reported that before their exclusion they experienced a gradual decline in school engagement (Brede *et al.* 2017).

Further evidence of the challenges that autistic learners experience with school engagement includes a study that found that these individuals spent less than half of the observation time being productive, independent or in well-regulated states within classrooms (Sparapini *et al.* 2016). This finding highlights the importance of a long-standing recommendation by the National Research Council (2001), which states that educators should engage autistic learners in 25 hours of meaningful and purposeful activities each week.

Why are autistic learners at a disadvantage in classrooms?

Autistic learners are at increased risk of exclusion and disengagement due to a combination of factors. Neurological differences in social understanding, communication, sensory processing, interests and information processing (Autism Education Trust 2021a) can all influence an autistic learner's ability to engage in busy school environments. Other factors that can be commonly experienced by autistic individuals include challenges with sleep, learning disabilities and poor mental health (*ibid.*) and these may also impact classroom engagement.

One environmental factor which may also contribute to challenges with engagement is a lack of reasonable adjustments at school. Some mainstream teachers feel that they do not have the appropriate training to support autistic learners (National Association of Schoolmasters Union of Women Teachers 2013); and in some legal cases school policy, such as zero tolerance behaviour systems, has been ruled discriminatory (HCB Solicitors 2018). The combination of characteristics related to autism, together with a lack of effective support, can result in children presenting with complex and challenging behaviour, which may then lead to disengagement and school exclusion. Indeed, disengagement and behaviour that is considered to be challenging often present as a result of unmet needs (Autism Education Trust 2021b). It is therefore crucial for the rights, education and well-being of autistic children that teaching staff can recognize factors that have a negative impact on learner engagement and can offer effective support at those times.

Applying bio-ecological theory to classroom engagement

Given the complexity and range of factors influencing the engagement of autistic learners, we present a model of engagement based on the principles of bio-ecological theory. By looking at engagement through a bio-ecological lens, we acknowledge that a child's experience of school will be shaped by a range of interdependent factors, such as their personal characteristics (biological, neuropsychological and psychological factors) and wider environmental influences (Bronfenbrenner & Morris 2006; Education Endowment Foundation 2020).

This model also includes an adaptation of five engagement domains that are specifically considered to be important for autistic learners (Sparapini *et al.* 2016): organization, spontaneous communication, social communication, emotional regulation, flexibility. Figure 4.1 illustrates a bio-ecological model of engagement.

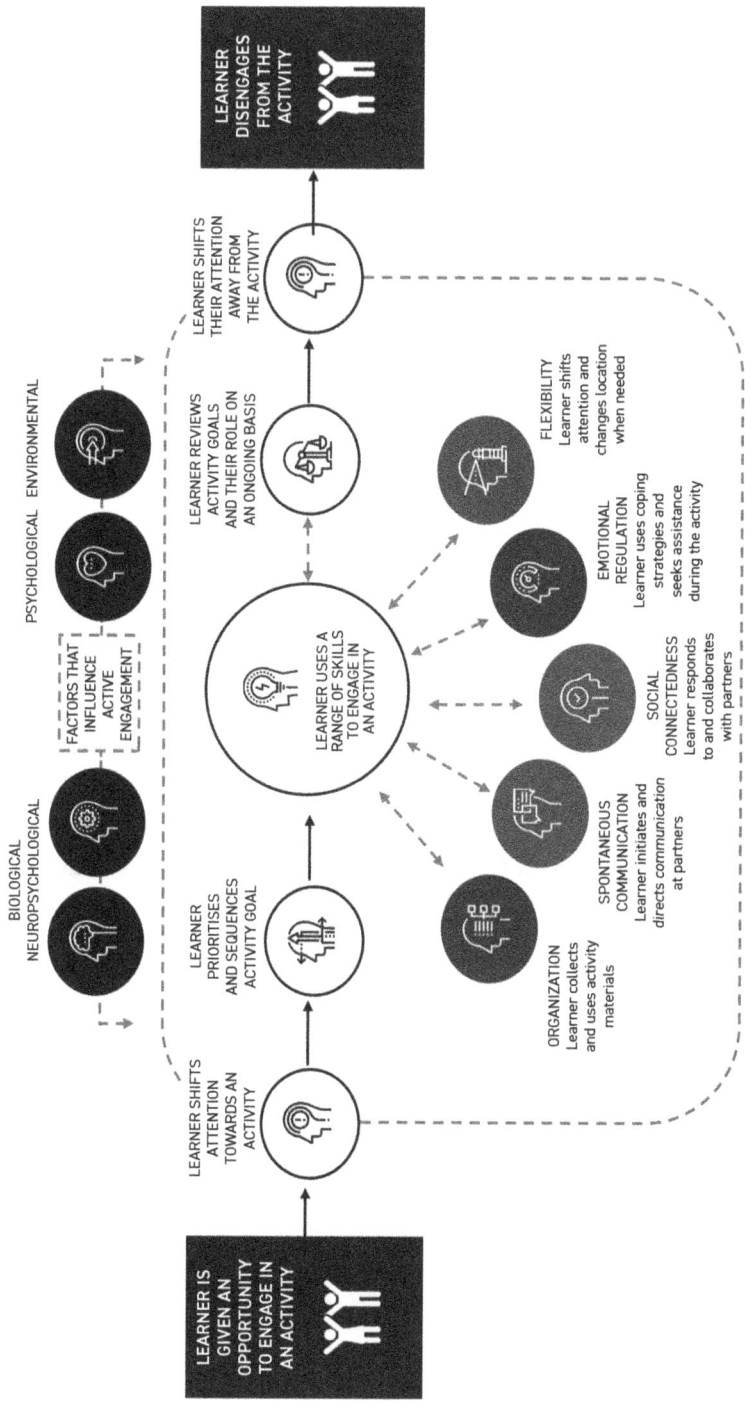

Figure 4.1: A bio-ecological model of the processes, factors and engagement domains which influence the nature of a learner's engagement within activities

The figure depicts the following process flow:

LEARNER IS GIVEN AN OPPORTUNITY TO ENGAGE IN AN ACTIVITY

→ LEARNER SHIFTS ATTENTION TOWARDS AN ACTIVITY

→ LEARNER PRIORITISES AND SEQUENCES ACTIVITY GOAL

→ LEARNER USES A RANGE OF SKILLS TO ENGAGE IN AN ACTIVITY

→ LEARNER REVIEWS ACTIVITY GOALS AND THEIR ROLE ON AN ONGOING BASIS

→ LEARNER SHIFTS THEIR ATTENTION AWAY FROM THE ACTIVITY

→ LEARNER DISENGAGES FROM THE ACTIVITY

FACTORS THAT INFLUENCE ACTIVE ENGAGEMENT:

BIOLOGICAL / NEUROPSYCHOLOGICAL

PSYCHOLOGICAL

ENVIRONMENTAL

Engagement domains:

ORGANIZATION — Learner collects and uses activity materials

SPONTANEOUS COMMUNICATION — Learner initiates and directs communication at partners

SOCIAL CONNECTEDNESS — Learner responds to and collaborates with partners

EMOTIONAL REGULATION — Learner uses coping strategies and seeks assistance during the activity

FLEXIBILITY — Learner shifts attention and changes location when needed

We use this bio-ecological model to inform practical methods of understanding and increasing the engagement of autistic learners. These methods include:

1. Reflective questions to facilitate discussion around (a) the different factors which may influence learner engagement and (b) the domains associated with increasing learner engagement.

2. An engagement checklist which combines the five engagement domains with developmental skills from the SCERTS (Social Communication, Emotional Regulation and Transactional Support) model (Prizant *et al.* 2006).

These methods are illustrated by a case study found at the end of this contribution.

1. Reflective questions

We have developed two tables that pose reflective questions and 'conversation starters' relevant for each factor and engagement domain outlined in Figure 4.1. These questions are designed to promote team discussion around a learner's engagement in specific activities. The aim of this is to build a picture of a learner's strengths and challenges and to identify opportunities and supports that will foster greater levels of learner engagement.

The first table (Table 4.1) explores a learner's personal circumstances, and the second table (Table 4.2) considers the way a learner engages in an activity.

Table 4.1: Factors that influence engagement, with questions to facilitate an understanding of a child's personal circumstances

Factors that influence engagement	Examples of reflective questions
Biological factors refer to internal factors, such as genes and hormones, which determine how children grow and develop.	1. What do we know about the learner's development (e.g., language skills, mobility) which might influence how they engage in this activity? 2. For teenagers, are hormonal and neurological changes influencing shared attention, emotional regulation and perspective taking?
Neuropsychological factors describe how the brain and nervous system 'work' and how this might influence cognition, including cognitive abilities associated with learning and executive functions, interoception and sensory processing. These factors may shape the learner's thinking, reflection and processing.	3. What is the learner's cognitive profile (e.g., verbal ability, visual-spatial, non-verbal reasoning, memory)? How do strengths and challenges influence classroom behaviour? 4. How might the learner's sensory processing differences, preferences or sensitivities influence their behaviour in this activity? 5. Are there strengths or challenges with understanding different perspectives, predicting social behaviour, and planning that need to be considered when designing activities?
Psychological factors relate to lived and social experiences that shape the learner's understanding of themselves, such as their sense of belonging, confidence, resilience and self-belief. These factors may influence engagement through the learner's mood, motivation and self-belief.	6. What is the learner's mood in this activity compared to other activities? 7. What are the learner's confidence levels around this task? What will make this activity challenging (but not impossible), fun and inviting for the learner? 8. Does the learner have any immediate or wider worries that are affecting classroom behaviour?

cont.

Factors that influence engagement	Examples of reflective questions
Environmental factors include the school and home settings. These factors refer to activities that children take part in and interactions they have with staff, peers and family members.	9. Does the classroom environment promote engagement? Consider how the classroom is organized, sensory properties, language and social demands. 10. Is the activity differentiated according to the learner's strengths and challenges? 11. Are learners paired with other children, or adults who set the stage for engagement – e.g., are they responsive, a positive role model, and able to adjust their interactions to promote reciprocal communication? 12. How might the learner's home and family life influence their school life?

Table 4.2: A description of key domains important for increasing engagement (Sparapini *et al.* 2016) and reflective questions designed to promote the learner's skills within each domain

Engagement domains	Examples of reflective questions
Learner is organized. **Learners with organizational** challenges might appear disorganized, forgetful or may not use materials in a meaningful way.	1. What supports are used to help the learner understand the way an activity is carried out? 2. Are there opportunities for the learner to (a) collect materials and (b) use them in an appropriate way?
Learner spontaneously communicates. If the learner has language and/or communication challenges they might find it difficult to initiate and direct communicative bids towards others. This can impact on how they build relationships, and influence and interact with those around them.	3. How is the learner supported to spontaneously communicate, and how is expressive language supported – e.g., are they provided with symbols/vocabulary/modelling? 4. Are there opportunities for the learner to use communication for a range of functions (e.g. commenting, requesting, turn-taking) within an activity)?

	Learner is socially connected. Learners might experience challenges when asked to collaborate with peers. Being socially connected involves being responsive to communicative bids and engaging in reciprocal interaction.	5. How do adults make a bid for the learner's attention? If the learner does not respond, how is this followed up and repaired by the adult? 6. How have activities been designed to support the learner to collaborate effectively (e.g., by structuring turn-taking and giving opportunities to practise different roles in interactions, such as giving and following directions)?
	Learner is emotionally regulated. As greater demands are placed on learners to engage in classrooms, then more demands are placed on their emotional regulation skills. A dysregulated learner may appear disruptive or withdrawn. Learners require skills in both self-regulation (coping on one's own) and mutual regulation (coping with another's help) to manage emotions when environmental demands increase.	7. Is the activity designed in a way which interests and motivates the learner to remain engaged, and persist in activities? 8. Are supports and opportunities available for the learner to (a) self-regulate and (b) seek mutual regulation when activities become more demanding?
	Learner has flexible attention. Challenges in this area may mean that learners miss cues to redirect their attention, to finish activities when immediately asked or to transition around the class.	9. Are supports used to help the learner shift their attention focus within tasks or between people, or when given directions from adults or other learners? 10. What support is available which enables the learner to transition independently around the classroom?

Once the range of factors and engagement domains have been explored, an engagement checklist can be used to understand the profile of an individual learner.

2. Using the SCERTS model as an engagement checklist

Over two years, action research groups consisting of representatives from the Pan London Autism Schools Network (PLASN) collaborated with the Centre for Research in Autism and Education (University College London) and Speech Therapy Services London Ltd. The aim of these groups was to implement the SCERTS model (Prizant *et al.* 2006) in their schools to increase levels of learner engagement. Indeed, a randomized control trial has previously shown that the SCERTS model does promote engagement of autistic learners (Morgan *et al.* 2018), as measured by the five engagement domains identified by Sparapini and colleagues (2016).

The SCERTS model is an educational approach which addresses the core challenges experienced by autistic pupils (social communication and emotional regulation). The model provides a curriculum which is presented as checklists so that adults can identify goals for learners at three different developmental stages. The SCERTS model has two additional checklists called 'transactional supports'. These describe modifications that adults can make to their interaction style and the classroom environment.

The PLASN groups identified learners for whom they would like to increase engagement. The groups explored factors that might impact learner engagement using reflective questions similar to those described in Tables 4.1 and 4.2. To support further changes for individual children, groups used an engagement checklist which was devised specifically for these projects. This checklist maps developmental skills from the SCERTS model onto an adaptation of Sparapini *et al.*'s (2016) five engagement domains. Like the SCERTS model, the engagement checklist is organized across three developmental stages (so that professionals choose the checklist that is developmentally appropriate for a child) and paired with a list of transactional supports.

The engagement checklist enables adults to create a profile for learners on an activity-by-activity basis. Adults mark on the checklist which skills they observe a learner using and, by looking at unchecked boxes, can see where there are opportunities to develop skills within specific engagement domains. For example, if an adult wants to increase a learner's social connectedness, they can choose from a range of 11 socio-emotional skills, as identified by the SCERTS model (see Table 4.3).

Table 4.3: An excerpt from an engagement checklist showing the social connectedness domain with skills from the SCERTS model (Prizant *et al.* 2006)

Social connectedness	
Learner collaborates effectively through reciprocity and taking turns	Learner responds to a communication partner when they make a bid for attention
Monitors the attention focus of a partner	Responds to advanced relational words ('wh–' questions)
Follows conventions for initiating conversations and taking turns	Responds to causal relationships (why–because)
Shows reciprocity in speaker and listener roles to share experiences	Responds to time concepts
Maintains interactions by requesting or providing information	Extracts meaning from spoken paragraphs
Takes a role and collaborates with peers in role play	Responds to non-literal language: humour, figures of speech, teasing, sarcasm, deceptions
Collaborates and negotiates with peers in problem-solving	

A case study

This case study describes Cyril, a Year 2 learner with emerging language skills, who was presenting with challenging behaviour at playtimes. It outlines how staff at Five Acre Wood School in Maidstone, Kent, applied the bio-ecological model and engagement checklist to increase engagement through fostering reciprocal relationships between Cyril and his peers. An abridged version of this case study, by Leanne Scott and Kelly Davies, appears in 'Implementing the SCERTS Model through appreciative inquiry' (Greathead & Crane, in preparation).

STEP 1: Teaching teams applied bio-ecological principles and used reflective questions to better understand factors that influenced Cyril's engagement during play.

- *What was happening?* Cyril communicated using short sentences supported by symbols. He enjoyed social interaction and games with his peers and adults but found it challenging to spend playtimes engaged in meaningful play. Rather than use toys for their intended purpose, he would throw items high in the air, risking injury to other children. Although Cyril enjoyed playing with people, he had challenges in requesting play; for example he might push them in the back. This resulted in negative responses from others and negative playtime experiences. When playtimes ended negatively, Cyril found it difficult to settle into his next lesson, which further disrupted his learning.

- *What do we want to be different?* For Cyril to spend his playtimes engaged in meaningful games with adults and peers.

- *Cyril's perspective:* Cyril was not able to explain his thoughts and feelings about this activity but, critically, the team wanted to consider his perspective. They interpreted his behaviour as being communicative and hypothesized that he was trying to initiate games with his peers, albeit in a non-conventional way. During team discussions, they asked the people who knew him best which games Cyril liked to play so that he could be given these as choices at playtime.

- *Biological factors:* Cyril experienced challenges with learning language at the same rate as his peers.

- *Neuropsychological factors:* Cyril was autistic and could initiate play in an unconventional way. He was also sensitive to busy, cluttered environments, which made it difficult for him to orient and maintain his attention to one meaningful activity.

- *Environmental factors:* Cluttered environments distracted Cyril and made it difficult for him to engage in play. Adults were not immediately available to pre-empt communication breakdown, and symbols that depicted Cyril's favourite games were not readily available.

STEP 2: Teaching teams identified adult and learner goals related to the domains of engagement through using the engagement checklist.

- *Using the engagement checklist:* Adults observed Cyril at playtime and completed the developmentally relevant engagement check-list. When they analysed the checklist, the adults recognized there were opportunities to build organization, social connectedness and spontaneous communication into this activity. From the checklists, the team were able to identify specific SCERTS goals for Cyril and his team. These are highlighted in Table 4.4.

Table 4.4: Increasing Cyril's engagement

Engagement domain	What will adults do to support Cyril?	How would we like Cyril's engagement to increase?
Organization:	Cyril enjoyed cause and effect games which involved anticipation. Adults will reduce the number of activities at playtimes and introduce toys with these features so that resources are developmentally meaningful to him.	SCERTS goal: *For Cyril to select and use toys in meaningful ways at playtimes.*
Social connectedness:	Adults will provide games that are structured and encourage turn-taking with other children. Adults will model how to play these games and gradually reduce their involvement as children begin to play more independently.	SCERTS goals: *For Cyril to take turns and respond to directions from adults and peers.*
Spontaneous communication:	The team want to generalize the language skills that Cyril uses in other activities. Adults will make available visual supports which enable him to use a range of subject, verb and object words so that he can communicate what he wants to play and who he wants to play with.	SCERTS goal: *For Cyril to initiate interaction with his peers and adults by using subject + verb + object sentences to make requests and give directions.*

STEP 3: Teaching teams reviewed the effectiveness of the supports in fostering engagement.

Following the implementation of these supports, the teaching team felt that Cyril engaged more positively at playtimes. Visual supports helped Cyril to increase his spoken language and initiate interactions with his peers in a way that would lead to play. Over time, he needed less adult direction and started to develop independent relationships with other children.

Staff reported they had a better understanding of Cyril's needs, which strengthened their relationships with him. Following the review of these supports, the class team worked with Cyril's family to set up similar games at home with his siblings.

Conclusion

Article 24 of the UN Convention on the Rights of Persons with Disabilities (United Nations 2006) supports the rights of autistic learners to access inclusive education with appropriate support that enables them to reach their potential. Research on the exclusion experiences of autistic children suggests that there is still a long way to go before we achieve this goal.

Within this bio-ecological model of engagement, we have presented ways of better understanding engagement through applying research, methods and resources that are specifically related to the core characteristics of autism (e.g., Sparapini *et al.* 2016; Prizant *et al.* 2006). We hope that this model and these methods can support educators to explore the range of factors that impact a learner's engagement in the classroom, including reflecting on their own role in supporting autistic children to be successful in their learning, and most importantly, to enjoy their time in school.

We would like to thank Emily Rubin and Dr Vicky Slonims for giving their time to discuss and guide earlier versions of this work.

Icons in the bio-ecological model are from Maxim Basinski at https://thenounproject.com/basinskimaxim/collection/thinking-and-brain-process.

UNDERSTANDING AND SUPPORTING PUPILS WITH A PDA PROFILE

Phil Christie

Introduction

When the government announced its forthcoming (and subsequently delayed) review of the Autism Strategy in 2018 (Department for Education/Department of Health and Social Care 2019), details of what the revision would encompass included a number of key points, one of which was 'improving understanding of autism and all its profiles, including recently identified forms such as Pathological Demand Avoidance (PDA)' (p.1).

The term 'PDA' was first used by Professor Elizabeth Newson in the 1980s to describe an evolving understanding of a group of children who had been referred to her clinic for diagnostic assessment, and were seen by the referring professional as complex and unusual in their developmental profile. These children reminded the referring professionals of children with autism or Asperger syndrome but were often seen as atypical in some way (Newson 1990).

However, it wasn't until 2003 that the first peer-reviewed publication about PDA appeared and Newson and colleagues described the central characteristic as 'an obsessional avoidance of the ordinary demands of everyday life' (Newson, Le Marechal & David 2003). This was combined with sufficient social understanding and sociability to enable the child to be 'socially manipulative' in their avoidance. Newson initially proposed that PDA should be seen as a separate syndrome within the pervasive developmental disorders, which was the recognized category used within the versions of the psychiatric classification systems that were current at the time (*ICD-10*, put forward by the World Health Organization 1995 and *DSM-IV* by the American Psychiatric Association 1994).

In the following years, it became apparent that the term 'autism spectrum disorder' was being used as though it was the same as pervasive developmental disorder. Indeed, the National Institute for Health and Care Excellence guidelines on autism spectrum disorders (2011; updated 2017) described the two terms as being synonymous. Following on from this, PDA has become increasingly understood as being a profile within the autism spectrum. Individuals who present with this particular profile are characterized by a drive to avoid everyday demands and expectations to an extreme extent. This is rooted in an anxiety-based need to be in control. Individuals share difficulties with others on the autism spectrum in terms of social aspects of interaction and communication, together with some repetitive patterns of behaviour.

The main features of PDA (adapted from Newson *et al.* 2003) include:

- Resisting and avoiding the ordinary demands of life, which might include getting up and joining a family activity or other day-to-day suggestions. This may be the case even when the person seems to want to do what has been suggested

- Using social strategies as part of the avoidance (e.g., distracting, giving excuses, negotiation)

- Appearing sociable on the surface, but lacking depth in their understanding

- Exhibiting excessive mood swings and impulsivity

- Being comfortable in role play and pretend, sometimes to an extreme extent

- Showing 'obsessive' behaviour that is often focused on other people.

As recently highlighted by an editorial in *Child and Adolescent Mental Health* (Ozsivadjian 2020), the debate around the place of the profile within classification systems and how distinct PDA is from other profiles are described as a 'nosological distiction'. Research, though, is now moving into more practical arenas, such as trying to understand why some children present with problematic demand avoidant behaviour and, recognizing that 'conventional ASD strategies' are often ineffective, how best to support children and their families.

Wider educational context

For a number of years those working across the education sector supporting children and young people with additional needs have noted that they have been seeing an increasingly complex group of learners. This prompted a Department for Education-supported project (Carpenter 2010) exploring the needs of children with 'complex learning difficulties and disabilities' (CLDD). The research group agreed that children with CLDD may:

- be working at any level of the national curriculum

- have conditions that co-exist, creating a complex profile of learning need

- show inconsistent attainment, presenting an atypical profile of learning

- have a range of 'layered needs', which may require informed specific support and strategies

- require personalized learning pathways.

These children were described as 'a wide and varied group of learners who do not simply require a differentiated curriculum...but who, at times, require further adaptation to teaching if they are to make progress' (Porter & Ashdown 2002, p.11)

More recently, a number of reports, including that by the All Party Parliamentary Group on Autism (2017), have concluded that many children with autism are being let down by the education system, and exclusions are rising significantly, with fewer than half of the children surveyed saying that they were happy at school. This is especially true for those with more complex presentations, such as those with a PDA profile. The PDA Society (2018) report, *Being Misunderstood*, points out that a significant proportion of children with a PDA profile are being excluded from school; it cites the Children's Commissioner's report (2019), *Skipping School*, which highlights the rise of exclusions more generally from an 'unforgiving school system'.

Such reports underline how a detailed assessment that leads to a greater understanding of an individual's profile and needs is the starting point to making the adaptations needed to improve the educational experience and outcomes for all learners on the autism spectrum.

While the debate about how the PDA profile should be best conceptualised and described within diagnostic systems continues, there is wide agreement about the need to recognize the particular education and support needs of these children. This was forcibly advocated in an article about PDA published by the British Psychological Society in 2016 (O'Nions, Happé & Viding 2016, p.iv); this concluded that 'It is essential that this help is provided to these very vulnerable individuals and their families.'

Guidelines for educational provision and support

Guidelines for supporting children with a PDA profile have evolved over time, promoting an approach based on a less direct and more flexible style than the more structured methods that are most often advocated for many other children on the autism spectrum. These guidelines have since been developed and adopted as part of the National Autism Standards, published by the Autism Education Trust (2012). The limited research that has taken place on educational approaches has supported the efficacy of this approach (Gore Langton & Frederickson 2015; Doyle, McNally & Kenny 2020).

In a later publication (Fidler & Christie 2019), this methodology was set out in more detail and given the title of *Collaborative Approaches to Learning*. This was very much about an approach and style, rather than a set of prescribed methods that can be consistently applied and adhered to. The core principle is about collaboration: working with the child or young person, finding a way to negotiate solutions, adjusting expectations, compromising on outcomes and collaborating closely with parents and others. Underpinning the approach is *the understanding that at the heart of PDA is an anxiety-driven need to be in control and avoid other people's expectations.* It is likely that on a day-to-day basis, expectations will need to be adapted according to the pupil's level of tolerance at the time. The key challenge is *getting the right balance between the expectations that adults have of the child and their capacity to cope.* Teaching and learning is a transactional process, and it is the role of the supporting adults to enable tolerance and confidence to grow so that expectations can be progressively increased.

Key principles

Children with PDA will be catered for in a range of different settings and with varying levels of support but *flexibility and adaptations* of one sort or another will be needed. These adaptations may be considerable and are likely to be needed at both an *organizational* level and in an adult's *personal* style. The timetable itself may need adjustment in terms of the amount of time spent on particular subjects, or where learning takes place. A major issue to take account of is likely to be the extent of the *adjustment to whole-school practice* or policy that is needed to include a particular pupil, such as the uniform policy and arrangements for assembly or break time. Classroom staff need to feel supported in ensuring that they are able to provide *sufficient personalization*, both in the curriculum offered and the way in which it is delivered. This is likely to mean finding a way of embedding the child's interests into the curriculum and allowing a significant degree of choice to give a feeling of control. The degree of adaptation and personalization needed for many children with PDA doesn't sit easily alongside inflexible whole-school policies.

Principles in practice

Putting these principles into practice requires a range of strategies in order to maintain the pupil's engagement. It is beyond the scope of this contribution to describe all of these in detail but a few of the key ones are given below.

Choosing priorities. What is important now and what can we come back to? Use of a simple priority rating scale completed by staff and parents together can be a useful starting point. Only a realistic number can be worked on at any one time.

Being indirect and avoiding unnecessary confrontations. Priorities will need to be put in place but with a child with PDA there is the potential for 'flashpoints' over a whole host of everyday expectations. Using indirect, invitational language and giving more choice can help to avoid unnecessary confrontation: for example, 'It would be great if we could get this done today. Shall we do it in the hall or the library?' and 'Oh this looks a bit tricky. Perhaps you might be able to help?' This may mean adjusting aspects of a typical teacher–pupil dynamic so as to create a sense of alliance.

Adapting visual strategies. Using visual strategies is very helpful to most children with autism, clarifying information in a way that gives them more time to process what is being asked. Schedules and systems can, however, come across as being too prescribed and seem to represent a 'to-do list', but they can be adapted in a flexible way that enables a pupil to better see choices and possibilities.

Providing extra processing time. This is important for all children with autism who are likely to need more time to fully process some of the information they are given. This may be the case for the child with a PDA profile too and they may also need additional time to process whether they can cooperate at this particular moment (this is likely to be linked to their level of anxiety).

Minimizing anxiety. Anxiety is at the heart of the child's difficulties with cooperating and meeting other people's expectations. As a result, it is critical to look at ways that anxiety can be reduced. In addition to the teaching approach being less pressurizing and more accommodating, it is also necessary to consider ways of moderating certain situations that might cause the child to be anxious in the first place. Additionally it might be helpful to consider introducing, or increasing, the amount of time that the child has access to activities that they find calming and regulating. These will be different for each individual but might include relaxation techniques, mindfulness, physical activity or quiet periods of engagement based on a favoured interest.

Foster emotional resilience and self-reliance

The strategies above are aimed at reducing the child's level of anxiety, helping them feel less pressurized and in turn more amenable to the expectations that people have of them. Improving this can make an enormous difference to children who have become extremely stressed and reluctant to engage. It is also likely to have a cumulative effect and, as the child participates more, they become less anxious and more trusting with a wider range of people and in more situations. At times, though, it seems that children with a PDA profile have a sense of fragility and lack of permanence in their learning. It is important to think carefully about how much progress is dependent on getting it right in the moment and how much is due to a more long-lasting change 'within the child'. In the longer term, thought and planning must be given to ways in which the young person can be enabled to become more self-aware, and better able to communicate their anxieties in an effective way and manage and regulate their own emotions.

Children will need help to develop *an understanding of their own emotions and those of other people* and then work towards how they might use that knowledge to manage their own personal regulation. Initial steps might include naming and categorizing emotional vocabulary, perhaps devising and updating their own personal dictionary. They are likely to need help understanding the emotions of others, how to look out for indicators of particular emotions in people they know, and think about what might have contributed to them. Many children are helped, by developing an understanding of social and emotional consequences, to recognize the importance of making accommodations and managing their own impulsive behaviour. They can begin to see how the impact they might have on others may bring negative outcomes for themselves. Emotional barometers, flow charts and spider diagrams can be helpful ways of representing this learning visually. It will also be helpful if they can work out what will calm them when they become dysregulated or anxious. This could lead to them grading and matching activities or techniques to different levels or types of situations and keeping access to these for use in emergencies.

One report, *Educational Provision and Outcomes for People on the Autism Spectrum* (Wittemeyer *et al.* 2011) recommended that guidance from the Department for Education to teachers, especially those in mainstream settings, should support achieving a balance between teaching key academic skills and those others which promote social and emotional development.

Developing emotional resilience in pupils with a PDA profile will require additional time and support. It is always going to be more effective if the approach to developing resilience is done proactively rather than in response to a crisis. Many opportunities can arise within the classroom for promoting these areas of learning when designing a personalized curriculum to meet the needs of any learner on the autism spectrum. In addition to this, though, it is likely that dedicated individual time will need to be allowed. This means that there needs to be a commitment by senior leaders, as well as classroom practitioners, to protecting time to work on this area of learning. A system of personal tutorials has been described in earlier publications (individualized one-to-one sessions between a pupil and their tutor which provide dedicated time to focus on social and emotional learning). For those wishing to find out more about this approach, detail can be found in longer accounts (Christie 2007; Christie *et al.* 2012; Fidler & Christie 2019).

Conclusion

As our understanding of the PDA profile grows, so does recognition of the implications for those who live and work with children and young people. Due to their high levels of anxiety and need for control, children with this profile respond better to flexibility, negotiation and a less direct style.

Putting this sort of learning environment in place requires significant adaptation from schools as organizations as well as in the individual style of those working directly with the pupil. When these adaptations are made, tolerance levels increase and lead to greater engagement in learning opportunities.

Reflecting on some of these adaptations one headteacher commented:

Using different strategies has made the world of difference to school staff. It's amazing how big an impact making small changes in emphasis and priorities can make... At school, we are so much better equipped to move forwards with a more flexible and positive education.

EMOTIONAL INTELLIGENCE AND PARENTING A PERSON WITH AUTISM AND BEHAVIOUR THAT CHALLENGES

Bola Abimbola

I genuinely believe that autism teaches us as parents to explore as if there are no boundaries, attending only to the things that bring our children happiness and showing love without needing words. In my personal and professional life – with over 20 years' working in psychology, disability and trauma – being a parent of a brilliant 24-year-old man who has autism with behaviour that challenges, has been the most profound experience.

It is often said that no two children with autism present the same way. Equally, no two parents of a child with autism present in the same way. As a special educational needs and disabilities (SEND) consultant as well as an independent care advocate for parents and carers, I come across parents facing, with courage, the stigma attached to disability and the isolation (emotional and physical), even as they enjoy the medal stripes of awesome parenting.

In our epic pool of knowledge, we do not share enough about our experiences. Yes, there are some things that feel too much to share, but this sharing would reduce the tangible pull of isolation, which threatens and sometimes breaks our resolve and strength, especially as we get on in years.

I chose to contribute to this chapter to share my experience as a parent, especially to share the two key factors that led to and continue to inform my son's transformation from the angry street-fighter champion he once was to the present yoga-loving gentleman who struggles with behaviour that challenges.

My son Shaun has been the key to the positive changes in his life. He has engaged time and time again with new ways to do things, despite his personal challenges. Let's face it: with the best will in the world, if a child refuses to engage in any intervention, there is no progress. Shaun's determination to keep learning and enjoying his life continues to inspire our family and those who know him.

Shaun has intellectual disability, autism, severe speech and language communication difficulties, sensory processing difficulties, anxiety, behaviour that challenges, dysphagia and oromotor dyskinesia. The presentation of his different diagnoses occurred at different times over the years.

His loss of words started at 18 months. The challenging behaviour quickly followed suit when he struggled to communicate and understand everything around him, even with attention at home and at nursery. He was diagnosed with autism before the age of two. We tried to keep up with encouraging him to listen, repeat and focus, but within one year we went from being a two-parent family to a one-parent family; from me having one au pair to paying for two au pairs at the same time; from au pairs giving some notice to leave, to me waking up to find the au pair had quit and left without notice during the night. One day, I got a call at work from my au pair to say she had to leave immediately, and I should come home otherwise she would be forced to leave the children. When I got home that day, Shaun was distressed and unharmed, thankfully. His brother Otto, less than two years younger, was upset but also unharmed. The living room window and TV were broken. Shaun had bitten off a piece of the au pair's skin. I was shocked and speechless. I soothed my au pair of seven months and tried to gather myself as she went to pack her things. I wrote her a cheque with a two-weeks' bonus and thanked her for her good service. She was quite distraught too and left within an hour. I took over my children, confused and very scared.

As the au pair left, there seemed to be a calm in our home. It was a turning point. I looked at Shaun and it seemed that there was relief on his face. Shaun and I had formed a bond from day one and it exists to this day. It took me a while to realize the impact of my consistency on him. I have learned only to promise him what I can deliver. I do try to keep my promises to him. On the occasions when I am unable to, I look him in the eye, explain what happened, and apologise for my part in it. He has come to trust me to a large extent.

These two factors – Shaun having the willingness to engage in interventions and the trust that he has in my consistency as his main carer – are key factors in dealing with a child with autism and behaviour that challenges.

A child's willingness to engage

What makes that child willing to engage in interventions is the degree to which they feel comfortable within themselves. I personally did not realize the impact of sensory processing difficulties and literacy (specifically comprehension) on behaviour that challenges.

Behaviours that challenge could be self-harm (e.g., biting wrists, picking skin, hitting body against wall), aggression to others (e.g., verbally abusing or kicking/punching/spitting at others) and damage to furniture (e.g., throwing objects, knocking over the TV, kicking radiators, breaking windows). Behaviours that challenge come in degrees, from requiring soothing or de-escalation to requiring hospitalization or even incarceration (temporary or long term).

There is a school of thought that states that if the person with challenging behaviour can be supported to comprehend what is going on around them, to feel included and cared for consistently, their behaviour that challenges will stop. I have observed this to be true myself many times. The behaviour that challenges can become a managed need, whereby interventions are put in place to build the capacity of the child. These interventions must remain consistent for progress to continue.

There was a time for six months when Shaun did not display one iota of behaviour that challenges. A lot of strategies were in place at the time, including not a single change in my work schedules/care/support staff around him. Also, intensive daily occupational therapy prescribed a sensory diet including:

- heavy weights for low muscle tone in his legs

- an iPod playing his favourite music, to soothe and comfort

- a tablet playing funny videos for soothing visual stimuli

- an iPad with a communication app, so he could communicate at times when speaking was a challenge (as is often the case, in line with his generalized anxiety disorder, autism spectrum disorder and severe speech and communication diagnosis)

- a sensory-therapy vibrating ball, providing vestibular stimuli to soothe and align his sensory perceptions

- Social Stories – daily and weekly schedules devised by the speech and language therapist

- appropriate chemical support, in his case anti-psychotic medication, from his consultant psychiatrist to help him understand his day and participate fully, making informed choices.

The willingness to engage for a child with autism, increases when they feel at ease within themselves. A lot of trial and error is involved in achieving this, so the key is to keep trying new interventions, most especially if what worked yesterday no longer seems to work.

The emotional intelligence of parents

It was a miracle that I 'showed up' in feeding, maintaining health and wellness, and schooling, considering my own childhood trauma. Nevertheless, I tried to step up to be a superparent and it was a struggle, especially with working, attending school meetings and managing expenses. In fact, I had a nervous breakdown. I was trying so hard to do the impossible and, at times, I failed at it. It was not possible to be in two places at the same time and so in the end I left work. This was the best thing I did, though at the time, I felt like a complete failure. I knew that I had no other choice, but I could not help thinking I had not played a good game somehow. I beat myself up mentally, cruelly.

As I stayed at home and kept doing my best with great determination, ongoing personal development and inner transformation, I continued to struggle with Shaun's challenges. However, my capacity for coping had increased and I began to make more informed decisions about his medication and schooling. Shaun went from state mainstream nursery to state-maintained autism specialist nursery, then from independent autism specialist primary to independent specialist secondary, and finally to independent autism specialist post-19 college. These school change decisions were vital and the early days were the toughest. Deciding to go from mainstream to specialist setting, especially, is a life-changing decision for your child, you and your family. School change decisions are best made with expert assessment and dialogue with an educational psychologist with specialist autism experience. I was lucky at key times, for many years, to have the advice and counsel of a remarkable educational psychologist. One of my very first key decisions about school was whether Shaun would be best in a residential school so he could have even more consistency. He did go to residential school, coming home at weekends for many years, and it was a win, without a doubt. Our best decisions are about what is informed and appropriate, rather than what we consider is right or wrong.

Personal development is how I sustained consistency in my parenting. I learned that personal development is vastly different from one's own self-care, which is still a journey. I discovered quickly that shouting at the top of my voice to calm Shaun down did not get us anywhere. I also discovered that the calmer I got, the calmer Shaun got. I faked it at first and when that did not work, I really began to work on my emotions.

Emotional intelligence is the ability to identify and manage one's own emotions as well as the emotions of others. Cultivating my emotional intelligence was my saving grace, because it helped me support my child better. Now I joke with my clients, who are parents of children with autism who have behaviour that challenges, that we all signed up for an imaginary but real, 'Fast Track Intense Parenting Class 101'. The fact is that there is a lot to learn and do, with transforming our own emotions and our thoughts to get the best out of our parenting experience – much more than there is for the parent of a neurotypical child. Our smile widens as we cultivate emotional intelligence: being able to take full responsibility, release guilt, shame, anger and our own traumas, so we can see and use the opportunities around us better for the well-being of our family. As we heal from the heartbreak of having a child who is perceived not only as different, but also as 'less than', we can begin to feel the joys of parenting, which are very tangible.

It is critical for a child to continue to receive collaborative, comprehensive assessments across educational, therapeutic and medical professionals, and for the parent to cultivate emotional intelligence, to keep an open mind, to continue to explore, even when significant change occurs.

The chaos around us persists. The one thing that can ensure sustainable change in our preferred direction – the significant progress of our child – is the way we respond to the chaos. Our response is determined by how we master our emotions. This is different from how well we speak and articulate; it is how we truly feel. Our children with autism do have high, laser-sharp radar around this.

Whether our child is living at home, in supported living, residential school or a care home (near or distant), the most important factor that determines their welfare is parental involvement, our informed advocacy. I define informed advocacy as the process of gathering information about the condition of you and your child and using this information to engage, cultivate and advocate with relevant professionals and establishments for the optimal education and well-being of your child.

Shaun is in his last year of independent specialist post-19 college, near his home, supported with local authority home-school transport, a sensory diet, medication, communication programmes, and a behaviour and support plan implemented by specialist autism personnel round the clock. Shaun receives reiki from me daily. He has a team of experts with whom I work closely, including a consultant psychiatrist, a general practitioner (GP), a speech and language therapist, an educational psychologist, a specialist teacher, an occupational therapist, a behaviour analyst, a dietician, a dysphagia specialist, a psycho-sexual behaviour specialist, a positive behaviour specialist, a physiotherapist, specialist leisure centre staff and an employment specialist.

Following the disruptions to schooling due to the Covid-19 pandemic, we are currently awaiting a decision from the local authority about Shaun starting two days' face-to-face home learning with a specialist teacher in maths and English. Remote online learning, which is now commonly being offered to our learners, is not appropriate for Shaun. He needs to consolidate key learning outcomes this last year, so he can be prepared to start his sous chef work placement at a cafe, 45 minutes from his home. The cafe is a social enterprise run by a charity for individuals with disabilities. Shaun's natural skills in cooking and baking continue to sustain his interest. He remains motivated, thankfully. He will continue to need support from specialist staff and appropriate aids and equipment to help him manage his emotions and behaviour, as he consolidates his knowledge of social norms, the value of money, food measurements, recipes, time and so on. Otto is doing well too, and studying medicine at university.

All in all, the uncertainty of parenting and life continues; we can only keep showing up, using the opportunities around and within us, as parents and carers. This makes our parenting and personal journey more palatable and even enjoyable, especially as time passes.

Chapter conclusion

The contributors to this chapter have described an ultimately positive and constructive outlook on the area of behaviour that is perceived to be challenging. The focus has been on understanding and explaining behaviour and planning adaptations and interventions accordingly.

There will always be a tension in mainstream schools between the delivery of the curriculum and the focus on social and emotional development. This issue was particularly pertinent after the 2020 lockdowns and school closures when schoolchildren, whether autistic or neurotypical, returned to school after lengthy periods at home. Reports from numerous sources have indicated that many children have struggled to engage positively, in terms of both classroom tasks and social activities. An emphasis on strategies to reduce anxiety and promote engagement is likely to lead to long-term benefits for everyone.

POINTS FOR REFLECTION

☞ A key target of interventions should include increasing engagement in meaningful activities in the classroom.

☞ Assessments should be holistic and take into account family factors and parenting preferences.

☞ Developing a clear and comprehensive understanding of the child's profile is a vital part of any assessment.

References

All Party Parliamentary Group on Autism (2017) *Autism and Education in England 2017: A Report by the All Party Parliamentary Group on Autism on How the Education System in England Works for Children and Young People on the Autism Spectrum*. London: National Autistic Society.

American Psychiatric Association (1994) *Diagnostic and Statistical Manual of Mental Disorders (Fourth Edition) (DSM-IV)*. Washington, DC: APA.

Autism Education Trust (2012) *National Autism Standards*. Accessed 20/08/2021 at www.autismeducationtrust.org.uk/shop/schools-standards-shop.

Autism Education Trust (2021a) *What is autism?* Accessed 25/02/2021 at www.autismeducationtrust.org.uk/what-is-autism.

Autism Education Trust (2021b) *Exclusions*. Accessed 25/02/2021 at www.autismeducationtrust.org.uk/exclusions.

Brede, J., Remington, A., Kenny, L., Warren, K. & Pellicano, E. (2017) 'Excluded from school: Autistic students' experiences of school exclusion and subsequent reintegration into school.' *Autism & Developmental Language Impairments, 2*, 1–20.

Bronfenbrenner, U. & Morris, P.A. (2006) 'The Bioecological Model of Human Development.' In W. Damon (series ed.) and R.M. Lerner (volume ed.) *Handbook of Child Psychology: Theoretical Models of Human Development* (pp.793–828). New York, NY: Wiley.

Carpenter, B. (2010) *Complex Learning Difficulties and Disabilities*. London: Specialist Schools and Academies Trust.

Children's Commissioner's Report (2019) *Skipping School: Invisible Children*. London: Children's Commissioner for England.

Christie, P. (2007) 'The distinctive clinical and educational needs of children with Pathological Demand Avoidance syndrome: Guidelines for good practice.' *Good Autism Practice 8*,(1), 3–11.

Christie, P., Fidler, R., Duncan, M. & Healy, Z. (2012) *Understanding Pathological Demand Avoidance Syndrome in Children*. London and Philadelphia, PA: Jessica Kingsley Publishers.

Department for Education/Department of Health and Social Care (2019) *Review of the National Autism Strategy 'Think Autism': Call for Evidence*. London: DfE/DHSC.

Doyle, A., McNally, S. & Kenny, N. (2020) *Mapping Educational Experiences of PDA in Ireland*. Dun Laoghaire, Rathdown: Prism.

Education Endowment Foundation (2020) *Special Educational Needs in Mainstream Schools: Guidance Report*. Accessed 25/02/2021 at https://resources.finalsite.net/images/v1589180181/bsmeorguk/x8vmwwdvv3boyefpvdbs/EEF_Special_Educational_Needs_in_Mainstream_Schools_Guidance_Report.pdf.

Fidler, R. & Christie, P. (2019) *Collaborative Approaches to Learning for Pupils with PDA*. London and Philadelphia: Jessica Kingsley Publishers.

Gore Langton, E. & Frederickson, N. (2015) 'Mapping the educational experiences of children with pathological demand avoidance.' *Journal of Research in Special Educational Needs, 16*(4), 254–263.

Greathead, S. & Crane, L. (in preparation) *Implementing the SCERTS Model Through Action Research: Experiences of Professionals Who Collaborate Using Appreciative Inquiry*. Accessed 28/02/2021 at www.speechtherapyservices.co.uk.

HCB Solicitors (2018) *Disability Discrimination and Zero Tolerance Behaviour Policies*. Accessed 28/02/2021 at www.educationlawadvice.com/2018/03/21/disability-discrimination-zero-tolerance-behaviour-policies.

Moore, C. (2016) *School Report*. London: National Autistic Society.

Morgan, L., Hooker, J.L., Sparapini, N., Reinhardt, V., Schatschneider, C. & Wetherby, A.M. (2018) 'Cluster randomized trial of the classroom SCERTS intervention for elementary students with autism spectrum disorder.' *Journal of Consulting and Clinical Psychology, 86*(7), 631–644.

National Association of Schoolmasters Union of Women Teachers (NASUWT) (2013) *Support for Children and Young People with Special Educational Needs*. London: NASUWT.

National Institute for Health and Care Excellence (2011) *Autism Spectrum Disorder in Under-19s: Recognition, Referral and Diagnosis*. NICE Guidance number 128. Accessed 10/12/2021 at https://www.nice.org.uk/guidance/cg128.

National Research Council (2001) *Educating Children with Autism*. Committee on Educational Interventions for Children with Autism. Washington, DC: National Academy Press.

Newson, E. (1990) Pathological Demand Avoidance Syndrome: Mapping a New Entity Related to Autism? Inaugural lecture, University of Nottingham.

Newson, E., Le Marechal, K. & David, C. (2003) 'Pathological demand avoidance syndrome: A necessary distinction within the pervasive developmental disorders.' *Archives of Disease in Childhood, 88*, 595–600.

O'Nions, E., Happé, F. & Viding, E. (2016) 'Extreme "pathological" demand avoidance.' *BPS DECP Debate, 160*.

Ozsivadjian, A. (2020) 'Editorial: Demand avoidance – Pathological, extreme or oppositional?' *Child and Adolescent Mental Health, 25*(2), 57–58.

PDA Society (2018) *Being Misunderstood – 2018 Survey: Experiences of the Pathological Demand Avoidance Profile of ASD*. Sheffield: PDA Society.

Porter, J. & Ashdown, R. (2002) *Pupils with Complex Needs: Promoting Learning through Visual Methods and Materials.* Tamworth: Nasen.

Prizant, B.M., Wetherby, A.M., Rubin, E., Laurent, A.C. & Rydell, P. (2006) *The SCERTS Model: Volume I Assessment.* Baltimore, MD: Brookes Publishing.

Sparapini, N., Morgan, L., Reinhardt, V.P., Schatschneider, C. & Wetherby, A. (2016) 'Evaluation of classroom active engagement in elementary students with autism spectrum disorder.' *Journal of Autism and Developmental Disorders, 46*(3), 782–796.

Standards and Testing Agency (2020) *The Engagement Model: Guidance for Maintained Schools, Academies (Including Free Schools) and Local Authorities.* Accessed 25/02/2021 at www.gov.uk/government/publications/the-engagement-model.

United Nations (2006) *Article 24 of the Convention on the Rights of Persons with Disabilities.* Accessed 29/03/2021 at www.un.org/development/desa/disabilities/convention-on-the-rights-of-persons-with-disabilities/article-24-education.html.

Wang, M.T. & Degol, J. (2014) 'Staying engaged: Knowledge and research needs in student engagement.' *Child Development Perspectives, 8*(3), 137–143.

Wittemeyer, K., Charman, T., Cusack, J., Guldberg, K. *et al.* (2011) *Educational Provision and Outcomes for People on the Autism Spectrum.* London: Autism Education Trust.

World Health Organization (1995) *International Classification of Disability – Version 10 (ICD-10).* Geneva: WHO.

CHAPTER 5

Supporting Anxiety and Well-Being

Editors: Diana Loffler and Erik Dwyer

Introduction

In the previous chapter, all the contributors showed us how looking beyond the outward behaviour, considering emotional regulation and reducing anxiety can result in greater well-being.

In recent years, there has been growing awareness and concern about the impact of anxiety on young people. Anxiety experienced by autistic individuals is often more intense and pervasive, yet its impact can go unrecognized, dismissed as a feature of the autism itself and so may lead to greater mental health issues. In recent years, the autistic community has redefined the understanding of autism by emphasizing that many so-called features of the condition are in fact secondary and a consequence of living in society. As Luke Beardon points out in this chapter, anxiety for autistic individuals is often pervasive through everyday life as a consequence of interaction with a social environment that is more inclined to suit neurotypicals.

We have clear evidence that anxiety is more prevalent among those with autism than neurotypical people. A recent study (Nimmo-Smith *et al.* 2020) analysing data from a Stockholm youth cohort has found that autistic young people were over two-and-a-half times more likely to have a clinical diagnosis of an anxiety disorder than a reference population without autism (20.1% of autistic individuals compared to 8.7% of controls). It should be noted that many studies indicate that the figures for generalized anxiety in autistic people are even higher. Furthermore, the figures are likely to be an underestimate given that measures of anxiety are not always sensitive to its presentation among autistic individuals.

Many studies show prevalence of anxiety is higher among autistic individuals who have greater social and linguistic engagement (Vasa & Mazurek 2015) and this is generally attributed to these individuals having greater insight, and, it is assumed, a greater awareness of their differences. However, much of the research assumes a neurotypical perspective of how anxiety is communicated or expressed. This requires not only linguistic competence but also an expectation that sharing will result in help. Additionally, those with greater difficulties in the areas of communication and social awareness may experience equal amounts of anxiety, but show it through repetitive behaviours, inflexibility and dysregulation.

From our experience as educational psychologists, we know that autistic young people are often referred to professionals because of concerns about their not being able to meet behavioural expectations. The SCERTS framework, as pointed out by Scot Greathead and Rhiannon Yates in the previous chapter, has helped to re-frame behaviour in terms of emotional regulation and the need for more positive experiences of engagement. Billy Parker, in the interview in this chapter, eloquently expresses for us the important role his interests have played in supporting his well-being and managing his anxiety. This is further addressed by Annie Etherington, who describes how we can become more aware of the perception and experience of autistic individuals and thereby make relevant adjustments in their environment and support.

Experience also tells us that autism is all too often identified after the individual is found to have a mental health issue. These mental health issues are likely to develop, at least in part, due to the pressure of suffering with unmanageable and pervasive anxiety. Increasingly, autism is being recognized among young people presenting with self-harm, eating disorders, obsessive compulsive disorder or depression.

In recent years, it has become apparent that the number of girls with autism has been underdiagnosed (Loomes, Hull & Mandy 2017). We know that autistic girls are less likely to be identified partly because they can present differently from many of the behavioural criteria and classifications that have been used in diagnosis. Girls tend to be more subject to social pressures, particularly during adolescence, and autistic girls may be more focused on trying to fit in and so copy the behaviours of others. In doing so, the stress and pressure they place on themselves, combined with their difficulty understanding the social interaction going on around them, can result in extreme anxiety and low self-esteem. Autistic girls have been found to be particularly vulnerable to social anxiety (Carpenter, Happé & Egerton 2019) and additionally it is not uncommon for them to be diagnosed later through interventions to support a mental health crisis.

Studies (Sharma *et al.* 2014) have also shown that autistic individuals have more negative expectations of the future, more negative beliefs about their abilities and a greater tendency to self-blame than neurotypicals. However, this is not surprising because we know that the feedback autistic individuals receive through their social engagement is often negative. In this chapter, Billy's testimony is remarkably generous in his perspective of others and at the same time he vividly describes how struggling to understand others and express himself have had negative implications for his emotional well-being.

The impact of pervasive anxiety, which can arise from simply going about one's daily life or from the overwhelming thoughts triggered by trying to understand and fit in to the social world, should not be underestimated. The onus, as Annie Etherington points out, is for us to listen and provide flexibility and support attuned to the individual.

HOW AND WHY ARE AUTISTIC PEOPLE ANXIOUS?

Luke Beardon

Identity-first language is used to reflect the majority of autistic preference (i.e., 'autistic person').

'Predominant neurotype' (PNT) is used to denote those who are not autistic or neurodivergent.

Imagine a life in which you simply cannot believe in yourself; you have lived a life in which you have constantly been told that you're in the wrong, that your way of doing things is 'the wrong way', that your thought processes, your belief systems, your sociality – *your very way of being* – needs to change to be more like everyone around you. This is what being autistic, for many people, is like within current society. This, among a plethora of other reasons, will lead to anxiety. This isn't to suggest that *being autistic* leads to being anxious – this is not the case at all. A more accurate statement would be that being autistic *within this current regime* will increase the risk of high levels of anxiety. As I have oft pointed out, autism + environment = outcome; *not* autism = outcome. Within the context of this contribution, the outcome that is the focus is anxiety. If one's autism cannot be changed (which it clearly can't) then surely the best way forward in terms of reducing anxiety would be to *change the environment*. Sometimes it's the simplest of things that can make such a huge difference – but the PNT *must* understand life through 'the autism lens' to appreciate the impact that change can have (positive or negative). Three examples:

1. The person for whom sending an email and awaiting a response equates to elevated anxiety until a response is made, but often the response can take days. Possible solution – to respond with a time frame within which a response will be made in full. While this may not eliminate anxiety, it is likely to at least decrease it.

2. The person who is highly anxious about an upcoming unavoidable social situation which appears to be 'open-ended' in terms of duration. Possible solution – provide the guarantee of a 'cut-off' point by which the engagement will end (or the person can leave); again, this will not remove anxiety altogether, but at least it lends some predictability to the situation.

3. The person at work for whom the phone on the desk causes panic whenever it rings (do not underestimate just how powerful this panic can be!). Possible solution – well, there are plenty, from taking the phone away altogether, to always having the phone on 'divert' so the person can listen to voice mail at a time that suits them. The important thing to note is that this apparently innocuous component of the working environment can be massively problematic to an autistic person.

Going back to the lack of belief in self; perhaps an analogy would be the colour-blind child who *actually* sees colours differently from others – but doesn't know it. Autistic children and adults will perceive the world around them in different ways to the PNT. This is what can often lead to the constant suggestions of those around them, that 'you are getting it wrong'. This can lead to astonishingly worrying levels of low self-esteem, not to mention long-term problems with physical and mental health. As adults, some people who finally recognize that they are autistic will still feel that maybe they aren't – not because they don't feel that they are autistic, but because it is so ingrained in them that their belief system is not to be trusted. This is how the environment can impact on autistic people (and this, usually, means people). And yet, what would it take to change the narrative for the autistic person, from as early an age as possible, to reduce that risk and increase the chances of a healthy and happy life, free from anxiety?

Anxiety is often linked to specific triggers – questions such as 'well, what is it that triggered your anxiety?' are not in the least bit uncommon. This is absolutely fair enough; but as a society, we need to understand that for many autistic children and adults, while specific triggers might explain some anxiety, they are far from the whole story. Much harder to 'see', and possibly harder to understand from a PNT perspective, is the complex anxiety that too often goes hand in hand with 'simply' living on a day-to-day basis in a world that is not suited to the person. Note – the world is not suited to the person, rather than the person is not suited to the world; there is a vast difference, and a hugely important one.

Feeling unstable in the world, pretty constantly, even at a low level, can do untold damage in the long term. This is the type of anxiety that this contribution will focus on. So, why do many autistic individuals feel unstable and, thus, anxious most of the time? Possibly the easiest way to explain is to turn the question around – how come so many of the PNT *don't* feel unstable most of the time? Well, it's all about 'fitting in' at a subconscious, intuitive level. And 'fitting in' goes way beyond fitting in at a social level – although sociality does play a big part.

Most people of the PNT have a good sense of how to effectively com-municate with each other. Most have a good sense of how to socialize with each other. Most share the sensory world with each other. Most understand how other PNTs think and behave. However, it is pretty rare to find someone of the PNT who is able, intuitively and effectively, to communicate, socialize, share the sensory world, and understand the thoughts and behaviours of the autistic population. And it's the same in reverse. Autistic people will often have issues over PNT communication, socialization, sensory experiences, and thought and behaviour. But just because the autistic population is in the minority, this should not make them 'in the wrong'; in reality, what happens is that the autistic popula-tion is the one that is deemed 'impaired' in these areas, despite the fact that that the flip side demonstrates pretty clearly that those same areas could easily be seen as 'impairments' in the PNT. However, this is not (yet!) the case – so it is left for the autistic to be the ones to conform, learn PNT 'skills' and fit in – all of which can cause ongoing and in-depth anxiety. Breaking it down, and giving some examples illuminates just how problematic the PNT world might be for some autistic individuals, and why they might suffer such high levels of ongoing anxiety.

Communication

Many people of the PNT really do not say what they think in a style that is conducive to the natural way in which many autistics process language. Rather than acknowledging that there are many linguistic flaws in PNT communication, the current trend is to assume fault with the autistic, accusing the individual of being 'pedantic', or 'too literal' in their interpretation of language. This is somewhat ironic – if language needs to be 'interpreted' then surely it is at fault in the first place? Surely, lack of ambiguity is something that all good communicators should be striving for?!

Socialization

Many people of the PNT seem to enjoy social chit-chat – small talk. In fact, many of the PNT seem to enjoy simply being in the company of all sorts of people, even when it appears that they might not even have that much in common. Many are perfectly chilled out chatting to one another in environments in which they should or could actually be doing something more constructive (such as studying or working). Many of the PNT find it effortless to make conversation, even when it's about a subject that they might not be particularly interested in. Where does this leave the autistic person who has no interest in social chat – in fact, it causes no end of anxiety? What about the autistic woman who finds being with others (aside from very close friends and family) anxiety-inducing in and of itself? What about the autistic man who can't stand time being wasted during working hours and finds it unduly stressful when others chat instead of work? What about the autistic pupil who loves nothing more than chatting about his passionate interest, but finds it painful to have to chat about anything else?

There is no 'right' or 'wrong' way to socialize, but it must be noted that autistic sociality very often differs to PNT sociality – and it's usually the autistic individual who ends up with social anxiety as a result, because they are forced into PNT sociality, and rarely allowed to bask in their own way of socializing. No wonder many autistic people choose simply to opt out of social environments. But that, again, puts them at a huge disadvantage.

Sensory

Autistic people very often have to exist in physical environments that are stress-inducing, but without anyone else in the same environment suffering from the same issue. From a sensory point of view, hypersensitivity to touch, noise, light and smell are often the main issues for the individual. Light touch that is processed as pain can cause unimaginable distress to the child in a school in which they are forced to have contact in the corridors every time they move from one class to the next. If one is noise sensitive, then every tick of the clock, every sneeze, every tap of the pencil – each and every one of these can be processed as noise to the point of pain; and yet, no one else may have an issue with it. If a child is sensitive to light but is not allowed to wear her lenses, then she is exposed to harshness that obliterates everything else. If an adult in a work environment has synaesthesia and certain smells are painful – perfume, for example – then he has to suffer on a daily basis.

These are very simple, individual examples; there are endless others that demonstrate just how disadvantaged an autistic person might be if their sensory needs are not taken into account.

PNT thinking and behaving

So many of the PNT population rarely have to consciously try figure out what is going on in the heads of others, or why others are behaving in the way in which they are. It is ironic indeed, then, that there are all sorts of training, writing, theories and the like about trying to explain to the PNT population what is going on in the heads of autistic people, or to explain why the autistic person is behaving in the way in which they are. Yet again, there is a massive imbalance here. Why all this support for the PNT people to help understand the autistic population, with so little (if anything) afforded to the autistic to aid understanding of the PNT world? And yet, seeing as the autistic individual is in the minority, they are the ones left to try figure it all out without any help.

These snippets are perfunctory at best; they exist to serve one main purpose – to identify just how disadvantageous it can be to be autistic within an environment that does not make adjustments, does not accept and does not understand. All of this will increase anxiety, and often create constant anxiety, which can be severely debilitating.

Can anxiety be seen?

Or, to put it another way – is it possible to ascertain signs of anxiety in order to subsequently do something about it? The answer, as it is so often in the autism world, is yes and no. Anxiety itself is an emotional state and, therefore, logically, invisible. However, the manifestation of any emotional state might take myriad forms. It is often changes in a typical pattern of behaviour that might indicate a change in an emotional state – this can be an increase in specific aspects of behaviour or a decrease. Examples might include an increased reliance on familiarity (whatever form that might take); a common cause for concern is when an individual shows a decrease in motivation. But it might be that a person masks their anxiety very effectively. This is why it is so important to have communication systems in place to gauge emotional states at all times if possible: many autistic individuals will not proactively let others know how they are feeling, so in some circumstances it can be down to others to try to find out for themselves.

Alexithymia

This term relates to difficulties in understanding emotional states (both in self and others); this categorically does not mean that autistic people do not feel emotions but that it might be more difficult for them to process and understand them compared to the PNT population. Many autistic people will process emotional states (including anxiety) incredibly intensely, to the point of being overwhelmed, at which point the only way to 'manage' the overload is to 'shut down'. Ironically, this then might appear that the person has no emotional response at all, when in fact the opposite is the case.

Ways forward

So, what can be done about anxiety? Possibly a better query would be: what *shouldn't* we be doing? Too many children are taught 'coping strategies' for their anxiety; while this might be useful for some children (or adults) some of the time, surely it is not an end goal itself. Surely a better end goal would be living without anxiety, not having to cope with it?

Teaching everyone about what causes anxiety is a good starting point to subsequently be doing something about it. And 'everyone' includes autistic people themselves! Teaching autistic children and adults about what it means to be autistic, and why they might struggle in environments that don't seem to affect others, could be a great way forward to increase self-awareness, understanding and self-esteem. Teaching the PNT population about just how anxiety can impact on autistic people could be a great way forward to effecting change.

Make no mistake – anxiety can destroy lives; long-term trauma is very real among the autistic population, and much of that trauma stems from ongoing anxiety as a child. High levels of anxiety might also lead to other long-term conditions, physical and mental. It is imperative that the wider society (not just autism provision) has a far better understanding of the variety of needs that the autistic population has. Not only does this come from an ethical perspective, but it also could be very much a lawful necessity. If anxiety puts autistic people at a substantial disadvantage (which it often does) then there is a requirement to make reasonable adjustments in order to balance out that disadvantage. If a reasonable adjustment is to not force a child into a PNT social engagement, or to adapt communication so that it is clear and unambiguous, or to remove the need for autistic children to have to eat in the canteen, or to provide appropriate sensory spaces, or to keep to timings within meetings – then this is what lawfully must happen. Instead of crippling autistic children and adults with anxiety, instead of autistics suffering because of a lack of knowledge, instead of long-term trauma – society could teach itself about autism, listen to autistic individuals, and adapt environments to make them work for everyone.

DOESN'T SOUND LIKE TOO MUCH TO ASK, DOES IT?

An interview with Billy Parker, by Diana Loffler

Billy first attended a mainstream primary school. He was diagnosed with autism in Year 2 when he was six years old and then moved to a primary school with a centre for children with autism when he was seven years old. He later attended a secondary school where he was supported at a newly opened centre for autistic pupils.

As an educational psychologist, I supported Billy (as the need arose) from his time joining the primary centre until the end of his time in the secondary school when his family moved out of the area. Involvement included individual work providing emotional and social support, discussion with his mother and advice to school staff.

At the time of the interview, Billy was 17 years old and studying for A-levels at a local sixth-form college.

Could you describe any difficult feelings you experienced as a child in your primary school years? (I know you first went to a mainstream school and then a primary school with a centre to help children with autism.)

During my primary school years, I had groups of people with whom I was good friends, and others with whom I did not properly connect. In my earlier years of primary school, my main difficulties were based on a general inability to properly interpret the nature of how other people were or weren't treating me, particularly because it was very difficult to distinguish between when people were either attempting to antagonize me, or simply trying to interact with me through comical means. I also did not necessarily share particularly similar interests to many other people, which made it difficult to engage with many individuals and form proper connections with them. In retrospect, I had good theoretical academic potential which did not end up expressing itself in practice until perhaps my last year of primary school (Year 6). Social obstacles before then prevented me from applying myself academically, but I always largely maintained a certain level of interest and curiosity for different areas of knowledge and information throughout much of that time, even if they were very different from that possessed by other children.

In my later years of primary school, I started to improve on a number of things, including my level of interaction and familiarity with other people, including (to a certain extent) both pupils and teachers. There were many other people, however, who I did not get on well with. A combination of dispositional factors concerning both myself and those individuals played a role in those difficulties, though I dare say that some of those people were preferably to be avoided, independent of any limitations there were within myself. I also had many issues in relation to sensitivity to noise and would often be very anxious and on edge whenever noise accumulated in different situations. This in turn made it very difficult for me to function adequately during many of my earlier years at school.

Can you remember when and where these difficult feelings happened?

In better contexts, if somebody was attempting to make physical contact in a friendly manner, I may have misinterpreted such gestures as being malicious in intent. To give an analogy, though not one to be taken literally by any means, I may very well have confused play-fighting for fighting. I would get extremely anxious around not being able to differentiate between when somebody was or wasn't agitated or angry at me. It was very challenging for me to properly and accurately interpret cues for the recognition of the emotions of others; and I often found that the behaviour of other individuals was inconsistent, complex and perhaps irrational in expressing how they truly felt, or whether they were actually feeling anything significant at all (which to be fair is probably true to a certain extent).

Can you describe some of the things at this time which gave you good feelings?

There were plenty of things which gave me good feelings during this time. As previously stated, I had groups of friends, many of whom were 'neurotypical' and, especially towards my last years of primary school, I started to be more productive academically (or at least educationally). I had already read lots about Ancient Egypt in my own time, so I was familiar with a lot of the theological and sociological history of Ancient Egyptian civilization prior to our classroom learning about it in Year 5, so I enjoyed a lot of the classroom topics which we ended up going through. I also enjoyed a lot of artistic activities that took place over the last couple of years. In a more effectively summarized conclusion, I always possessed an interest in different areas of knowledge that I was able to connect to different parts of my primary school life in order to obtain a lot of positive experience and pleasurable appreciation for many years of my primary education.

You have given an excellent description of the subtleties involved in interaction and difficulties that can occur. You also sound very reflective and understanding about other people. Do you think you were so at the time, and was your anxiety hard to manage?

At the time, I found the behaviour of other individuals too ambiguous to properly interpret and accurately infer from. Consequently, I struggled to both understand other people accurately and express myself to others effectively. This in turn had negative implications for my emotional well-being, as the complexity of the way people behaved and the unpredictability of how they would behave towards me left me in a situation where I didn't really know what to think, but it still caused me to feel excessive anxiety.

At secondary school, you were initially supported in their centre for autistic students and gradually, as you grew older, you spent more time in mainstream lessons. What situations and environments were troubling and upsetting for you, either in or out of school? What experiences were positive and gave you good feelings?

I possessed a passionate desire to engage in mainstream lessons, which led me to originally fail to recognize the importance of the centre. At first, I wrongly perceived it as a mechanism of separation between me and wider social circles. Over time, however, I gradually succeeded in understanding the centre as a mechanism by which I was to be socially prepared for my progression into further mainstream lessons. The initial idea of me being separated from the wider community did trouble me to begin with and clouded my judgement of the centre to a significant degree. Over time, my acceptance of the necessary assistance I received at the centre enabled me to progress more successfully into mainstream education. I possessed, and still do possess, a passion for science, which enabled me to display a positive attitude towards the subject. However, I still faced problems in relation to extreme anxiety. I would often fail to distinguish between someone attempting to antagonize me or simply engaging with me through comedic means. This often drained my mental energy just contemplating the possibility that somebody may be angry at me about things which were simply irrational to even remotely stress about. The complex and ambiguous nature of how people behave meant it was difficult for me to understand why people behaved in different ways, and consequently what emotions their behaviours were supposed to indicate. This again generated extreme anxiety which was piled on top of the already existing nervousness that everyone faces when first entering secondary education.

There were many things which made me feel good during these times. The centre had very good-natured and understanding teachers, and although I originally struggled to accept help from them, they were fantastic people who had a strong understanding of my anxiety, and helped me to cope significantly. I made multiple friends too (some also on the spectrum and others 'neurotypical') who remained such throughout the rest of my time in secondary school. There were some who were especially accepting of me as a unique individual and also understood any significantly abnormal behaviours of mine as being a product of the social anxieties I struggled with. Those friends, and those teachers, both made very important contributions towards my productive experiences at secondary school which followed.

It is helpful how you describe your feelings and frustration about being separated from mainstream lessons. It seems that your views were not fully understood and taken account of. Also, it is useful to know that your academic interests were so motivating for you and helped with your emotional well-being. I know that sometimes anxiety became more overwhelming and persistent for you. Can you explain how this affected you and what things helped you overcome it? Looking back, what could have happened differently that might have helped you?

I experienced excessive anxiety throughout many different areas of school life. I recall worrying significantly about how I would be perceived by mainstream friends as a member of the centre. I also formed strong friendships with many people who were in the centre, but I had many anxieties about whether I had done something to upset them, even though there was not sufficient evidence to suggest that there was any tension between me and others under such circumstances. I would often become overwhelmed by anxieties about social interaction both inside and outside the mainstream sector of the school, which resulted in me struggling relentlessly to maintain a productive level of concentration in classrooms. In many ways, this helped to strengthen my relationship with the centre, as I received lots of help with managing these problems from the teachers there. They were excellent in talking with me and helping me to reason things out to a degree that my anxiety was able to be reduced. Their help allowed me to function much better in the mainstream and therefore I see the staff as being one of the most important factors in my improvements in emotional health. They took an idiographic approach towards helping me, as did staff in the mainstream too, meaning that not only was the centre fantastic in helping me, but also the school was fantastic for helping people in general. As well as this, I focused on trying to postpone anxieties until I had the opportunity to discuss them with the staff in the centre, which allowed me to once again be more productive in mainstream lessons. Another key thing that enabled me to cope well with anxieties was some of the friendships which I formed with mainstream individuals. I had many, but there were some who understood me as being particularly unique compared to others and different in my perception of the world and my key interests. They helped me greatly. In retrospect, if there was anything that could have happened differently that might have helped me, it would have been for me to open up more about myself earlier on and appreciate and accept the help given to me sooner than I did. Nonetheless, in spite of my initial hesitation to accept such help, those offering it succeeded in helping me greatly regardless.

I also benefited significantly from the help I received from CAMHS (child and adolescent mental health services) which included both CBT (cognitive behavioural therapy) and, for a time, medication. During my experiences with anxiety, I prioritized finding psychological means of managing my anxiety over biochemical means, and therefore considered biological therapies to be a last resort. However, the help received at school and the CBT were very important, along with some medication, and I consider all of the factors collectively to have helped me to improve as much as I have. It is my view that if you were to remove any one of them from the equation, my levels of improvement would have significantly decreased. It is a combination of all the things I was fortunate enough to receive which led me to the levels of improvement I have achieved.

What advice would you give to someone in a similar position to you who was struggling to manage anxiety?

I suppose the best strategy may vary for the specific individual, but the overall responses which are most beneficial from my perspective are to first find people who you can talk to about the problems. Individuals who hold a good amount of knowledge about you in terms of your character and their familiarity with you make a significant difference. There is no objective way of assessing who to talk to, but those who you have formed the most trusting relationships with are obviously preferable (more to the point, necessary). One of the biggest obstacles for people with Asperger syndrome is that they often have special interests which, while they very much have highly productive potential implications for many important parts of society, can make it much harder to form strong relationships with other people. I have found that there are neurotypical people who are much more understanding than others, and also more interested in understanding particularly unique individuals. The social connections that people form are, as far as I am concerned, vital for overcoming any issues someone is facing, and these particular issues should be no exception. Furthermore, I believe that one thing that helps people to cope with any struggles they are facing is to invest time in channelling their interests and passions. It may sound like a vague and bizarre proposition at first, but when somebody channels their interests (whatever they may be) into something productive then they are shifting attention away from whatever the theoretical anxiety is and are instead developing themselves by expanding on the things which make them most happy.

Another important thing to take into consideration is the issues that surround the social anxieties. Autistic individuals are often influenced significantly by the interactions they have with other people and the concerns they have over how they come across to others. Many people are feeling increasingly pressurized to maintain a level of popularity and likability with others, leading these people to conform to the behaviour of others around them, and this pressure amplifies social anxieties overwhelmingly, particularly during adolescence. People on the spectrum are likely to find it the most difficult to conform to the behaviour, language and hobbies of others, which can increase the extent to which they feel isolated from other people. As well as this, both autistic individuals and neurotypicals recognize the qualitative differences between one another and consequently are likely to feel uncomfortable around each other. This feeling of discomfort and, in turn, anxiety is perhaps felt by a very large proportion of people. What can make it especially problematic for autistic individuals is that they are surrounded by an environment of mostly neurotypical people, which means they not only deviate the most from others but also may experience further anxiety over the fact that they are outnumbered in most social environments. This accumulates to produce large amounts of excessive anxiety and can be a serious challenge for autistic individuals when attempting to maintain relationships with others.

The reason this is all relevant is that a key step towards addressing these sorts of anxieties is to remember that, whether you are autistic or not, there is nothing explicitly wrong with you. Don't view yourself as being an anomalous or abnormal person who is at fault for any worries or general problems you have with other people. If you do view yourself in that light, then it is likely to make any issues you face with anxiety much worse. Another important thing to keep in mind in terms of the availability of help is that different things end up working for different people. Interventions such as CBT and some types of medication have, I understand, been shown by various studies to be effective and make a significant difference for many people, but not for others. If you do talk to a professional, though, make sure that you are fully open about the severity of the issues you are experiencing. All in all, having confidence and compassion for your own self (independent of what others may or may not think about you), maintaining communication with those with whom you have formed the most trusting relationships, and investing time in your most upheld passions, as well as talking to a professional, if necessary, are some of the main solutions.

UNDERSTANDING AND RESPONDING TO AUTISTIC ANXIETY: LEARNING TO LISTEN

Annie Etherington

The importance of sensitive adjustments and adaptations to the learning environment, with a particular emphasis on the role of the professional, is well highlighted in the exploration of anxiety by both Luke and Billy in this chapter. A critical element is the refocusing of attention away from the autistic learner in favour of a consideration of other elements – the educational professional, or carer, and the physical learning environment. There are existing frameworks which support such refocusing. Central to their model, Prizant and colleagues (2006) pay close attention to the developmental stage of the child/young person in relation to social communication and emotional regulation which is then linked to the transactional support which can be put into place (SCERTS, *ibid.*). The transactional element considers the interpersonal support (what the adult can do) and the learning support (how the environment can be adapted or modified). This model significantly builds on, and extends, some of the key principles of the well-established Treatment and Education of Autistic and Related Communication-Handicapped Children (TEACCH) framework which acknowledges some of the strengths of autistic processing (autistic culture) to create a supportive structure by creating a 'prosthetic' learning environment to address potential areas of need (Mesibov, Shea & Schopler 2005). The National Autistic Society has developed a framework over many decades which also considers the transactional elements of support. Devised in collaboration with autistic individuals, the principles embrace: Structure; Positive approaches and expectations; Empathy; Links; and Low arousal (SPELL 2020). These frameworks, and in particular SPELL, along with the reflections on anxiety by Billy and Luke, will inform this section exploring responses and support in relation to anxiety and autistic learners.

Structure

One of the valuable lessons from TEACCH is the essential role of structure to provide a predictable environment which may address the tension, and ultimately anxiety, created by uncertainty, and draw attention to what is salient in an activity or interaction, and clarify expectations across a day or parts of a day. While following certain established principles, such supports need to be personalized to reflect the preferences and learning strengths of the individual. The role of the adult in adapting the interpersonal and environmental supports is paramount, and key questions to consider have been expressed most effectively by the SCERTS in the form shown in Table 5.1.

Low arousal

Both Billy and Luke have commented on the impact of the sensory environment and the profound distress it can create for those who may be highly sensitive to everyday aspects of the learning environment. For many on the spectrum, the anticipation of aversive sensory experiences can create high levels of anxiety which can interfere with all aspects of engagement and learning. The Autism Education Trust (2018) has produced a range of helpful materials and resources, and the Enabling Environments section of the School Programme includes two sensory audit tools (see Standards, Resources, p.34), one for reviewing the environment for potential sensory issues and the other for creating a basic, personalized sensory profile for a student. It can be very helpful to conduct both of these in *collaboration* with pupils as this can develop an understanding of their particular stress points. Addressing the sensory sensitivities identified through this process can positively influence decisions and choices made about the learning environment on a general level (e.g., organization and clarity within the classroom, nature of displays, creation of low arousal areas within the learning space) as well as personalized responses for some (e.g., ear defenders, position in classroom, provision of a sanctuary space – pop-up tent, workstation, screened area).

Empathy

In Billy's exploration of some of the challenges he has faced, particularly in understanding the intentions of others, and throughout Luke's section, the significance of the allistic (non-autistic) understanding of the autistic perspective is emphasized. This can often be an issue as autistic academic and writer, Damian Milton, has described in the 'double empathy problem'. For too long, he argues, we have failed to recognize the bi-directional flow of empathy and have ignored the failure of the allistic population to understand, and have empathy for, the autistic perspective (Milton 2012). In order to support, understand and address autistic anxiety, we need to understand it from the lived perspective of the autistic individual. This requires close listening, attention to communication (often beyond words) and allowing a safe space for the inner world to be expressed. A crucial element may be creating a dialogue which is informed and influenced by the autistic individual rather than the imposition of a particular 'strategy' by the allistic supporter. This may begin with facilitating the development of self-awareness using some of the following approaches and ideas.

The Know Your Normal project (Crane *et al.* 2017) arose from a community-based participatory research approach involving young autistic adults alongside academic researchers. A number of significant findings emerged from their survey, in particular the perceived demand from the neurotypical community to conform and suppress autistic behaviour, a point strongly made by Luke. This is a view endorsed across multiple online autism forums, created and run by individuals on the spectrum, where the demand for social conformity is seen as a persistent source of stress and anxiety and a cause of masking and camouflaging responses. The general position is captured powerfully in a paper by Milton and Moon (2012), who make the link with a normalization agenda, which is alienating for the autistic individual and potentially impacts on mental health.

Table 5.1: An excerpt from SCERTS in Action Observation and Planning Form by Emily Rubin, SCERTS Online Training (https://scerts.com/training)

Do you think the learners know…	What supports are working? How have partners effectively supported the learners?	What are some next steps? Action plan
Why they have to do something? The desirability of the task; hands-on materials/purposeful endpoints/tied to special interests or real-life events/role play/humour		
When to take part (when to initiate)? The activity includes opportunities for participation, responsive partners and a range of communication functions (e.g., requesting, commenting and asking questions)		
How to communicate (what to do)? Visuals such as objects, photos, pictures and written words/sentence starters to remind the child how to ask for help, comment and respond to questions (e.g., modelling and visuals indicating expectations)		
What is happening next? The sequence of activities; objects of reference, activity baskets, photo/picture schedules and written day planner		
What the steps are within the activity? Materials laid in sequence, count-down strips, visual timers and written help boxes		
That others are responsive and a source of emotional support? Interactive partners who adjust tone of voice, expectations, and the environment to soothe or engage		
How to soothe or engage by themselves? How to regulate their emotions; access to sensory supports and visual choices of coping strategies		

A positive and practical outcome of the Know Your Normal research was a toolkit which can serve as a helpful guide for the autistic individual to establish what is familiar, normal behaviour for them. It provides a potential tracking system to identify both when there are changes in their personalized 'normal' (a possible early indicator that their mental health may be in decline) and when they may need additional support. It is also a powerful tool to help the professional gain greater insight into the experience and emotional world of the young person. Some adaptation of the toolkit may be needed for younger children.

In a similar vein, the *Molehill Mountain* app offers a personalized, daily opportunity to reflect on and understand anxiety, and develop some self-help tools using daily 'tips'. The app was developed from a psychoeducational toolkit using adapted cognitive behavioural therapy principles for children and young people on the autism spectrum. In a pilot trial involving 8–18-year-olds (all on the spectrum and with significant anxiety) and their parent(s), there were some positive findings in terms of improvement in the child's level of anxiety (Kent *et al.* 2018). Subsequently the app, currently for use on smartphones and tablets, was developed and is under continuing development by Autistica, a national UK research charity led and managed by a neurodiverse team. Currently focusing on independent learners on the spectrum (teenagers and older), it offers the opportunity for a 'supporter' to engage with the young person and offer feedback and acknowledgement either through the app (if nominated) or in person.

Both the toolkits may offer a useful starting point for working with an autistic young person to support self-reflection and strengthen self-awareness in terms of their emotional health. However, currently, all require access to relatively sophisticated language skills – and this can be compromising for individuals who find language processing challenging when feeling anxious or distressed, or for those whose communication tends to be non-language based. Where this is the case, greater ingenuity may be required on the part of the supporter. A number of systems have been developed which capitalize on strengths in the visual processing of learning and systemizing. A number of these capture some of the elements of adapted CBT. An example may be found in five-point scales; Table 5.2 shows a scale that was devised by an advisory teacher working with a ten-year-old boy on the autism spectrum and illustrates some of the potential areas which could be explored in this systematic rating system.

Table 5.2: Example of a five-point rating scale to support self-reflection

Rating	Looks/sounds like	Feels like	I can try or others can help by
5	Completely silent. Can't usually see me because I've hidden my face. I am sometimes crying.	I am a giant volcano about to explode. I want to go outside and throw tiles on a stone floor. I am extremely upset. I feel like I'm going to throw up. I don't want to be in this world any more. I want to be alone.	Staff say, 'You need a break.' I may take a while to leave. Staff can say, 'I am going to walk with you to take a break.' They could hold my hand. I will try to walk with them to the calm space. I can sit there and do my relaxation.
4	My head in my arms. Completely silent. I have stopped flapping my arms. I'm so worried. I'm ignoring most people who are not my friends or teacher.	Don't feel good; tense all over, and slightly sick. I feel like I've turned into a statue. I'm invisible. Feel like I want to get away from here. Very worried.	Staff give me my calm card. I can do my breathing and counting routine. After two minutes, staff can say, 'Do you need more time?' I can try to say 'yes' or 'no' or nod or shake my head.
3	Flapping my arms quite a lot. Almost stop talking. My eyes get bigger. Look quite nervous. Fidgeting. Stretching.	My arms and body feel tense. I try to ignore everything else. Feel quite worried, like I want to get away from the class.	Staff can say, 'Tell me what is wrong?' I can try to tell people what is worrying me. I would like people to listen and try to take action.
2	I might start flapping my hands. I might be a bit quieter. You can see a hint of nervousness in my face. I usually bite my teeth.	There's a small trickle of worriedness and panic going through my body. My arms start to feel tense.	I can show my worry card to my safe person. I can say what is making me worried. I can work out how to solve my worry. I can remember, 'I can ask for help.'
1	Working well, looking happy, laughing, very chatty, humming.	Excited, really happy, a nice feeling inside me, calm.	Enjoy the time I feel happy. People can try not to remind me of anything bad that has happened.

An additional column could be used to identify what engenders those feelings, with some linked solutions. So, for example, if level 2 anxiety may be caused by uncertainty about task requirements, this could be identified alongside a proactive solution (such as asking for more information). In addition, explicitly identifying the feeling experienced in relation to each level can be helpful. The example shown requires access to both receptive and expressive verbal language of some sophistication. A picture/colour-based scale (shown in Figure 5.1) was developed with a six-year-old girl who used little spoken language. She selected the colours (to represent feeling good, okay and bad) for a reduced scale linked to positive actions (walk, pop-up tent, work).

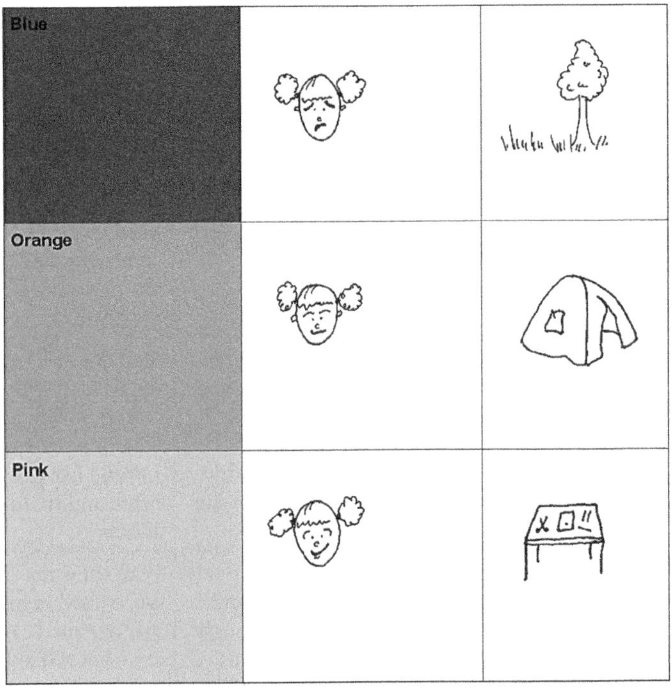

Figure 5.1: Example of a picture/colour-based scale for use with children with little spoken language

There are a number of published resources which can support the understanding of using scaling systems. The link between this visual, systematic approach and adapted CBT has been acknowledged: Dunn Buron (2012), has noted that scales can support the recognition and identification of internal emotional states which can, ultimately, be linked to useful self-regulating responses (or regulation with support from another).

Establishing and developing trusting relationships with a child or young person on the autism spectrum is essential and, potentially, a powerful tool in engagement that is meaningful, reassuring and purposeful. Barry Prizant, one of the SCERTS creators, has stated, 'the absence of anxiety isn't calm, it's trust' (Prizant 2016, p.73). Such trust (as noted earlier by Billy) is precious and requires considerable thought, understanding and awareness on the part of the allistic individual. It requires exquisite attention to detail in observing and learning about each individual child and their anxieties. As Prizant reminds us: listen, observe, ask why (*ibid.*). As well as learning to read the many and sometimes minute signs that signal anxiety, we need to find personalized ways of listening to the autistic voice. Sometimes it may be possible to have a language-based exploration but often words may interfere with such communication. There are some innovative approaches which may elicit the autistic voice and experience that do not depend entirely on spoken language. This may be critical in exploring the inner emotional experience of some autistic children and young people. Digital Stories, as a method for empowerment for non-literacy/language-based communication, has been very successful in capturing the perspective of very young autistic children through, among other digital approaches, using video footage from small wearcams (Parsons *et al.* 2020). Talking Mats, while not autism-specific, has much to offer in terms of providing a format for interaction which uses visual rather than spoken communication, allowing the thinker – in this case the autistic individual – to express (visually) their views, preferences and experiences to a listener. Mundt (2020) has provided a helpful overview of the theories underpinning the approach.

The process of enabling the expression of self-reflection and the sharing of emotional experience may also be supported through the use of photography. Its use as a participatory and collaborative tool in research is gaining momentum and has a particular value for individuals who may find challenges in conventional ways of articulating complex inner states, views and experiences (Doronzenko, Bishop & Roberts 2014). In an interesting and current project at Curtin University, Australia, researchers and autistic adults collaborated to understand important aspects of quality of life from an autistic perspective (*Quality of Life of Autistic Adults*, Curtin Autism Research Group 2021). An online

Photovoice gallery has been created, consisting of photos and word commentary from the participating adults. This captures powerful insights into the meaning that participants ascribed to the photos taken, and a number of important themes emerging from them. Several of these resonate with issues raised by Billy: the importance of relationships, emotional well-being, socializing and sensory issues. Engaging in this way requires commitment and sensitivity from the allistic professional/supporter. In another study, conducted with nine autistic children, the researchers highlighted the responsibilities and challenges involved:

> The interactive process in the photovoice project required the researchers to spend more time to observe, engage with, listen to and experience the children's lives while also acknowledging our differences and accepting the limitations of our abilities to fully understand another's perspective and the inadequacies of our representations. (Ha & Whittaker 2016, Discussion)

Photovoice has the potential to facilitate the exploration of the autistic child/young person's lived experience and create a communicative interaction offering some insight into the child's inner world, allowing for an exploration of their anxieties. For example, a young autistic boy aged six with very little spoken language was given a camera and went on a tour of his primary school with his teaching assistant. He took many photographs and his teaching assistant made notes as they walked, to try to help with understanding if he seemed to have positive or negative feelings about different features as he took the photographs. It was difficult for her to be certain, but she did note that there were a series of pictures taken when he appeared excited and happy. Reviewing the photos with him later, she paid particular attention to these, but could find very little to link them (bookcase, door, notice in the corridor and so on), until she noticed that all included, in some form, a green rectangle. Conjecturing this was something of importance and pleasure to him, a green rectangle was introduced as part of his activities, and his engagement and interaction significantly improved. What the research and this simple example suggest is that the use of an indirect approach (in this case, the use of a camera, but other options could be considered) may open a channel of communication which gives expression to feelings beyond words but requires close attention and attunement from the listener/viewer:

For human beings to engage with one another we must move in syn-chrony, pausing at appropriate times, observing, listening, not judging or jumping to conclusions, but paying close attention to the other's expression. All of this allows us to respond appropriately and share meaning. (McCreadie & Milton 2020, p.160)

Links

Billy has described the importance of friendships in his life, and it is a theme he revisits frequently. Research supports this: there is a link between anxiety and social isolation and loneliness for some on the spectrum (Lau *et al.* 2020). Attention to supporting, or at times facilitat-ing, social contact in a non-invasive way may be helpful for some. Joshua Muggleton (2011), an autistic psychologist and author, has pointed to the importance of 'secondary socialization', creating opportunities to socialize around a shared interest or passion rather than creating groups which only focus on learning how to be 'social'. With this in mind, adap-tations of approaches such as Circle of Friends, or similar, can provide a format for creating a network of support linked to shared interests (and, potentially, developing understanding and empathy among the neurotypical supporters). A helpful meta-study by Locke and Harker (2017) outlines a range of peer support programmes.

SPELL, SCERTS and TEACCH all emphasize the importance of collaboration between professionals and family members to create a rounded and shared network of support with the child/young person at the centre. When addressing issues of well-being, this shared per-spective, starting with the focus on the individual and their views, is of particular importance.

Positive approaches

Finding joy through irresistible learning experiences and interactions is a powerful antidote to anxiety. This may start with engaging with the child/young person's passion and interests (Kluth 2008) as the focal point of an activity. Child-centred approaches such as Intensive Interaction (Caldwell *et al.* 2019; Frith 2006) and Attention Autism (Marsh 2019) can provide principles for utilizing the child's interests or focus as a way of building meaningful and positive contact. In addition, Vermeulen (2014) suggests creating positive sensory preference scales and activities where the individual identifies the sensory experiences which are pleasurable. Creating personalized sensory resource boxes in collaboration with the child/young person, with their preferred items, can be calming and may reduce anxiety.

All of the ideas explored here do not require specialist training, but they may need us to think about education in a broader sense and acknowledge that ongoing anxiety will erode the capacity to engage in learning over time. Consider this key recommendation from a well-researched project conducted in Australia:

> Educational settings should support the social emotional wellbeing of students on the spectrum, as an essential element of programming. This has been widely recognized as a protective factor for wellbeing and mental health, as well as a key to educational success. (Saggers *et al.* 2018, p.152)

Chapter conclusion

Autistic adults have made clear how dysregulation and anxiety are a constant part of their lives. Luke described how this is linked to the lack of stability and predictability in the environment. All the contributors have shown how stress can build through interacting with and trying to understand the subtle complexity of the social world. All have emphasized how neurotypicals need to develop and extend their own empathy skills to recognize this experience. Events and interactions, which may seem everyday and incidental to many, can be overwhelming, intrusive and negative for those with autism. This has recently been recognized in research on post-traumatic stress disorder where it has been shown that the so-called 'triggers' for autistic people can seem more apparently benign than those that generally affect the allistic population.

Billy talks in illuminating detail about the pressures and self-doubt engendered in his search to understand the intentions of others. He also refers to his distractibility in the classroom, which can all too often be seen as a behavioural problem, rather than a consequence of trying to process and understand the meaning behind the myriad of complex social interactions which can exist within a school environment. Using individualized and innovative approaches, as illustrated by Annie in her examples of intervention, can be powerful in understanding the emotional world of others and enabling more positive experiences.

Billy and Annie have also highlighted the importance of 'trust'. As a result of negative social experiences, autistic individuals often do not perceive others as a source of help. To develop trust requires time and sensitivity, which then builds respect and understanding for the others' emotional state and can lead to greater engagement and reciprocity. This idiographic approach, relying on empathic observation, rather than applying a theoretical knowledge of autism (as Annie points out), is essential for reducing anxiety and enabling individual emotional well-being to develop.

Many traditional interventions rely on inference and abstract thinking skills; however, the work of Attwood and Vermeulen and of the 'Social Thinking' approach[1] have shown us how such interventions can be adapted to suit the autistic individual. Inherent in all these approaches are strategies which start with a recognition of the valid coping mechanisms already used by those with autism, including interests and strengths, which can support emotional well-being and reduce anxiety. In fact, those of us who have supported autistic young people are aware that the right interventions and adaptations can make a massive and positive change.

From this chapter, we have learned that the causes of anxiety in autistic individuals can go unrecognized and are often a consequence of the demands and inflexibility of our neurotypical world. It is important for professionals and carers to listen to and observe the individual, to clarify and make intentions clear in the social world, to provide both structure and flexibility in the environment and to facilitate a sense of control for autistic individuals. We need to become more alert to differences and diversity in terms of individual processing and perspective, and broaden our means of communication so that we can understand and support effectively and reciprocally. We need to value and give space for the interests and relationships which enable positive feelings and encourage those calming strategies which are already used effectively by autistic young people. In reading this chapter, we should remember that, as professionals and carers who work/live with autistic young people, too much focus and emphasis on the word 'anxiety' can be a problem in itself, in that we may inadvertently signal that to experience anxiety is something bad and to be avoided. We should remind young people that to have emotions and feelings is a normal part of life, and it is our

---

1   www.socialthinking.com

response to these that is key. As Billy reminds us, it can ease anxiety just to tell the autistic person that 'There is nothing wrong with you.'

POINTS FOR REFLECTION

☞ It is important to recognize that anxiety for autistic individuals is often pervasive across their day, due to issues with the lack of consistency in everyday social interactions and the lack of clarity in context.

☞ When supporting an autistic person, it is important to take account of what that person already uses and needs to support their emotional regulation and to develop and work around these as much as possible.

☞ Sensitive observation (including, when they are young, striving to understand and respond to their communicative efforts) is key to understanding the autistic individual's perspective and thereby developing a trusting and reciprocal relationship.

Resources

www.ambitiousaboutautism.org.uk/what-we-do/youth-participation/youth-led-toolkits/know-your-normal
www.autismeducationtrust.org.uk
www.autistica.org.uk/our-research/research-projects/anxiety-tools-for-autistic-people
www.autistica.org.uk/molehill-mountain
www.autismcrc.com.au/news/latest-news/photovoice-gallery-event-recording-now-available
www.autism.org.uk/advice-and-guidance/topics/strategies-and-interventions/strategies-and-interventions/spell
https://scerts.com
www.socialthinking.com
www.talkingmats.com

References

Autism Education Trust (2018) *Schools Programme: Autism Standards, Enabling Environments*, Resources (1). www.autismeducationtrust.org.uk.

Caldwell, P., Bradley, E., Gurney, J., Heath, J., Lightowler, H. & Richardson, K. (2019) *Responsive Communication: Combining Attention to Sensory Issues with Body Language (Intensive Interaction) to Interact with Autistic Adults and Children*. London: Pavilion Publishing.

Carpenter, B., Happé, F. & Egerton, J. (2019) 'Where are All the Autistic Girls? An Introduction.' In B. Carpenter, F. Happé & J. Egerton (eds) *Girls and Autism: Educational, Family and Personal Perspectives*. London and New York: Routledge.

Crane, L., Adams, F., Harper, G., Welch, J. & Pellicano, E. (2017) *Know Your Normal: Mental Health in Young Autistic Adults*. London, UK: UCL Institute of Education.

Curtin Autism Research Group (2021) *Quality of Life of Autistic Adults*. Accessed 19/08/2021 at https://carg.curtin.edu.au/quality-of-life.

Doronzenko, K.P., Bishop, B.J. & Roberts, L.D. (2014) 'The use of photovoice with people with intellectual disabilities: Reflections, challenges and opportunities.' *Disability and Society, 29*(6), 1–15.

Dunn Buron, K. & Curtis, M. (2012) *The Incredible 5-Point Scale* (second edition). Shawnee, KS: AAPC Publishing.

Frith, G. (2006) 'Intensive Interaction: A research review.' *Mental Health and Learning Disabilities Research and Practice, 3*(1), 53–63.

Ha, V.S. & Whittaker, A. (2016) 'Closer to my world: Children with autism spectrum disorder tell their stories through photovoice.' *Global Public Health, 11*(5–6), 546–563.

Kent, R., Carruthers, S., Bridge, L., Ozsivadjian, A. & Simonoff, E. (2018) 'Managing Anxiety in Autism: A Pilot Trial of Newly Developed Psychoeducational Toolkits.' Poster presentation, International Society for Autism Research, Rotterdam.

Kluth, P. (2008) *Just Give Him the Whale! 20 Ways to use Fascinations, Areas of Expertise and Strengths to Support Students with Autism*. Baltimore, MD: Brookes Publishing.

Lau, B.Y., Leong, R., Uljarevic, M., Lerh, J.W. *et al.* (2020) 'Anxiety in young people with autism spectrum disorder: Common and autism-related anxiety experiences and their associations with individual characteristics.' *Autism, 24*(5), 1111–1126.

Locke, J. & Harker, C. (2017) 'Using Typically Developing Peers as Support for Social Inclusion of Children and Adolescents with Autism.' In C. Little (ed.) *Supporting Social Inclusion for Students with Autism Spectrum Disorders*. London: Routledge.

Loomes, R., Hull, L. & Mandy, W.P.L. (2017) 'What is the male-to-female ratio in autism spectrum disorder? A systematic review and meta-analysis.' *Journal of the American Academy of Child and Adolescent Psychiatry, 56*(6), 466–474.

Marsh, F. (2019) 'Attention Autism for children and young people on the autism spectrum: A critique of the current evidence-base.' Academic critique, Doctoral Programme in Educational Psychology, University of Southampton.

McCreadie, M. & Milton, M. (2020) 'Autism: Understanding Behavior.' In D. Milton (lead ed.) *The Neurodiversity Reader*. London: Pavilion Publishing.

Mesibov, G., Shea, V. & Schopler, E. (2005) *The TEACCH Approach to Autism Spectrum Disorders*. New York, NY: Springer.

Milton, D. (2012) 'On the ontological status of autism: The "double empathy problem".' *Disability and Society, 27*(6), 883–887.

Milton. D. & Moon, L. (2012) 'The normalisation agenda and the psycho-emotional disablement of autistic people.' *Autonomy, 1*(1).

Muggleton, J. (2011) *Raising Martians – From Crash Landing to Leaving Home*. London: Jessica Kingsley Publishers.

Mundt, I. (2020) *Theories that Underpin the Principles and Strategies of the Talking Mats Tool*. Copenhagen: University College.

Nimmo-Smith, V., Heuvelman, H., Idring, S., Carpenter, P. *et al.* (2020) 'Anxiety disorders in adults with autism spectrum disorder: A population-based study.' *Journal of Autism and Developmental Disorders, 50*(1), 308–318.

Parsons, S., Ivil, K., Kovshoff, H. & Karakosta, E. (2020) '"Seeing is believing": Exploring the perspectives of young autistic children through Digital Stories.' *Journal of Early Childhood Research*. https://doi.org/10.1177/1476718X20951235.

Prizant, B. (2016) *Uniquely Human: A Different Way of Seeing Autism*. London: Souvenir Press.

Prizant, B., Wetherby, A., Rubin, E., Laurent, A. & Rydell, P. (2006) *The SCERTS Manual: A Comprehensive Educational Approach for Children with Autism Spectrum Disorders, Volumes 1 and 2*. Baltimore, MD: Brookes Publishing.

Saggers, B., Klug, D., Harper-Hill, K., Ashburner, J. *et al.* (2018) *Australian Autism Education Needs Analysis: What are the Needs of Schools, Parents and Students on the Autism Spectrum?* Full Report and executive summary, Version 2. Brisbane: Cooperative Research Centre for Living and Autism.

Sharma, S., Woolfson, L.M., Hunter, S.C. *et al.* (2014) 'Maladaptive cognitive appraisals in children with high-functioning autism: Associations with fear, anxiety and theory of mind.' *Autism, 18*(3), 244–254.

SPELL (2020) Strategies and interventions. Accessed 19/08/2021 at www.autism. org.uk/advice-and-guidance/topics/strategies-and-interventions/strategies-and-interventions/spell.

Vasa, R.A. & Mazurek, M.O. (2015) 'An update on anxiety in youth with autism spectrum disorders.' *Current Opinions in Psychiatry, 28*(2), 83–90.

Vermeulen, P. (2014) 'The Practice of Promoting Happiness in Autism.' In E. Hurley & G. Jones (eds) *Autism Practice: Autism, Wellbeing and Happiness* (pp.8–17). Birmingham: bild.

CHAPTER 6

Transition to Adulthood

Editors: Charlotte Hatton and Jane Park

Introduction

This chapter examines the complex transition to adulthood for autistic people. Their voices and those who support them are shared. We consider their journey during this turbulent period of change through the lens of the particular difficulties associated with the autism spectrum. Various ways that support can be provided are suggested. We also look to the progress that has been made in response to negative experiences via the implementation of new legislation. We consider a more hopeful path for autistic young people in the future.

TRANSITION: AN OVERVIEW

Carol Povey

Throughout time, and reflected in art and literature, transition from childhood to adulthood is recognized as a pivotal life stage but can also be one of turmoil and turbulence. This is particularly true for autistic young people and their families who may already be managing a multitude of challenges and are expected to navigate a complicated, and at times inflexible, system.

Successful transition to adulthood means having opportunities to participate in work and further education, and to become more independent, all of which are interlinked. However young people on the autism spectrum too often experience difficulties throughout their lives, especially when moving from children's services to adult life. The National Autistic Society's Transition Support Service states that families and young people report feeling that they have fallen through the gap between these two services (Babbage 2021). Fewer than one in four young people on the autism spectrum continue their education beyond school (Ambitious about Autism 2011) and only 16 per cent of autistic adults are in full-time employment (National Autistic Society 2016). This results in many young people being disconnected from work, education and their community, and lacking independence in adult life.

Roux *et al.* (2015) found that poor future outcomes are influenced by several factors. These include parents' uncertainty regarding their role during transition, non-individualized support, and a lack of comprehensive and integrated services. Similarly, Snell-Rood *et al.* (2020) found that inadequate involvement of key decision-makers, overburdened services and ineffective services negatively affected post-school outcomes. *Moving Forward?*, a report by Ofsted published in 2016, noted that for learners with high needs, the careers guidance was weak, provision was not sufficiently focused on preparing them for adult life, and the effectiveness of commissioning arrangements varied considerably.

So why do young people on the autism spectrum so often miss out on the opportunities their peers take for granted? And what can be done on an individual, organizational and structural basis to change things?

Routine, consistency and knowing what to expect all help to give confidence and stability to autistic young people. Therefore, the prospect of this significant change to their lives can be daunting for both the individual and their family. Many young people on the autism spectrum experience difficulties in imagining and planning for the future due to the particular nature of their needs. Thus, to minimize the difficulties young people experience through transition, support should focus on preparation, partnerships and person-centred practice.

The SPELL framework (Beadle-Brown, Roberts & Mills 2009), developed within National Autistic Society schools and services, can be useful in ensuring that the transition process is as positive as possible. While primarily a framework for good autism practice, it can be used to support the transition process. SPELL stands for:

Structure: There should be timely planning, effectively communicated to all parties.

Positive approach: Linking with person-centred planning, a positive approach ensures that the individual is at the centre of the process and aims to build their strengths rather than being defined by their difficulties.

Empathy: Recognizing how the young person and family feel is vital for a successful transition. Acknowledge any fears and anxieties they have, and work on what is important to them.

Low arousal: Many young people are already feeling very pressured, so while the importance of planning for the future should be recognized, this needs to be done in a way that doesn't provoke further anxiety.

Links: The vital links between different agencies, the young person, their families and the professionals around them must be open, respectful and positive.

Structure

Many of the systems through which autistic young people and their families have to navigate are immensely complicated, such as accessing specialist provision or applying for additional support, with the move from child to adult services being especially complex, as detailed below.

Preparation for adulthood typically starts from age 14, but eligibility and obligation differ in each of the devolved nations (Department of Health 2015). The age at which different agencies move from child to adult teams also varies according to which agency is involved, the service used and where the family live. For example, some mental health services transition at 16, and some at 18. The more thorough the planning for transition, the better the outcomes are likely to be. Future placements risk breakdown should there be inadequate transition planning (Hendricks & Wehman 2009).

In England, the Special Educational Needs and Disability (SEND) Code of Practice (Department for Education/Department of Health and Social Care 2014) states that local authorities must ensure that the Education Health and Care Plan (EHCP) review at Year 9, and every review thereafter, include a focus on preparing for adulthood. The situation is the same in Wales (Welsh Government 2013). In Northern Ireland, the first annual review after the young person's 14th birthday should include a transition plan (Northern Ireland Assembly 1996), and in Scotland this should be at least 12 months before the young person is due to leave school (Scottish Government 2017).

In England, every local authority has to publish their 'local offer' (Department for Education/Department of Health and Social Care 2014) which gives information on SEND resources for young people extending up to their 25th birthday, and most will have a section detailing what support and services are available within that authority. Yet, in its 2016 report, *Moving Forward?*, Ofsted found that most of the local authorities reviewed failed to provide sufficiently detailed information.

There is also, simply, a lack of post-education options, and the absence of any meaningful daytime occupation has been found to be an enormous worry for parents (Beresford *et al.* 2013). Where there are services, they may be unable to adapt sufficiently to be able to meet the individual needs of the young person on the autism spectrum.

It is important that the young person knows what the transition process is, and when things are going to happen. Where there is uncertainty, or situations where there is a possibility that they could be let down, such as a placement that may or may not take place, this should be explained clearly. The use of visual or written aids and technologies can be useful. Simple strategies, such as making sure adequate notice is given for meetings, having a clear agenda, and following up with minutes, can help to minimize anxiety.

Positive approach

In teenage years, many young people struggle to understand and assert their identity. There can be difficulties with low self-esteem, and for autistic young people, whose strengths and talents may be in areas poorly valued by society, this may be more pronounced. In a review by Hebron and Humphrey (2015) a shockingly high number of young people on the autism spectrum were reported as having been bullied, with the highest rate reported as 94 per cent. There are similarly concerning accounts of numbers of autistic pupils excluded from school. In England in 2018/19, 5607 autistic pupils received at least one fixed-period exclusion and 155 autistic pupils were permanently excluded (Department for Education 2020). This means that autistic pupils are twice as likely to be excluded from school than pupils with no special educational needs (SEN), and autistic pupils are given three times as many fixed-period exclusions as pupils with no SEN (*ibid.*).

By the time many autistic young people reach their teenage years, they may be acutely aware that many things they struggle with seem to come easily to other young people. The importance of peer acceptance is often far stronger than it was in younger years. Peers may be starting to develop romantic relationships, appearing to be able to navigate the complex web of hidden rules and nuances involved in such fluid social relationships. These pressures can lead to a great deal of anxiety – not only for the young person themselves, but also their family.

Positive role models of successful autistic adults can be helpful, whether from the media, business or from the local community, as can peer mentoring or being part of a mixed-age social group where they can see autistic adults living fulfilled, purposeful lives. It is important to talk positively and realistically about both the young person and autism. For example, the use of terms such as 'high' or 'low functioning' are thought to be offensive by many people, and at the very least unhelpful, and do not help to describe people's individual needs (Kenny et al. 2015).

Good person-centred planning is crucial for a successful transition. The principles of person-centred planning are simple, but in practice, we see it being carried out far more rarely than it should be. It is vital that the young person is at the centre of the process, but it is important to recognize that this may have to be adapted to meet that person's needs. For those young people who struggle in more formal, group settings, which is the most traditional way of getting people together to do joint planning, there are many creative ways to support their involvement. This can include photos, video or other mixed media. Sensory challenges can create barriers to the young person being fully involved in their own planning so these must be taken into consideration.

Empathy

Around the time of transition to adult services, autistic young people may already be having to deal with numerous pressures. Hormones are surging, and they may be having to manage not only the formal curriculum, with all its inherent pressures, but also the ever-changing 'hidden' curriculum. This comprises the rules and conventions that are not formally taught, but which neurotypical children seem to pick up instinctively, and this makes it particularly challenging for autistic students (Myles & Simpson 2001).

Both young men and women experience challenges through transition, but these pressures are likely to differ. In general, girls are diagnosed later than boys (Giarelli et al. 2010) and may have had to struggle, feeling that they are quite different from their peers without having an explanation for this. They may, either consciously or unconsciously, camouflage or mask their difficulties (Hull, Petrides & Mandy 2020) so people's expectations of what they can cope with may be unreasonably high. Many young autistic women and girls may feel they have to meet others' expectations of them and be unable to ask for help and support when it is needed (Sproston, Sedgwick & Crane 2017). All these issues can exacerbate the difficulties of transition.

Low arousal

It is estimated that around 50 per cent of autistic children experience significant anxiety (Simonoff *et al.* 2008). Along with a positive approach, it is important that the transition process, with its inherent uncertainty, does not exacerbate any anxieties. One of the ways of doing this is to focus on lowering arousal. While often regarded as a method for managing challenging behaviour, strategies such as recognizing arousal levels, adapting one's interactions, and ensuring meetings are planned, structured and well organized all help to enable the young person to contribute fully to their own plans. This does not mean that expectations are lowered – it is important that young people on the autism spectrum are exposed to a wide range of experiences, but this needs to be done in a planned and sensitive way.

Links – with *families*

Throughout the transition period, families are a vital source of information and should be regarded as partners, yet very often at this time they feel excluded, and worry about both the transition from school and their long-term future. The transition process may trigger parents to become very aware of their own mortality, and the need to plan long term for what needs to happen when they are no longer around, recognizing the impact this may have on siblings and wider family.

Once their child legally becomes an adult, it may come as a surprise that regardless of the intellectual ability of their child, they are no longer officially the decision-maker. Some families may feel that professionals are dismissive of the very deep and detailed knowledge they have of the issues their son or daughter experiences. This is particularly true if the young person struggles to express these themselves, either because they are non-verbal and struggle to identify their own strengths and challenges, or because, naturally, they wish to portray themselves as they would like others to see them. Families have vital understanding and experience of how the young person has navigated stressful situations before. This is likely to be enormously helpful, as the same emotions and possibly distressed behaviours may re-emerge when the young person is once again exposed to the stressors of transition. Knowing what strategies have been successful before is very helpful.

Conversely, Beresford and colleagues (2013) report that some parents feel that they had had to become the primary or sole planner for their son or daughter, finding information about what is available regarding further education or paid work, and researching and visiting these opportunities. Parents who were largely positive about service support felt that their role was to make informed decisions alongside the young person, which was complemented by services, particularly in the information and advice they gave.

In England and Wales, from age 16, the Mental Capacity Act comes into play which deems that:

> Mental capacity is present if a person can understand information given to them, retain the information given to them long enough to make a decision, can weigh up the advantages and disadvantages of the proposed course of treatment in order to make a decision, and can communicate their decision. (Care Quality Commission 2019, p.3)

In Scotland, the equivalent legislation is the Adults with Incapacity (Scotland) Act 2000, and in Northern Ireland the Mental Capacity Act (Northern Ireland Assembly) 2016.

Links – with *other agencies*

The concept of person-centred planning is that the different agencies, friends and family involved in a young person's life should focus on the needs of that person, listen to what they want and aspire to, and work together to make this happen. Sadly, my experience suggests that this rarely happens, and one of the reasons is that our systems are set up in a way that makes it exceedingly difficult even for dedicated, skilled and enthusiastic professionals to work together!

It is important that any school also has strong relationships within the wider community, and knows what opportunities are available. For some young people, success may not lie in traditional routes of college or work, and professionals supporting young autistic people into adulthood need to think very creatively, utilizing the young person's interests, talents, and passions to find occupations that will engage them. In some cases, exploring less traditional areas can be beneficial. Sometimes the creative industries can value difference and appreciate the talents of autistic young people.

Conclusion

The transition to adulthood should be an exciting time, full of possibilities and opportunities. Sadly, for many autistic young people and their families it is characterized by anxiety and further battles to access what so many take for granted. Yet it need not be like this. By getting the transition right, by all working together, keeping the young person at the centre, not only will the future be better for autistic young people, but also society will benefit from the immense contribution these young people have to offer as fully included citizens.

MY TRANSITION EXPERIENCES

Robyn Steward

I am 34 years old. I am autistic and have nine other disabilities. I run a successful business and have done for 11 years. I work doing various things including making music, broadcasting, autism training, consultancy and research. As a young person, I thought I would fail in life, because I was failing in school. My transition from primary to secondary school was managed really well. At the time, I had a fear of toilets, specifically of being locked in. I think this was more about my dexterity as I also have cerebral palsy (CP). We had a lot of visits to the school, and the special educational needs coordinator was really kind. However, I was a long way behind my peers with my emotional social development. I wasn't really well equipped to cope.

I started off okay, making friends, but then when a friend said we couldn't play together after school, I was really upset. I couldn't see what I would do instead. This issue created a rift between me and the girl's family. The older brother got his friends to prey on my anxiety around toilets and stop me from leaving by holding the door; other kids in their year would pick me up by the handle on my backpack and dangle me in mid-air. The girl's younger brother would scrawl things like 'Robyn's a spaz!' on the bus shelter at the playground. As I had been drawn to the bullies' attention, they told the teachers (who hadn't noticed) that I was wearing very dark navy-blue sandals. This was because my mum and dad had been unable to find sandals with a back that I needed due to my CP and so my parents had put black shoe polish on them so that they met the black shoe requirement. (It had been acceptable until the bullies noticed.) The bullies also took to looking over the cubicles when I was on the loo. I didn't have any of the skills needed to hide in plain sight and the more anxious I was the more difficult my behaviour became. I got headaches and was often in the sick room. After a year, my parents took me out of the school.

The missing piece I feel in the transition was the whole school having disability training, not simply singling particular children out but making sure that staff and pupils knew about disability. While this might not have deterred the bullies, it may have helped create allies for the disabled children as the high school contained the area special needs unit. However, my social emotional skills may well have been beyond the school's remit.

The next high school was where my mum worked. There was less bullying and because it was further from home the bullying didn't follow me home. It was still miserable. My mum had advocated for me to have an extra year in primary school, which meant when the high school had had enough of me in Year 10, I was old enough to leave and start college. Looking back, I can see that secondary school was overwhelming for me. I don't think I learned anything at all during this time.

I think parents and educators should remember that children *must* go to school. They often can't take a break from lessons when they need it, and they can't leave the premises. However, staff can. They can change their jobs. When they are not teaching, they can go and sit outside or take a short walk. They can choose to work while wearing headphones when not teaching, for example. College was instantly better. When I needed to, I could listen to music, take a walk, or eat a snack. I also was studying a subject I enjoyed – IT (information technology).

When I moved to another college, the bullying started again. A learning support assistant took me to an autism support group. As a group, we said we wanted a safe space to go to within college, and training for staff. I suggested that the students deliver the training and so along with two other students we did just that. This is where my interest in autism came from.

Transitioning to adulthood was very difficult. I was highly vulnerable and this made me easy to manipulate. This resulted in me being raped when I was 20. I just wanted to be loved and cared about and to do the same for someone else, but it went horribly wrong. I only understood what had happened when I saw it happening to someone else and realized that the man was targeting autistic people. It took me a long time to get over it (about ten years). I learn by experience so with some cognitive behaviour therapy that focused more on behaviour than cognition (this can work better for autistic people), and the help of a couple of friends, I overcame it. The situation was not as bad as those that many autistic people face. I have two parents who love me, and I had a stable childhood but without that I think it would have been much harder.

I think it is important to give young people information and practical activities around theory of mind (putting yourself in someone else's shoes) (Baron-Cohen, Tager-Flusberg & Cohen 2000), and understand the developmental path that people follow when developing theory of mind skills.

From experience, I know I could get a date from an online website but, just like everyone else, I'd have to go through a lot of people to find the one. I know now that being in a relationship does not always equate to happiness, and it's better to be single and happy than in a relationship that doesn't work.

I thought I was stupid until I wrote half of my first book in ten days in June 2012. Then I understood I just worked differently but this difference could be useful.

Since the start of secondary school, I had struggled with my mental health. This didn't really get sorted until I was 32, when I got the right combination of medication (mainly dealing with anxiety and regulating sleep) and I also learned to have more confidence in myself. Sometimes I have done things other people would perceive as risky, but I actually think things through deeply, and research and seek information from others. I am now able to make decisions, not feel bad if things don't work out, and have help to assess what can be learned from it.

I can't stress enough how having time to process information is important. Like many autistic people, I am described as having a 'patchy profile', meaning I am good at some things and not at others. Part of my profile is having problems with short-term memory and processing speed. Probably, like many people, I needed others to give me different options rather than telling me off. For example, I learned how to be reactively tidy by paying a professional organizer to help me learn how to categorize things and not get overwhelmed. I am lucky to have the life I have now and I hope more autistic people can have the life they choose.

TRANSITION EXPERIENCES IN AUTISTIC INDIVIDUALS: CHALLENGES AND OPPORTUNITIES FROM A PRACTITIONER PERSPECTIVE

Irina Roncaglia

Introduction to transitions

Throughout over 15 years' experience as a school psychologist at the Sybil Elgar School, I have learned how important it is to identify clearly the particular needs of each autistic individual and their families, and to think about various ways these can be met to ensure transitions are successful. This can be achieved through the development of appropriate interventions. Well-being is also at the core, and (specifically when gathering information about an autistic individual) a positive, strengths-based framework becomes the guiding light to design successful transitions. Therefore, I aim to illustrate here some brief theoretical understanding and more widely practical approaches to transitions with young autistic people and their families. I also share ways in which practical support can be consistently implemented through different transitions and life stages, focusing on school environments and examples from my work with the National Autistic Society.

Transitions occur throughout our lives and these pivotal periods can cause significant disorientation and stress. For autistic people and their families, it is well documented that transitions can be challenging as routines are often relied on to navigate and cope in social situations. Sudden or unpredictable change to schedules can spark uncertainty, stress and high levels of anxiety (Friedman *et al.* 2013; Rydzewska 2016). Transitions from child to adult services can be fraught and are also associated with high anxiety (Transition Information Network 2020; National Autistic Society 2016, 2020). The challenges in making transitions are often worsened by difficulties with cognitive adjustments and inflexibility, thus leading to frustration, stress and high levels of anxiety.

Transitions: A psychological perspective

To provide meaningful support through the phases of any transition experience, I find it useful to give equal weight to both the actual change from and the change to the new situation, provision or even task. The development of an awareness and understanding of the psychological impact of transitions needs to take place in order to provide meaningful support to autistic people, so that they may better and more positively cope with the uncertainties and level of experienced anxiety.

Role transition

A role transition involves a role loss, which generally precedes a reconsideration of one's behavioural, psychological, and social make-up. During role transitions, the individual might lack a self-defining connection such that the role identity of an individual becomes ambiguous. By presenting practical transition management tools, I use Ashforth's (2001) psychological framework, which helps to inform the what, why, who and when of role transitions.

He suggests four psychological motives that are aroused by the process of a role transition:

1. *Identity* – defined by the process of learning to locate oneself while maintaining the integrity between self and behaviour, attaining a positive sense of self through differentiation, and keeping a sense of self-growth, which are all essential elements for the formation of identity.

2. *Meaning* – the sense-making process that we ascribe to ourselves and the context in which we happen to be part. This sense-making process through transitions is even more significant for autistic people who often refer to and understand their social world in concrete, visual and literal ways.

3. *Control* – a sense of agency and self-empowerment, where having control over one's actions creates a sense of involvement and responsibility (Ashforth 2001). Perception of control can be considered here as a psychological process during the transition process and as a fundamental element of the individual's psychological make-up during the coping stage of the transition. Whether an individual perceives being in control (or not, as often is the case for autistic individuals) will determine whether the transition process will be experienced as positive.

4. *Belonging* – interlinked to the previous three motives, belonging is expressed as the need to maintain a certain amount of positive and meaningful interpersonal interactions. This can be incredibly significant to the autistic individual and often important to the

circle of people around them, which can include immediate and extended family, siblings, friends, professionals and carers.

More recently I have adopted the self-determination theory (SDT) (Ryan & Deci 2000). This provides a useful framework through which changes, challenges and responses can be better structured. This provides a sense of autonomy and empowerment in the decision-making process of any type of transition, a sense of belonging (and relatedness) and a sense of competence. Beytien (2009) suggests that transitions can be experienced as a challenge by families and carers alike. She recommends that strategies and advice also be shared. Additionally, I have observed the collaboration and partnership within the circle of people around a young person to be a key element for positive outcomes.

Transitions: Practical understanding in supporting autistic individuals

To present positive examples of how transition experiences can be supported with autistic people, the process will be presented through the following stages:

1. Transition experiences: Role entry

2. Transition experiences: Coping with change

3. Transition experiences: Role exit

The objective is to ensure that transition experiences are not addressed as one single event (or one change) but are experienced and presented through different stages of transitions: a *process of change* rather than an *event in time*. The resources discussed are individualised according to the information-gathering process applied overtime, and its stages can be adapted to any type of transition as illustrated in Figure 6.1.

1. Transition experiences: Role entry

During transition, such as between primary and secondary school, and joining early years or moving on to adult services, autistic individuals can experience substantial changes in relation to their environment, routines and teaching staff and within their support network. The young person must be prepared and supported in leaving what has been familiar and meaningful to them. This can be achieved by understanding the particular profile of each autistic individual using a positive framework. This should identify their strengths, abilities, likes/dislikes, styles of communication, and what is important *to* them and also *for* them.

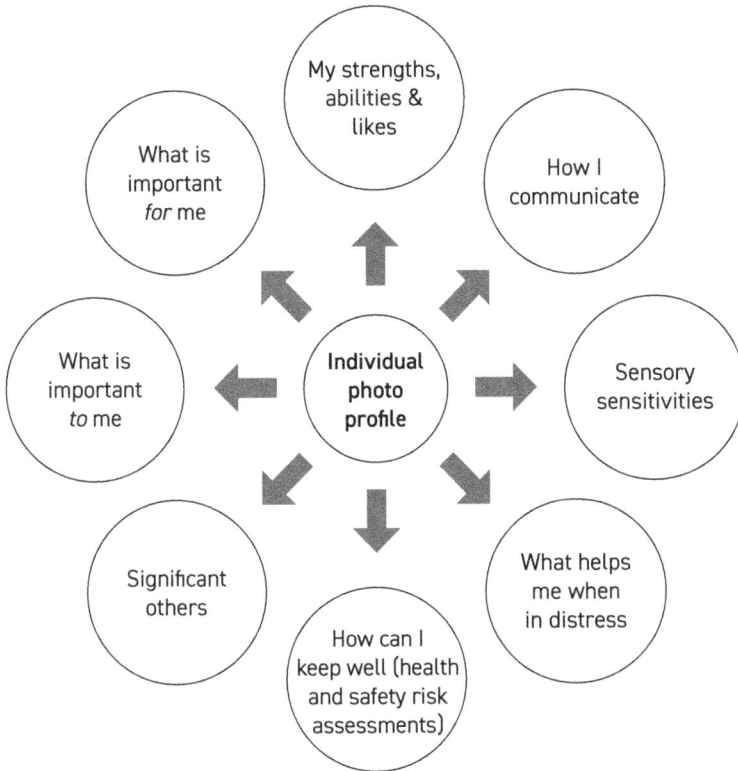

Figure 6.1: Framework for individualized transition booklets

Figure 6.1. illustrates a framework for a personal passport, transition booklet or identity card – whichever matches best the autistic individual. This can accompany them when entering their new role and environment. What is important to the individual, including potential issues of control and a sense of belonging, can be gradually addressed by encouraging the young person's full participation in this process alongside other significant figures in their lives. Visual representations, drawings, photos, pictures, symbols, and journals can be organized in a creative and informative manner that fits the individual's strengths and abilities. Professionals should develop a good knowledge of the young person to provide a true reflection of the individual's characteristics.

2. Transition: Coping with change

As individuals gradually adjust to new structures, micro-transition experiences will continue to be part of the challenge. I have successfully used the Lazarus and Folkman (1984) transactional model in managing psychological stress and anxiety. It suggests two types of coping mechanisms: problem focus skills and emotion focus skills.

Coping with change can be addressed, for example, by introducing a small 'unexpected' event within a well-structured visual timetable, on either a daily or weekly basis. This aims to introduce an element of novelty and 'surprise' without significant interruptions to daily routines. The change becomes embedded in a structure which can be better coped with as part of a predicable timetable. As an individual builds on experience and coping skills, small adjustments can be translated in bigger and more significant changes.

More recently, researchers at Newcastle University have been developing a programme that seeks to teach and support parents how to help their autistic children to cope better with uncertainties in life (Rodgers *et al.* 2017). The main aim of the CUES (Coping with Uncertainty in Everyday Situations) programme is gradually to introduce children to uncertainty and help them develop strategies for tolerating it. Within the emotional skills, the autistic individual ought to be supported in identifying how they are feeling about the change, how they respond if sad or upset, and how they respond when others are sad or angry. I have certainly included examples with families which included the use of symbols, photographs, Talking Mats and Social Stories to name a few (Cameron & Matthews 2017; Gray 2015, 2020). The information that we should capture is not limited to the risks or challenges but based on a positive framework, on well-being and on life-long learning.

3. Transition experiences: Role exit

The next significant transition is the move into adulthood. There is still a certain level of debate on how to measure the success of these transitions reliably (Rydzewska 2012, 2016). Opportunities for the young person to make choices, express preferences and build their own future are critical in managing some of the psychological impact of these transitions. Visiting potential future placements helps to prepare further for this move. The development of close links between professionals in both settings to promote a clear understanding of the individual's requirements is vital. This should involve comprehensive multiagency working as well the full participation of the individual and their families (Transition Information Network 2020).

In order to address different preferences and abilities of the young people involved, opportunities are encouraged for the use of photos, personal or collaborative drawings, writing, communication devices (such as tablets) or anything else that supports participation, engagement and motivation in the decision-making process.

This can be provided through individual and group sessions led by key workers or staff who have, over time, built positive relationships with the young person. Sessions can be scheduled throughout the school day, curriculum, and personal, social, health and citizenship education or other taught subjects, and opportunities for discussion at annual reviews where multiagency involvement and transdisciplinary support can be fully integrated. Members of a transdisciplinary team cross professional discipline boundaries to achieve service integration by consulting, collaborating and jointly formulating with one another. They do not work in isolation, or abandon their discipline, but blend specific skills with other team members to focus on and achieve integrated outcomes through shared aims, clarity of communication, collaboration, and cooperation and role clarity (Roncaglia 2016). Transition 'champions' for autistic individuals can also be engaged to enhance and support the process. These individuals can be identified within the school environment and ideally need to provide a 'good fit' with the autistic individual's profile. There have been instances where the autistic individuals themselves have chosen who they want to work with as part of their support team, which has provided a great sense of control.

Conclusions and take-home messages

As a practitioner psychologist, I have presented practical reflections on transition experiences for autistic individuals, with the adoption of individual support packages and personalized service provisions. Within the four psychological motives (Ashforth 2001), I have illustrated how these can help us to implement practical support more effectively regarding transition experiences. In summary, any transition needs to include:

- Full participation of the autistic individual and their families/carers

Chronological age 11–19+

YR7 YR8 YR9 YR10 YR11 FEU1 FEU2 FEU3

* EHCPs
* Referral admission procedures
* Multiagency involvement – information gathering
* Participation of young people – direct observations
* Transition planning prior to admission
* Transition visits
* Transition booklets

* Participation of young people and families
* Video clips/DVD at annual reviews with families
* Multiagency involvement – annual reviews
* Personal training days through POP
* Transition Action Group (TAG) in service
* Young people supported to contribute
* Personal passport information
* Planned visit to SES further education
* Participation and facilitation of prospective teachers

* Participation of young people and their families, including siblings
* Multiagency involvement – Connexions, adult services, social services
* Involvement of future placement – supporting visits
* Individual passport transition booklet-exit
* Facilitation and participation of prospective professionals – school visits and shared information

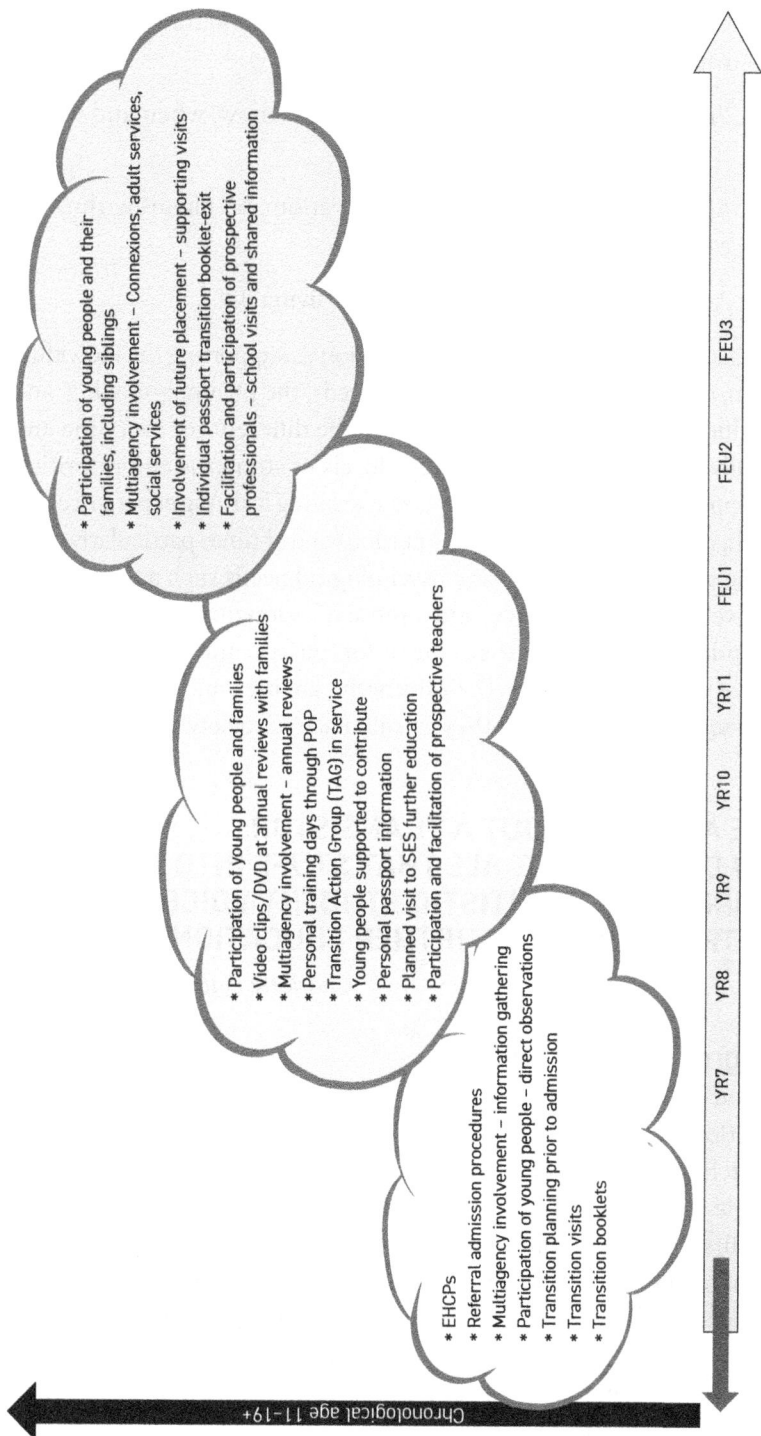

Figure 6.2: Transition steps through secondary and further education college.

Note: EHCP, Education, Health and Care Plan; PIP, 'Parents in Partnership' groups run at the school; SES, Sybil Elgar School.

- Comprehensive multiagency engagement (and transdisciplinary support)

- Provision of high-quality information – how, when and where this is collated

- Effective positive transition preparation and planning through a well-being framework

- An array of opportunities for (fully) living life.

What is significant, is the ability of professionals supporting the individual 'in transition' to really tune in to their needs, the meaning-making, and the values of each individual, which will be different for everyone and carefully acknowledges the different levels of strengths and priorities. New opportunities are then embraced as exciting learning experiences for growth, rather than experienced as perilous and at times particularly challenging stages. Addressing basic psychological needs such as autonomy, empowerment, competence, and a sense of belonging, while exploring and understanding what these mean for autistic individuals, helps to creatively tailor strategies to their strengths, abilities, and differences and harnesses the contributions they can all make to society.

'LIKE A MIC WITHOUT A TRANSISTOR: HOW DO I CONVERT ALL THAT STUFF INTO INFORMATION?!' AUTISTIC STUDENT VOICES ON THE TRANSITION TO FURTHER EDUCATION

Charlotte Hatton and Jane Park

Background to our research

Charlotte: My main motivation for studying transitions into further education (FE) for young autistic people was the personal experience of watching both my brother (who is on the spectrum) and his peers struggle after completing university. The post-16 educational transition is the first step into adulthood for many young autistic people, and I felt that the issues they experienced at this time were likely to be related to unmet needs at key transition points earlier in their lives. The vivid descriptions of the challenging experiences that the parents and young autistic people shared as part of my research were a privilege to hear. I was driven by a commitment to them, a passion for their voices to be shared and amplified, and a certainty that educational psychology as a profession could certainly do better. I felt that the common misman-agement of transition processes had massive implications for the future of these young people's lives. Geller and Greenberg (2009) describe the situation well by identifying that 'our support systems have been slow to respond to the needs of individuals with typical dreams and aspirations but atypical development' (p.92).

Jane: My doctoral research was motivated by a call for inclusive research which takes a strengths-based perspective on the experiences of young autistic adults and which promotes the inclusion of autistic people in the research process (Billington 2013). My research was situated in a period of significant legislative change, which meant that EPs were now tasked with working with children and young people from birth up to 25 years. This led to a greater emphasis on person-centred approaches, featuring exploration of each young person's aspirations and supporting their transition to adulthood. Current research highlights further benefits, such as a greater emphasis on independence for young autistic people (including self-management strategies for anxiety), the value of reliable and well-informed support staff, and greater use of academic accommo-dations (Gaona, Palikara & Castro 2019; Toor, Hanley & Hebron 2016).

In the UK research literature, accounts of the views of young people with autism on their transition experiences are clearly underrepre-sented. Edwards and Holland (2013) describe how enabling the voices of marginalized groups to be heard on their own terms is the aim of emancipatory research. Charlotte and I were united in our eagerness to magnify the voices of young people with autism, through our own doc-toral research. We hoped that using creative ways to elicit the richness of individual views and experiences, from which helpful suggestions may arise, could be truly emancipatory. This required both of us to remain mindful and appreciative of the uniqueness of each young person's indi-vidual experiences as a whole. This is what we hope to convey in our contribution to this book. We have both shared our research at EP-ASIG study days, which provided a welcome opportunity to communicate our participants' stories and our passions to a sympathetic audience. Now is our chance to share those stories further afield. The aim is to inform effective and successful transition experiences for all young autistic people aspiring to further education or training, by amplifying the voices of those with lived experience of successful transition to FE.

The following contribution contains no personal, identifiable information. All sensitive information has been anonymized throughout.

Prioritizing autistic voices

We were privileged to be able to work with seven young autistic people to learn from their experiences of successfully transitioning to further education. We interviewed two young women, Anna (aged 17) and Samantha (18), and five young men: Stephen (22), Jamie (18), Ben (21), Bobby (18) and Chris (17). Bobby and Jamie were the only participants without an Education, Health and Care Plan (formerly Statements of Special Educational Need). All but Stephen and Ben had previously attended mainstream secondary settings before transitioning into their local FE colleges.

For all participants, the idea of resilience was a recurrent theme, including the process of overcoming fears and challenging experiences at the point of transition to FE. Stephen began his interview with some passionately articulated words of encouragement, which related to personal experiences of being dissuaded from pursuing further education, saying *'Don't let people...don't let people say you can't do it. Don't waste a human mind.'* Over the course of the interview, it became apparent that Stephen had had some difficult experiences as he moved from secondary school to his first FE college, and his positive words were rooted in his own capacity to overcome challenges and demonstrate resilience: *'And there are some people who said that I couldn't do this...but I've proved them wrong.'*

Our participants also had to overcome a range of anxiety-provoking challenges to successfully access FE. Anna expressed feeling nervous about keeping up with academic demands as *'My writing's not that fast.'* Explaining some of the issues he had faced attending FE, Bobby said, *'I just found it really difficult I guess to get there, to get motivated enough to walk out the door and walk to the lesson and sit down and take concise, accurate notes.'* Chris talked about issues with recalling information, which was compounded by a lack of breaks: *'So it's the same with a computer if the connections are different: it wouldn't put them back together in the right order. So, you'd have to manually put it back and sometimes you can't because you've already done four or five more lessons, so there's a big traffic [jam].'* Chris explained this with feelings of sadness and frustration at being disabled by his environment and not able to learn as he had the potential to.

The idea of transitions offering the possibility of growth and development in various ways was a recurrent theme, such as having new experiences, learning new academic and life skills, and building independence. For Stephen, the idea of 'transition' led him to reflect on development from being a child into a teenager: *'The thing is, when you transition, for example, when you transition from a child into a teenager, think about it, you...there is no...rule book in terms of, you know, when you're a child you need to follow certain rules. When you're a teenager, you experience the world differently, and the same if you're an adult: you take matters into your own hands when you turn into an adult.'* Stephen also described how important learning practical life skills (such as interpreting a bus timetable and managing the journey into college) had been for his personal growth when planning the transition from secondary school to college: *'They always made sure that we figured out a bus timetable and knew where we were going, and looked on a map to make sure that we knew where we were going, before we left... We got the bus and stuff as part of independent training. But they didn't expose us to the trains and the tube... I think they should have; not just buses, but they should have just got us used to other types of public transport as well.'*

Ben associated transition with 'learning', including developing his academic and practical skills, and he described how he enjoyed *'learning new things...and new skills...like, maths and English and learning cooking at the moment'.* Ben also felt he had learned how to manage and understand his emotional responses and developed his social skills: *'Like, learning how to feel and what to do in situations...instead of, like, feeling scared, I just...feel a bit nervous'.* Despite having been enrolled on a second-choice course, Ben was still keen to pursue computing and described having the confidence to try something new: *'I might try something a bit different... maybe computers or something.'*

A sense of optimism regarding new social relationships on transitioning to further education was expressed. Anna looked forward to new friendships: *'I was going to make new friends, which I did, which I'm really happy about.'* Ben also talked about having experienced a feeling of readiness to *'move on'* from school to college and had confidence in his belief that he would be able to make new friends: *'Happy to move on...happy that I made friends at the school before...and happy I'll make new ones at the next one.'* In contrast, Chris struggled far more: *'I just couldn't mix with them [other students]. It's like putting lithium with water: it just does not work, it wouldn't work.'* For Chris, the transition served to highlight his lack of friends, feeling that he'd been 'completely isolated from everyone for years and years'. Family relationships emerged as key. Bobby presented as less reliant on his parents while Anna and Chris were more dependent. Anna frequently referenced her mother and her role in helping her 'make my decision [about further education placement]'. Chris felt that his mother played a vital role in his life, saying, 'She's my interpreter.'

Relationships with staff were mainly seen as positive and helpful, a significant protective factor in overcoming the 'scared' or 'anxious' feelings that were experienced at transition points. For Samantha, the feeling of being excited was also associated with meeting new people and being understood by staff: 'Excited! At college, like, meeting new people, teachers understanding you, if you need help you go to them, not to be scared to ask for help.' Ben also described the importance of forming new friendships in mediating feelings of anxiety about having a new start: 'When I left school and, like, joined different ones I was happy, like, I made new friends and stuff, and, like...scared, it's like a new school and new teachers.'

All participants spoke about issues regarding their mental well-being. Concerning their own coping strategies, Anna described asking her mother for help with transport whereas Bobby explained, 'I didn't draw attention to myself as much really. Learned to sort of just stay on the sidelines a bit rather than attracting attention all the time by doing stupid things.' Sadly, Chris struggled to cope with the many demands of college life, explaining, 'I used to get panic attacks in the corridor. I just used to randomly feel so anxious I'd just break down into tears in the corridor uncontrollably.' Stephen described his struggle and frustration at not being able to secure appropriate support while enrolled on a course in a different FE college: 'I tried so hard to ask for help and their idea of help was to bring in a – they finally did – they brought in a learning assistant, but that assistant was a bit like an assistant when you go into school who helps every single person in the class. I needed somebody to just be assigned to help me.' Stephen also described the longer-term impact of mental health difficulties experienced at an earlier stage in his life: 'I did have quite bad anxiety when I was younger. I received therapy and counselling for my anxiety. And, basically, what they did was – they gave me coping strategies. And I still follow those coping strategies today.'

Interactions between our research participants, wider systems in school/college and the local authority were shared. When Charlotte's element of the research was conducted there were issues regarding statutory funding extending into post-16 education; consequently, Chris lost his funded support. This deeply affected his ability to engage with learning: '*So now I have no statement. I'm just a guy stuck in this big circle of events. I don't know where to go now, in which direction...don't know.*' Bobby experienced frustration, saying '*It [the support in school] wasn't really helpful, though; it was sort of a waste of time.*' He presented as disengaged from the support, whereas Chris was considerably more dependent on the help available, explaining: '*All thanks to these people that helped me. If I didn't have those people helping me, I can't function. It's like a mic without a transistor: how's it going to convert all that stuff into information?*' Chris was left bereft by the removal of support: '*Why does it end? Because I mean they've spent all that money supporting me from primary school to secondary school and if I want to go further, they won't – they won't do that any more. They just throw me away. Why?*'

Broadly, participants communicated a clear sense of self-efficacy and control. Hopes of better exam results, academic progress and genuine inclusion were expressed; for example Chris commented that he anticipated accessing '*a specialist... course designed for people with disabilities who have interpretation problems specifically designed so they can do the same things as everyone else can do but in a different environment, a different way*'. Ben and Stephen described how their choice of college course had been limited by availability of places, though both young men had tried to make the best of the courses they got places on. Anna was pleased with her FE choices, and Bobby felt he was able to change his situation.

All participants indicated a desire to be understood, especially by support staff, to feel valued and to progress in education. Feelings of frustration and resentment were noted when this did not happen. Chris was most fearful about not being understood and the issue of being judged by those who should be supporting him, '*and that's not good because it means they...they'll be affected by their opinions on people. They'll judge people by how they act and they won't have any background knowledge of autism and anything. They won't know that. They'll just think something else of me. Which they did.*' Stephen was clear that staff should be the ones to learn and make adaptations to accommodate the needs of '*people who are different*': '*I don't think anyone should let anyone else define who they are. I think that we should just learn to work with people who are different.*'

Psychological theories

The findings of our research into the transition experiences of young autistic adults moving into further education are underpinned by psychological theory and may be understood through the lenses of Ryan and Deci's self-determination theory (SDT) (2000), Bronfenbrenner's ecological model (1977) and Seligman's 2011 multidimensional PERMA model of well-being. These three theories highlight the need to keep in mind individual and systemic factors when transition planning with young autistic people. These theories also speak to the way we need to work across different levels to ensure positive life outcomes for young autistic adults.

As mentioned earlier, Ryan and Deci's (2000) SDT focuses on three innate psychological needs – competence, autonomy and relatedness – which they consider essential for supporting optimal functioning, facilitating the process of natural development and promoting social well-being (all of which can be related to the themes which emerged from our research). Self-determination is important to people with autism, since the SDT emerged as a result of related social movements such as self-advocacy, self-determination, disability rights and the independent living movement (Ward 1996).

Bronfenbrenner's ecological model (1977) enables consideration of the systems around a young person that shape and influence their development, such as those found within a family, school or college. This model provides both a helpful framework for understanding the importance of the social context in which transitions to further education take place, and the bi-directional influences between an individual and their environment. In relation to effective transition planning for young people with autism, this could be interpreted as a call for arrangements to reflect the unique needs of each individual, matching their profile, and giving due consideration to how they may best be supported through the process of change and adjustment to a new environment and context.

PERMA (see Seligman 2011) is an acronym that stands for what Seligman describes as the five 'pillars' or core elements of positive human functioning which contribute to lasting well-being, and which people pursue for their own sake: 'Positive emotion' refers to subjective feelings of happiness and positive emotion; 'Engagement' refers to the psychological connection between a person and activities or organizations; 'Relationships' includes feeling socially integrated, cared about and supported by others, and satisfied with one's social connections; 'Meaning' refers to being part of something larger than oneself; and 'Accomplishment' refers to the progress an individual makes towards goals, their feelings of competence, and experience of a sense of achievement. According to Seligman (2011), these elements are subjective, meaning that different individuals value different aspects of PERMA and give different weight to individual elements. Seligman proposes that positive relationships and a sense of feeling understood (with differences accepted) support and deepen an individual's feelings of security, self-esteem, and subsequently self-acceptance. This relates to our participants' narratives of being negatively judged and the impact of this on their feelings of anxiety and depression, and to their expressed sense of being accepted and understood by teaching and support staff at college, which contributed to their sense of well-being.

Practical implications for professionals

Key protective factors facilitating a positive transition into further education which emerged from our research included the value of having healthy relationships with peers and with teaching and support staff, having a positive outlook and a resilient mindset, accessing appropriate tailored support, learning practical and emotional life skills, and being understood in terms of skills and strengths. Difficulties with receptive language and processing and organizing information occur within autism; however, these are often overlooked due to more obvious social difficulties (Howlin 2004). Adaptations to teaching approaches should be made, including consideration of language demands and use of visual supports, to improve access to the learning environment. Recent research indicates that good quality support can positively influence the success of transition (Gaona *et al.* 2019). More consistent relationships with support staff were signposted by the young people we worked with as an area for improvement.

Concluding reflections

It was truly a privilege to work with all the young people who contributed to our studies. With the aim of modelling good practice, we prioritized the narratives of young autistic people and operated with the view that they are valid interpreters of their own experiences. Focusing exclusively on the accounts of young autistic people deepened our understanding and offered insights that both support and challenge normalized versions of the processes of transition. The consideration of the transition experiences of young autistic adults, gathered from a research paradigm which adopted a strengths-based perspective, has been positioned here as central to bridging the gap between autism policy and applied practice.

Chapter conclusion

Underpinned by relevant psychological frameworks, this chapter draws together first-person accounts from autistic voices and practitioner perspectives and research, to move towards a multi-dimensional model of transition. Motivated by the call to listen to and amplify autistic voices, the chapter highlights the impact of both effective and less successful transition processes on the lived experiences of autistic people, emphasizing throughout the need for personalized support, collaboration and partnership. In the past, the picture of transition into adulthood has been far from positive. However, since the EP-ASIG study day on this topic in 2013, we have come a long way in terms of good autism practice in post-16 education. While it is too soon to evaluate fully the impact of various legislative changes and approaches, the progress we are observing is encouraging. It is our hope that this trajectory continues to ensure that young people can fulfil their potential and live the future they aspire to have.

POINTS FOR REFLECTION

☞ Strengths-based, person-centred working, including collaboration with families, is crucial for successful transition.

☞ Creative, visually oriented approaches must be prioritized to elicit autistic views and voices, with active participation appropriately facilitated.

☞ It is vital to respect and appreciate the uniqueness of every individual's profile of strengths, interests and areas for development to ensure they can truly fulfil their potential.

Further reading

Anderson, K.A., Sosnowy, C., Kuo, A.A. & Shattuck, P.T. (2018) 'Transition of individuals with autism to adulthood: A review of qualitative studies.' *Pediatrics, 141*(4), S318–S327.

Bridges, W. (1980) *Transitions: Making Sense of Life's Changes*. Reading, MA: Addison-Wesley.

George, L.K. (1993) 'Sociological perspectives on life transitions.' *Annual Review of Sociology, 19*, 353–373.

Hebron, J. & Humphrey, N. (2014) 'Exposure to bullying among students with autism spectrum conditions: A multi-informant analysis of risk and protective factors.' *Autism, 18*(6), 618–630.

Levinson, D.J. (1986) 'A conception of adult development.' *The American Psychologist, 4*(1), 3–13.

Matthews, N.L., Smith, C.J., Pollard, E., Ober-Reynolds, S., Kirwan, J. & Malligo, A. (2015) 'Adaptive functioning in autism spectrum disorder during the transition to adulthood.' *Journal of Autism and Developmental Disorders, 45*(8), 2349–2360.

National Audit Office (2009) *Supporting People with Autism through Adulthood: Report by the Comptroller and Auditor General (HC 556)*. London: The Stationery Office.

Smith, J., Donlan, J. & Smith, B. (2012) *Helping Children with Autism Spectrum Conditions through Everyday Transitions: Small Changes – Big Challenges*. London: Jessica Kingsley Publishers.

Wehman, P., Datlow Smith, M. & Schall, C. (2009) *Autism and the Transition to Adulthood: Success Beyond the Classroom*. Baltimore, MD: Paul H. Brookes.

Welsh Government (2014) *Social Services and Well-Being Act (Wales) 2014*. Cardiff: Welsh Government. Accessed 26/01/20 at www.legislation.gov.uk/anaw/2014/4/contents.

References

Ambitious about Autism (2011) *Finished at School: Where Next for Young People with Autism?* London: Ambitious about Autism.

Ashforth, B.E. (2001) *Role Transitions in Organizational Life: An Identity-Based Perspective*. Mahwah, NJ: Lawrence Erlbaum Associates.

Babbage, R. (2021) Discussion regarding transition with Carol Povey. Unpublished.

Baron-Cohen, S., Tager-Flusberg, H. & Cohen, D.J. (2000) *Understanding Other Minds: Perspectives from Developmental Cognitive Neuroscience*. Oxford: Oxford University Press.

Beadle-Brown, J., Roberts, R. & Mills, R. (2009) 'Person-centred approaches to supporting children and adults with autism spectrum disorders.' *Tizard Learning Disability Review, 14*(30), 18–26.

Beresford, B., Moran, N., Sloper, P., Cusworth, L. *et al.* (2013) *Transition to Adult Services and Adulthood for Young People with Autistic Spectrum Conditions*. Working Paper, no: DH 2525, Social Policy Research Unit, University of York.

Beytien, A. (2009) 'You too? Common stories from an uncommon parent: Transitions.' *Autism Spectrum Quarterly*, Autumn, 38–42.

Billington, T. (2013) 'Constructing critical resources for research and professional practice with young people: Feeling, thinking, learning, and neuroscientific narratives.' *Qualitative Research in Psychology, 10*(2), 174–188.

Bronfenbrenner, U. (1977) 'Toward an experimental ecology of human development.' *American Psychologist, 32*(7), 513–531.

Cameron, L. & Matthews, R. (2017) 'More than pictures: Developing an accessible resource.' *Tizard Learning Disability Review, 22*(2), 57–65.

Care Quality Commission. (2019) *BG004: Brief Guide: Capacity and Competence in Under-18s*, (BG004). London: CQC.

Department for Education (2020) *National Statistics: Permanent and Fixed-Period Exclusions in England: 2018 to 2019*. London: DfE. Accessed 15/01/2021 at www.gov.uk/government/statistics/permanent-and-fixed-period-exclusions-in-england-2018-to-2019.

Department for Education and Department of Health and Social Care (2014) *Special Educational Needs and Disability Code of Practice: 0 to 25 Years*. London: Office for National Statistics. Accessed 15/01/2021 at www.gov.uk/government/publications/send-code-of-practice-0-to-25.

Department of Health (2015) *Statutory Guidance for Local Authorities and NHS Organisations to Support Implementation of the Adult Autism Strategy*. London: DoH. Accessed 15/01/2021 at https://assets.publishing.service.gov.uk/government/uploads/system/uploads/attachment_data/file/422338/autism-guidance.pdf.

Edwards, R. & Holland, J. (2013) *What is Qualitative Interviewing?* London: Bloomsbury.

Friedman, N., Erickson Warfield, M. & Parish, S.L. (2013) 'Transition to adulthood for individuals with autism spectrum disorder: Current issues and future perspectives.' *Neuropsychiatry, 3*(2), 181–192.

Gaona, C., Palikara, O. & Castro, S. (2019) '"I'm ready for a new chapter": The voices of young people with autism spectrum disorder in transition to post-16 education and employment.' *British Educational Research Journal, 45*(2), 340–355.

Geller, L.L. & Greenberg, M. (2009) 'Managing the transition process from high school to college and beyond: Challenges for individuals, families, and society.' *Social Work in Mental Health, 8*(1), 92–116.

Giarelli, E., Wiggins, L.D., Rice, C.E., Levy, S.E. *et al.* (2010) 'Sex differences in the evaluation and diagnosis of autism spectrum disorders among children.' *Disability and Health Journal, 3*(2), 107–116.

Gray, C. (2015) *The New Social Story Book*. Arlington: TX: Future Horizons.

Gray, C. (2020) *What is a Social Story?* Accessed 10/07/2020 at https://carolgraysocial-stories.com/social-stories.

Hebron, J. & Humphrey, N. (2015) 'Bullying of children and adolescents with autism spectrum conditions: A "state of the field" review.' *International Journal of Inclusive Education, 19*(8), 845–862.

Hendricks, D.R. & Wehman, P. (2009) 'Transition from school to adulthood for youth with autism spectrum disorders: Review and recommendations.' *Focus on Autism and Other Developmental Disabilities, 24*(2), 77–88.

Howlin, P. (2004) *Autism and Asperger's Syndrome: Preparing for Adulthood*. London: Routledge.

Hull, L., Petrides, K.V. & Mandy, W. (2020) 'The female autism phenotype and camouflaging: A narrative review.' *Review Journal of Autism and Developmental Disorders 7*, 306–317.

Kenny, L., Hattersley, C., Molins, B., Buckley, C., Povey, C. & Pellicano, E. (2015) 'Which terms should be used to describe autism? Perspectives from the UK autism community.' *Autism, 20*(4), 442–462.

Lazarus, R.S. & Folkman, S. (1984) *Stress: Appraisal and Coping*. New York, NY: Springer.

Myles, B.S. & Simpson, R.L. (2001) 'Understanding the hidden curriculum: An essential social skill for children and youth with Asperger syndrome.' *Intervention in School and Clinic, 36*(5), 279–286.

National Autistic Society (2016) *The Autism Employment Gap: Too Much Information in the Workplace*. London: NAS.

National Autistic Society (2020) *Transitions Tips*. Accessed 30/7/2020 at www.autism.org.uk/advice-and-guidance/topics/transitions/transition-tips.

Northern Ireland Assembly (1996) *The Education (Northern Ireland) Order 1996*. Stormont: Northern Ireland Assembly.

Northern Ireland Assembly (2016) *Mental Capacity Act (Northern Ireland) 2016*. Stormont: Northern Ireland Assembly.

Ofsted (2016) *Moving Forward? How Well the Further Education and Skills Sector is Preparing Young People with High Needs for Adult Life*. London: Ofsted.

Rodgers, J., Hodgson, A., Shields, K., Wright, C., Honey, E. & Freeston, M. (2017) 'Towards a treatment for intolerance of uncertainty in young people with autism spectrum disorder: Development of the Coping with Uncertainty in Everyday Situations (CUES©) Programme.' *Journal of Autism and Developmental Disorders, 47*(12), 3959–3966.

Roncaglia, I. (2016) 'A practitioner's perspective of multidisciplinary teams: Analysis of potential barriers and key factors for success.' *Psychological Thought, 9* (1), 15–23.

Roux, A.M., Shattuck, P.T., Rast, J.E., Rava, J.A. & Anderson, K.A. (2015) *National Autism Indicators Report: Transition into Young Adulthood*. Philadelphia, PA: Life Course Outcomes Research Program & A.J. Drexel Autism Institute, Drexel University.

Ryan, R.M. & Deci, E.L. (2000) 'Self-determination theory and the facilitation of intrinsic motivation, social development, and well-being.' *American Psychologist, 55*, 68–78.

Rydzewska, E. (2012) 'Destination unknown? Transitions to adulthood for people with autism spectrum disorders.' *British Journal of Special Education, 39*(2), 287–293.

Rydzewska, E. (2016) 'Unexpected changes of itinerary: Adaptive functioning difficulties in daily transitions for adults with autism spectrum disorder.' *European Journal of Special Needs Education, 31*(3), 330–343.

Scottish Government (2017) *Additional Support for Learning: Statutory Guidance 2017*. Edinburgh: Scottish Government.

Scottish Government (2000) *Adults with Incapacity (Scotland) Act 2000*. Edinburgh: Scottish Government.

Seligman, M.E.P. (2011) *Flourish*. New York, NY: Simon and Schuster.

Simonoff, E., Pickles, A., Charman, T., Chandler, S., Loucas, T. & Baird, G. (2008) 'Psychiatric disorders in children with autism spectrum disorders: Prevalence, comorbidity, and associated factors in a population-derived sample.' *Journal of the American Academy of Child and Adolescent Psychiatry, 47*(5), 1164–1176.

Snell-Rood, C., Rubie, L., Kleinert, H., McGrew, J.H. et al. (2020) 'Stakeholder perspectives on transition planning, implementation and outcomes for students with autism spectrum disorder.' Autism: the International Journal of Research and Practice, 24(5), 1164–1176. https://doi.org/10.1177/1362361319894827.

Sproston, K., Sedgwick, F. & Crane, L. (2017) 'Autistic girls and school exclusion: Perspectives of students and their parents.' *Autism and Developmental Language Impairments, 2*, 1–14.

Toor, N., Hanley, T. & Hebron, J. (2016) 'The facilitators, obstacles and needs of individuals with autism spectrum conditions accessing further and higher education: A systematic review.' *Journal of Psychologists and Counsellors in Schools, 26*(2), 166–190.

Transition Information Network (2020) *Information and Support: Transition Guides*. London: Council for Disabled Children. Accessed 25/07/2020 at https://councilfordisabledchildren.org.uk/transition-information-network/about-us.

Ward, M.J. (1996) 'Coming of Age in the Age of Self-Determination: A Historical and Personal Perspective.' In O.J. Sands and M.L. Wehmeyer (eds) *Self-Determination Across the Life Span: Independence and Choice for People with Disabilities*. Baltimore, MD: Paul H. Brookes.

Welsh Government (2013) *Special Educational Needs Code of Practice for Wales*. Cardiff: Welsh Government.

CHAPTER 7

Autism and the Criminal Justice System

Editors: Judith Gainsborough and Ken Greaves

Introduction

The researcher Katie Maras and the National Autistic Society Criminal Justice Coordinator, Clare Hughes, have chosen to collaborate on the content of their contribution to this chapter and to extend the range of perspectives still further by involving colleagues from other agencies. Adam O'Loughlin is an autistic police officer with responsibility for autism in his police force, and Alexandra Lewis is a consultant forensic and child and adolescent psychiatrist, working with autistic youngsters in prisons. The resulting piece is impressively comprehensive, as well as being hugely informative and helpful for parents and all educators and agencies. The collaborative nature of their contribution perfectly reflects the need for a similar collaboration of all agencies in order to ensure that autistic youngsters are kept safe and treated appropriately by the criminal justice system (CJS). Their piece is brought poignantly to life first by Juliet Gittens's heart-breaking story of her autistic son's involvement with the CJS and the impact on him and his whole family; and then by John-Paul Horsley, who chronicles the lack of appropriate understanding and support for his difficulties through childhood and adolescence which culminated in a year spent in an American state penitentiary at the age of 14. John-Paul's reflection on whether the colour of his skin had contributed to a misinterpretation of his difficulties is deeply concerning and links to the exploration of issues of autism, culture and ethnicity explored in Chapter 9.

AUTISM AND THE YOUTH JUSTICE PATHWAY

Katie Maras, Clare Hughes, Adam O'Loughlin and Alexandra Lewis

Introduction

The criminal justice system (CJS) can be challenging for any young person, but navigating its social, procedural and legal complexities can be particularly challenging for autistic young people. In this contribution, we outline anecdotal and research-based evidence regarding how differences in the way that autistic people perceive, process and interact with the world around them can lead to difficulties within the CJS unless appropriate adaptations are made. We also outline what such adaptations might look like, and how an autistic young person (and those who support them) can ask for them.

Autistic involvement in the CJS

Autistic people come into contact with the CJS for a number of reasons. Sadly, autistic people experience higher rates of victimization and exploitation (e.g., Brown-Lavoie, Viecili & Weiss 2014; Weiss & Fardella 2018), which can precipitate contact with CJS as victim or witness. Behavioural differences may also result in an autistic person experiencing arrest and questioning as an innocent suspect, for example, where behaviours such as stimming are misinterpreted as intoxication or an act of aggression (Salerno-Ferraro & Schuller 2020).

For a minority of autistic people, characteristics associated with autism – such as obsessional interests, sensory sensitivities, emotional dysregulation, misinterpretation of rules, people and events, may also be associated with engaging in offending (e.g., see Allen *et al.* 2008; Helverschou *et al.* 2015; Rava *et al.* 2017; Tint *et al.* 2017; Woodbury-Smith *et al.* 2005). These factors alone are rarely enough to result in offending, but when exacerbated by triggers such as family issues, a deterioration in mental health, disruption to routine, stress or sensory overload, they can occasionally lead to contact with police (Allen *et al.* 2008; Helverschou *et al.* 2015; Mouridsen *et al.* 2008). Finally, some autistic people may offend for reasons unrelated to autism but might struggle to cope once in the CJS due to factors relating to their autism.

A mainstream school environment can be a challenging one for autistic students. For instance, Critchley (2019) concluded that the behaviour of autistic pupils is often the result of sensory overload resulting in the fight, flight or freeze responses. School exclusions, as a result of such behaviours, have been increasing in recent years. (Cooke 2018; Rogers 2019). In her research, Rogers spoke to mothers of autistic people who had been considered to be 'a challenge' in school. These parents had asked for help and support but had either not received it, or it had not been enough to address the issues. School exclusions can often cause children's self-esteem to plummet and can create mental health issues, while other autistic children can find being out of this stressful environment a huge relief (Critchley 2019).

Some autistic young people can be vulnerable to being exploited in a range of ways. Tamsin Gregory from St Giles Trust has said that hidden disabilities and neurodevelopmental differences can leave children more at risk of being targeted by criminal gangs, especially if they have been excluded from school. Through a project they have in place to support young people who have been exploited, up to 60 per cent of the young people had a diagnosed or undiagnosed condition such as autism, attention deficit hyperactivity disorder (ADHD), deafness or dyslexia (Devine 2019). Access to the internet and forums can also put people at risk.

For some young people, these issues regarding their behaviour, school exclusions, low self-esteem and being targeted by criminal groups can progress to the young people being involved with the CJS. Frustratingly, this trajectory is often predicted by parents and others who have been in contact with the child.

The youth justice system (YJS) is the part of the wider UK CJS that deals with children and young people aged under 18 years old. It refers to community and custodial services. The age of entry into the youth justice system (sometimes referred to as the age of criminal responsibility, ACR) varies across the UK. The age of criminal responsibility in England, Wales and Northern Ireland is 10 years old and in Scotland it is 12 years old. This means that children under 10 (12 in Scotland) cannot be arrested or charged with a crime; children between the minimum ACR and 17 can be arrested and taken to court if they commit a crime. However, the CJS treats children differently from adults, and significant weight is attached to the age of the suspect if they are aged under 18.

At 10 and 12 years old, the UK ACR is among the lowest in Europe and is out of step with what is known about brain maturation (Blakemore 2008; Shannon *et al.* 2011). This has been criticized by the United

Nations, which advocates a minimum ACR no lower than 14 years old (United Nations Committee on the Rights of the Child 2016, 2019).

A landmark report commissioned by the Children's Commissioner for England (Hughes *et al.* 2012) examined the prevalence of neurodisability within the youth justice system. It found a high prevalence of all types of neurodisability, including autism, plus significant co-morbidity. This prompted improved screening for neurodisabilities across the YJS in England and Wales.

Autistic experiences in the CJS

An accumulating body of research suggests that autistic people's experiences with the CJS are often negative (e.g., Crane *et al.* 2016; Gibbs and Haas 2020; Maras *et al.* 2017; Salerno-Ferraro & Schuller 2020). Autistic people often report feeling that they do not receive sufficient explanations of procedures, and that appropriate adaptations, such as changing the physical location to alleviate their sensory issues or adapting communication techniques, are not made often enough. It is important to note that a majority of autistic people also report they do not always disclose their autism diagnosis to police due to perceived lack of understanding and fear of stigmatization and discrimination by police (Crane *et al.* 2016; Gibbs and Haas 2020). Yet not disclosing one's diagnosis may have actually had the opposite effect, precluding both police understanding for their differences and the provision of adaptations.

Crucially, if an individual discloses their autism diagnosis, they are entitled to receive mandatory support provisions and reasonable adjustments, in addition to being eligible for a range of discretionary provisions (throughout engagement with the CJS) to ensure that their personal support needs are met. Indeed, respondents in the study by Crane and colleagues (2016) who did disclose their diagnosis often reported that this was helpful for the provision of support and adjustments, such as ensuring that an Appropriate Adult was present (see further information below). Further, several studies have shown that informing others about an autism diagnosis results in more positive perceptions of them in CJS contexts, as both child (Crane *et al.* 2018) and adult witnesses (Maras *et al.* 2019a), and as defendants (Maras, Marshall & Sands 2019).

First response

While the vast majority of interactions with the police that are experienced by autistic children are positive, there are a number of situations where there is the potential for these interactions to go badly. This is particularly the case when an autistic young person is suspected of having broken the law and the police are called, which is an inherently stressful situation for most people. Sensory sensitivities are common in autism (e.g., Ben-Sasson *et al.* 2009; Liss *et al.* 2006) and are often worsened under new or anxiety-provoking situations (Neil, Olsson & Pellicano 2016). Exacerbated sensory sensitivities during initial police response have been highlighted in several studies, for example, with shouting, sirens and restraints being overwhelming and, in some cases, resulting in a 'meltdown' (e.g., Crane *et al.* 2016; Gibbs & Haas 2020; Salnerno-Ferraro & Schuller 2020). Some of these things can be mitigated against by the police; however, some cannot. For example, in an emergency situation, responding police officers will often use the warning instruments in their vehicles (such as lights and sirens) to attend an incident promptly, and it is the expectation of society that they do so.

Anecdotally, the most successful interactions between police officers, police staff and autistic children occur when the police have a personal understanding of autism and adjust their behaviour accordingly (see also Crane *et al.* 2016). However, autism-specific training is not currently provided by the College of Policing, and so it is left to individual police forces to develop and maintain autism-specific training (although at the time of writing there are discussions about developing UK-wide police training). This leads to inevitable disparities across police services and individual officers and staff.

The police have a framework they use for all decisions, whether that's when responding to spontaneous incidents or planned operations, by an individual or team, and to both operational and non-operational situations; this is called the National Decision Model. This model is suitable for all decisions and should be used by everyone in policing, and it allows decision-makers to structure a rationale of what they did during an incident and why. Managers and others can use it to review decisions and actions and promote learning.

In dealings with autistic children, it is often a failure to recognize and understand the key facets of autism by police officers and staff that can lead to situations deteriorating quickly, creating adverse incidents that can affect autistic people for a long time afterwards. The first of these is communication difficulties, particularly when police first arrive. Very often, this is a moment of heightened stress for everyone involved, and the first impulse of the police is to try to quickly establish what has happened. However, research by Salerno-Ferraro and Schuller (2020) indicates that the ability of autistic people to communicate under the stress of a police interaction is impaired, making following instructions and articulating what has happened to them quite challenging. It is possible that in these situations, police may misinterpret these communication difficulties as non-compliance and react accordingly.

It is in these situations that autism alert-card schemes can be extremely beneficial. Many police services now offer autism-specific card schemes such as the Metropolitan Police Autism Passport scheme, or more generic schemes such as Safe Places. The value of these schemes is not to be underestimated, as they provide autistic people with a way of helping the police to understand not just that they are autistic, but also how they can best be communicated with. This is particularly important for those who may become non-verbal when under stress, and in many cases a simple understanding of the person they are dealing with can mitigate against any further stress caused and lead to more successful interactions.

However, there will always be times when police have to detain people against their wishes, either to keep them safe or if they are to be placed under arrest. These are often the occasions of maximum stress, both for detainees and the officers and staff involved. The use of coercive powers is not something police take lightly, and they should always aim to use the minimum amount of force that is appropriate. Again, a simple understanding of the effect that police tactics such as handcuffing techniques can have on an autistic person can go a long way to ensuring that longer-term harm is not caused.

It is also worth remembering that the use of force is something that each officer or staff member has to justify. The Police Code of Ethics sets out the policing principles that members of the police service are expected to uphold and the standards of behaviour they are expected to meet. It states that throughout a situation, decision-makers should ask themselves:

- Is what I am considering consistent with the Code of Ethics?
- What would the victim or community affected expect of me in this situation?

- What does the police service expect of me in this situation?

- Is this action or decision likely to reflect positively on my professionalism and policing generally?

- Could I explain my action or decision in public?

In a fast-moving incident, the police service recognizes that the main priority is to keep in mind their overarching mission to act with integrity to protect and serve the public. These standards originate from the Police (Conduct) Regulations 2012 (for police officers) and the Police Staff Council Joint Circular 54 (for police staff). They reflect the expectations that the College of Policing and the public have of the behaviour of those working in policing.

Appropriate Adults (AA)

A key safeguarding provision for young people and vulnerable adults in police contact is the Appropriate Adult (AA) role. It exists in England, Wales, Scotland and Northern Ireland but there are differences between the four nations. An AA provides active support and assistance in understanding and asserting rights, intervenes if they observe improper treatment, and assists with communication and understanding.

In England, Wales and Northern Ireland, police are required to make contact with an AA 'as soon as practicable' when detaining, voluntarily interviewing or issuing out-of-court disposals (where an offender has to admit they are guilty to be issued with an out of court resolution) to any under-18-year-olds. The police must start by asking a parent or legal guardian to undertake the AA role. If this is not possible, an AA will be provided.

AAs exist in Scotland and are statutorily provided but only for vulnerable victims, witnesses, suspects and accused persons who are aged 16 and over (Criminal Justice (Scotland) Act 2016). It is the presence of vulnerability rather than age that triggers allocation of an AA for 16- and 17-year-olds. This highlights the importance of disclosing an autism diagnosis. AAs are not provided in Scotland for young people aged under 16 years old. Instead, a parent, guardian or local authority must be present during any interview but does not undertake an AA role.

Using family members as AAs brings both advantages and disadvantages. Research indicates that issues may arise through misunderstanding the complex AA role and undertaking it in circumstances that are likely to be personally distressing (Dixon *et al.* 1990; Pierpoint 2006). However, family members are also likely to be most knowledgeable about the young autistic person's needs and communication style and be comfortingly familiar to them in a stressful situation. Professional AAs undergo formal training and will be more knowledgeable about the young person's rights and entitlements. Guidance is available from the National Appropriate Adult Network for parents, carers and untrained AAs.

Youth Justice Liaison and Diversion Services (YJLD)

An English Youth Justice Liaison and Diversion (YJLD) scheme started in 2008 both to enhance mental health screening through the use of structured validated tools at first contact with the youth justice system, and to provide help for young people with mental health and developmental issues. Evaluation (Haines *et al.* 2015) found an autism prevalence of 18.6 per cent. Interventions led to reductions in overall need, depression, and self-harm, and a delay and possible reduction in reoffending for all participants.

Youth Liaison and Diversion (YL&D) services are now available across all regions of England and Wales. This is an NHS service, the aim of which is to make contact with all young people who come into contact with the police, for whatever reason. The role has changed to screening and signposting only. Information gained from assessments is shared, with consent, with other health and CJS agencies, so that they can consider what reasonable adjustments are required. Training for YL&D workers is variable and some may have little understanding of autism and its related needs.

Police custody

Police custody suites can be noisy, frightening and unpleasant places for any detainee. However, there are specific features of police custody that are particularly challenging for autistic detainees, who report finding sensory information such as lighting or noises almost painful and can have difficulty screening them out (Rogers & Ozonoff 2005). Fortunately, however, many if not all of these issues can be mitigated for or designed out.

The first of these is timing. By its very nature, custody can be unpredictable, as the demands on staff vary quite considerably and complex investigations can take a long time. It is therefore not uncommon for detainees to be kept waiting for some time before they are 'booked in', and also for detainees to be kept in police cells prior to interview for a number of hours. For an autistic detainee who doesn't know what's about to happen, this can be particularly unsettling. However, when clear communication systems are in place describing the likely length of the wait, this can be managed successfully.

Second, the environment itself presents particular challenges for autistic detainees. Holloway and colleagues (2020) identified that sensory sensitivities could be particularly exacerbated by the unfamiliar physical surroundings, such as the noise levels and lighting which is very bright or fluorescent. Some police services are actively considering how to modify lighting to make the environment more comfortable, and also how to reduce the amount of noise.

Booking-in can cause further issues. At the start of the process, the arresting officer/staff is required by law to explain to the custody staff why a detainee has been arrested and is in custody in the first place. This requires the officer or staff to explain or 'justify' the circumstances of the arrest, for which subjective opinions can vary considerably. For example, an autistic detainee may disagree with the narrative given or even the allegation against them, leading to higher levels of anxiety and stress. It is for this reason that all officers and staff should be at pains to remind autistic detainees that at this point nothing has been decided and that no decisions have been made about what will happen to them. The increasing use of American vernacular is particularly unhelpful in this case, and many people, autistic or not, will often misunderstand that they have not been 'charged' with anything at that time.

Moving through the booking-in process, Holloway and colleagues (2020) also identified the use of non-specific questions as problematic. For example, autistic detainees have noted that social communication difficulties are intensified when ambiguous language is used, for example, 'Where do you live?' rather than 'What's your address?'

Autistic detainees also describe that the way in which other questions are phrased during the booking-in process is unlikely to lead to them disclosing their clinical diagnoses, because there are no obvious questions alluding to this. Indeed, the standard risk assessment does ask detainees if they have any mental health conditions, and also about learning disabilities, but it does not specifically ask about autism. As a result, those detainees who do not have co-morbid mental health conditions or learning disability may not advise about their autism. Custody staff are entitled to ask follow-up questions if appropriate; however, this relies on the officer or staff member in question to identify if a detainee may be autistic and probe further.

Unsurprisingly the most positive outcomes usually rely on the custody staff member having specific understanding of autism through personal experience. This is a risk for policing, as the failure to identify a detainee as autistic and therefore vulnerable during booking-in can lead to the detainee being denied access to an Appropriate Adult and further well-being support.

Interview

Police interviews are, by definition, formal social interactions that require the narration of a past, personally experienced event. A suspect interview is an especially complex social situation which can be particularly challenging for an autistic person. Crucially, however, the social communication and memory difficulties associated with autism do not have to negate the reliability of an interviewee's account if appropriate adaptations to the interview process are made.

When suspects are interviewed in England and Wales, the PEACE (Preparation and planning; Engage and explain; Account, clarify and challenge; Closure; Evaluation) model of investigative interviewing is employed where the focus is on information gathering and hypothesis testing (Home Office 2017). Specifically, the use of very open questions is the 'gold standard', to avoid leading an interviewee or constraining their recall (Milne & Bull 1999). However, standard police interview techniques have been developed based on neurotypical models of communication and memory. For an autistic person, the open-ended interview structure can be problematic for several reasons. First, it requires mentalizing (or 'theory of mind') processes to infer which details would be of interest to the interviewer and how much to recall, which autistic people find challenging (see Baron-Cohen 2000). Second, autistic people often have difficulties freely recalling specific past, personally experienced events under such open-ended situations (see Crane & Maras 2020), particularly in regard to monitoring the source of information in order to recollect when, where or with whom an event occurred (Bowler, Gardiner & Berthollier 2004; Bowler, Gaigg & Gardiner 2008). Finally, executive functioning difficulties can limit their ability to generate a coherent narrative under these conditions (Tager-Flusberg, Paul & Lord 2005).

Although autistic people can have trouble freely recalling specific past events (particularly pulling together all of the contextual details of an event into a coherent whole narrative), they are able to recall this information to a similar level to a non-autistic person when more supportive retrieval procedures are used such as specific cued questions (see Maras, in press). However, the use of closed questions is often inappropriate within a legal framework as it can lead an interviewee. This is important because although autistic individuals are no more *suggestible* to memory distortions based on interviewer suggestions (Bruck *et al.* 2007; Maras & Bowler 2011, 2012; McCrory, Henry & Happé 2007), they may be more *compliant* to knowingly acquiesce to suggestions; for example, in order to terminate the interview earlier (Chandler, Russell & Maras 2019). It is crucial, therefore, that interviews are non-leading.

Preliminary findings indicate that a novel 'witness-aimed first account' (WAFA) interviewing technique may be fruitful in supporting autistic people to recall events within a legally compatible non-leading framework (Maras *et al.* 2019b). Here, the interviewee self-segments their memory of an event into their own discrete parameter-bound 'topic boxes' at the outset, before engaging in an exhaustive free recall retrieval attempt (followed by interviewer probing) within the parameters of each topic box in turn. Thus, the interviewee still self-directs their recall, as would happen during a typical free narrative account, but rather than having a free-flow verbalization of the entire event – which is often difficult for autistic people – they provide their own segmentation of the event. Displaying the topic boxes on post-it notes can serve as a reminder of the structure of the event and reduces the amount of event information the interviewee has to remember at once, which frees up cognitive resources for the witness to focus their search and retrieval strategies within individual segments. Findings indicate that the WAFA interview elicits more detailed and accurate recall from both autistic and non-autistic individuals than a standard best practice interview (Maras *et al.* 2019b).

A particularly pertinent issue for suspect interviews is the manner in which evidence is disclosed to the suspect. For example, an interviewer may reveal evidence in a tactical manner, forcing the interviewee to respond to challenges without an opportunity to rehearse a response, or they may strategically withhold evidence until after the suspect has provided an account (see Bull 2014). An interviewee who has difficulty reading others' intentions and finds it difficult to predict their responses will naturally be at a disadvantage in such a context. No research to date has empirically examined how autistic individuals fare under these sorts of demands in a police interview, but the heightened cognitive complexities, shifting social demands and stress of being interviewed as a police suspect (Vrij, Fisher & Blank 2017) are likely to be problematic. It is therefore imperative that an interviewer is aware of an interviewee's social, communication and cognitive difficulties and differences, so that they can plan and conduct the interview accordingly in order to obtain a reliable and detailed account.

It is not realistic to expect all police officers to be experts on autism and currently they are provided with very little guidance on how to interview vulnerable suspects (O'Mahony *et al.* 2012; O'Mahony, Milne & Grant 2012). Officers can, however, be guided by expert advice in tailoring their questioning strategies based on the individual charac- teristics of the person they are interviewing. An intermediary (whose role it is to protect the rights and welfare of a suspect throughout their time in police custody, for example by facilitating communication) can be invaluable in this. In most cases, adaptations will be needed to the wording of questions, particularly bearing in mind that questions are likely to be interpreted literally by an autistic person (Salerno-Ferraro & Schuller 2020).

It also critical to consider sensory issues. Police environments are often loud, brightly lit (e.g., with fluorescent strip lighting) and strong-smelling environments. Many of the autistic respondents sur- veyed by Crane and colleagues (2016) were dissatisfied with the location in which their interview was held and the number of breaks provided during interviews. These are simple adaptations that can often be easily accommodated by police – if they are made aware of an individual's diagnosis and the need for particular adjustments before the interview is conducted. It is important to have a discussion between the individual, their support person, AA (appropriate adult) or intermediary, and the police regarding what particular sensitivities, triggers and other stressors they may experience, and where possible the timing and location of the interview should be planned around these. This may be as sim- ple as removing a ticking clock from the wall of the interview room, but at other times it may be appropriate to conduct the interview in a familiar environment such as the interviewee's own home in order to elicit best evidence (see Maras *et al.* 2019b). It is also important that any self-stimulatory behaviours (often used as a soothing mechanism and a way of regulating sensory input) are not stopped, and that if the individual carries a particular calming object (e.g., a fidget spinner), that they are allowed to keep this during the interview. A witness who feels more relaxed and comfortable can provide more detailed and accurate evidence (Geiselman *et al.* 1984).

Court

Youth courts are specialist courts dealing with criminal cases against children aged 10–17. They are less formal than adult courts. Children are called by their first names and the judge or magistrates speak directly to the child and may ask questions. They are designed to make it easier for children to understand what is happening and feel less intimidated. Children under 16 must attend with a parent or guardian who sits next to their child. More serious cases may subsequently be sent to the Crown Court, which is not specifically designed for young people, although adaptations are made. A parent or guardian is required to be present in the Crown Court for defendants aged under 16 and may be required by the judge to attend for 16- and 17-year-olds, if deemed desirable. Guidance regarding Crown Court adaptations for young defendants has been recently updated by the Judicial College (Branston & Norton 2021).

However, even with these adaptations, courts are unfamiliar, formal and high-stakes environments that can be stressful for most people, but there are a number of aspects of courtroom proceedings that are likely to be particularly problematic for an autistic person (Crane & Maras 2020).

Research has shown that autistic people often feel dissatisfied with their experiences in the courtroom, particularly regarding the way in which they were questioned (Maras *et al.* 2017). The aim of cross-examination is to discredit the witness (Stone 1988), with widespread use of suggestive (e.g., 'He was wearing a red hat, wasn't he?'), leading (e.g., 'Did he have a knife?'), multiple-part (e.g., 'Did you leave the house and was this before or after you received the phone call?'), complex (e.g., 'Is it not the case that when you saw John his demeanour was shifty which led to you to believe that he must have done something untoward?'), negative and double negative (e.g., 'Is it not the case that he did not go outside?') and tag questions (e.g., 'You got the bus here, didn't you?'). Such questioning persists despite evidence that even typical adults are susceptible to the negative effects of cross-examination and become less, rather than more, accurate (e.g., Ellison & Wheatcroft 2010; Kebbell, Evans & Johnson 2010; Valentine & Maras 2011; Wheatcroft & Ellison 2012). Unfortunately, the effect of the sort of adversarial, leading, negative and complex questions favoured by barristers on individuals with social communication difficulties is likely to be even worse.

The appointment of an intermediary can be critical in facilitating communication between the court and a defendant (O'Mahony 2010). The 1999 Youth Justice and Criminal Evidence Act in England and Wales enables a range of 'special measures' to be used to assist the provision of testimony from vulnerable witnesses and victims. These include the use of screens in court (so that the witness cannot see the defendant), evidence via live video link to the courtroom, video-recorded evidence-in-chief (e.g., the previously video recorded investigative interview with the police, if appropriate), the use of a registered intermediary, and communication aids – to enable a vulnerable witness to give their best evidence (see Bull 2010; O'Mahony *et al.* 2012). Witnesses may also be permitted to attend a familiarization visit to the court ahead of their trial. It has been argued that these special measures should also be offered to vulnerable suspects (Jacobson 2008; O'Mahony *et al.* 2012), and a recent development in England and Wales is that defendants will now be eligible for the provision of an intermediary to support them in giving evidence in court, although clearly the legislation needs to go further. Registered intermediaries are routinely available in Northern Ireland for vulnerable young defendants (Department of Justice 2015). 'Special measures' are employed in Scotland for vulnerable individuals, but this has not so far involved the use of intermediaries.

Contrary to some lay beliefs, jurors' perceptions of a vulnerable defendant are often improved if they are accompanied by an intermediary (Collins, Harker & Antonopoulos 2017; Ridley, van Rheede & Wilcock, 2015; Smethurst & Collins 2019). A critical factor in improving others' perceptions is also whether jurors are aware of an individual's autism diagnosis. Autistic individuals often display behavioural differences that others may erroneously rely on when judging their credibility. However, several studies have shown that if a witness (Crane *et al.* 2018; Maras *et al.* 2019b) or defendant (Maras *et al.* 2019b) disclose their autism diagnosis they are perceived as more credible. For example, Maras and colleagues (2019b) presented mock jurors with a written vignette about a hypothetical defendant who was described as displaying autistic-like behaviours. Mock jurors who were informed that the defendant had autism (and were provided background information about autism), rated him as significantly more honest and likeable, and less culpable for his actions, relative to mock jurors who received no diagnostic information about him. Disclosing one's autism diagnosis is also important to enable reasonable adjustments to ensure fair access to trial, for example with the provision of an intermediary.

The Advocate's Gateway provides practical guidance for judges and lawyers on vulnerable witnesses and defendants, including a range of toolkits (two specifically about autism) which provide general good practice guidance across the criminal, family and civil courts when preparing for trial in cases involving a witness or defendant who is vulnerable.

Community-based youth offending services

In England and Wales, the main services in contact with young people charged with or convicted of offences are youth offending teams (YOTs). These are community-based multiagency teams (local authorities, health, police and probation are statutory members) that deliver out-of-court disposals, provide a service to courts and manage court orders. In Northern Ireland, multiagency youth justice teams carry out a function similar to YOTs. In Scotland, there is an initial multiagency screening panel which identifies needs and decides which partner agency should take the lead in managing the young person.

Restorative justice

There has been increased use of restorative justice interventions across all four nations. However, there is no guidance on how this may need to be adapted for use with autistic young people (Restorative Justice Council 2015). Autistic individuals have a different style of social communication and it is possible that, if this is not understood by staff and explained to the victim, the autistic young person may be perceived to be insufficiently remorseful or lacking in sincerity in any apology, with unfair adverse consequences.

Youth detention

The number of young people detained in secure care has fallen substantially in all four nations over the past decade.

Broadly, youth detention takes place in three types of accommodation: small, highly staffed secure children's homes; large, young offender institutions with lower staff numbers; and secure training centres which fall between the two (the latter in England only). Northern Ireland has a single juvenile justice centre which most broadly resembles a secure children's home. A secure school will open in England in 2022 and this represents a new approach to secure care.

In England and Wales, placement decisions are made on the basis of YOT recommendations (Youth Custody Service, 2017). It is the YOT's duty to assess and communicate a young person's needs. Autism alone will not necessarily lead to placement in a secure children's home, although it could be considered that a small, highly staffed placement may be advantageous.

Young offender institutions (YOIs) (in Wales and England) have implemented adaptations to meet the needs of autistic young people to achieve Autism Accreditation from the National Autistic Society (Lewis *et al.* 2015; Lewis *et al.* 2016). These changes were introduced after recognizing that autistic children in the YOIs often struggled to cope. Some adult prisons are also achieving Autism Accreditation.

Regardless of the type of secure accommodation, all young people in England, Wales and Northern Ireland are assessed on reception using the same CHAT health assessment tool[1] as is used by YOTs, which includes a specific screen for autism (Lennox 2014). Findings inform subsequent psychological formulations and care plans. Some of the larger placements are able to provide autism assessments and post-diagnostic interventions.

Planning for the return to the community is particularly important for autistic individuals who are likely to find the transition challenging. Changes introduced by the revised Special Educational Needs (SEN) Code of Practice (January 2015) and Special Educational Needs and Disability (Detained Persons) Regulations 2015 mean that children detained in England who have an Education and Health Care Plan (EHCP) must continue to have this supported by their home local authority. These new regulations represented an acceptance by the government that a

---

1   The Comprehensive Health Assessment Tool (CHAT) collects key information about a young person's mental health, including key events, professionals involved, current risk assessment and coping strategies: www.chat.mentalhealth.sg/mobile/chat-assessment-service/chat-assessment.

new approach was needed to tackle the disproportionately high rates of SEN among children in the secure estate.

Local authorities are not obliged to fund EHCPs while the young person is detained, but they should be involved in a review of EHCP prior to transition back into the community and provision of ongoing support. Unfortunately, this is often delayed until after release or does not occur at all, jeopardizing successful resettlement.

Conclusion

We all want to avoid autistic young people having any contact with the CJS, but as for the non-autistic population, this can be difficult and complex. There needs to be better support available at the earliest opportunity for autistic young people, their families and those working with them, at the earliest opportunity to avoid the potential negative spiral that can result in their getting in to trouble. Post-diagnostic support varies from area to area, but it is crucial that plans are in place to address the presenting issues that brought the young person to the diagnostic pathway in the first place. Addressing behavioural concerns as early as possible and having clearer, consistent strategies in place across all settings, including the home, has to be part of the solution to avoiding the negative trajectory foreseen for some of these children. It is hoped that the forthcoming revised Autism Strategy will address both the factors that predispose contact with CJS as well as making the CJS more sensitive to the needs of autistic people.

Should autistic young people come into contact with the police or other CJS professionals, there are a number of adaptations that can be made to improve their experiences and to facilitate equal access to justice. Many of these are precluded, however, by an individual not disclosing their autism diagnosis in the first instance. Disclosing one's autism diagnosis (and how it affects them individually) is a key action that an autistic person or, with consent, their parent or guardian can take in order to enable adaptations and understanding throughout the CJS process, along with proactively requesting support.

A MOTHER'S STORY

Juliet Gittens

Lee had been brought up within a strong family unit with both parents and three brothers. In primary school, he did well academically and socially, but struggled in secondary school, as many of his teachers did not understand his needs as an autistic youngster. In spite of this, Lee strived and did extremely well, leaving school with a number of GCSEs, and was also offered a job. Lee's extended families were a tight network, looking out for him and accommodating his additional needs. He had never been in trouble with the law.

As an adolescent, Lee was very trustworthy and trusting and was easily manipulated by other young people. He was stopped and searched by the police on numerous occasions. This became the norm to him. He was arrested for allegedly attacking a pizza delivery man, but investigations concluded it was a case of mistaken identity. Then, Lee was arrested and charged in October 2012 with 'aggravated burglary with firearms' and found guilty by joint enterprise. He was stabbed several months before the trial in early 2012. It was believed that this was an attempt to silence him as he would not say who the other youths involved in the burglary were, even though he could describe the events of that day and explain why he was in prison.

I believe that the portrayal of Black youths as highlighted in the media is very unhelpful. This whole experience has made me see the legal and criminal justice system in a new light. I believe that my son did not get a fair trial, and everyone present was shocked by the verdict. He was a very vulnerable young person.

When Lee was sentenced to seven years it had a massive impact on the family. We struggled to understand how he could be sent to prison. His elderly grandparents missed him dearly and felt distressed about him being in prison, and his older brother felt that he had failed him, as Lee was the life and soul of the household.

I worried how he would cope in a different environment. I had many sleepless nights. I just wanted my son home. The day he was sentenced he called me from the prison and said, 'When can I come home?' I cried. He was in an environment that was unfamiliar to him. We found it very hard to function: my household was broken. Lee's brothers didn't know what to say to make it better. Later, they told me that they thought that I loved Lee more because I was so preoccupied with him.

I was so angry; I felt that no one understood what my family was going through. I don't make excuses for Lee but I know that he was confused about what had happened. I don't have any answers, because this was not part of my plan. He was always the nearest child to me.

One day I decided to ring the governor of the prison. I was actually surprised that I was connected. I was so geared up for a negative reaction, but he was very understanding. I explained Lee's condition and, eventually, he was given a key worker. We spoke once a week. Visiting was very hard as I had to leave him looking at me as though he wanted me to get him out. It has been very hard to talk about his time in prison.

When he was finally released the whole family turned up to welcome him home. It has been a long hard road as he still has some of the prison tendencies in him, but we are a strong family and we will always be there for Lee.

The question I ask myself repeatedly is: how many others are in prison right now who have a diagnosis of autism or who have missed being diagnosed or been misdiagnosed? I feel strongly that there must be more awareness about the needs of autistic youngsters who can be easily manipulated and used by their peers.

AN INTERVIEW WITH JOHN-PAUL (JP) HORSLEY

JP Horsley is an award-winning musician. He has worked with autistic youngsters and is the father of two autistic boys. JP featured in a television documentary with Simon Baron-Cohen, who confirmed a diagnosis of autism when JP was 38 years old. The following account is taken from an interview that JP gave to Judith Gainsborough.

My childhood was really fun. I was very close to my parents, especially my mum. I had difficulty speaking to people. At home, I could speak to a level that I was comfortable. When I went to kindergarten when we were living in America, if people spoke to me, my anxiety wouldn't let the words come out. I was very anxious and couldn't speak. I didn't really have friends at school and people would stay away from me because I didn't talk. I remember one time playing in the sand box and hearing children say: 'We can't be here anymore, because John-Paul Horsley is here.' That was an eye-opening moment for me. I moved to the UK when I was six years old. We were living in a hotel in Kensington. I didn't really have friends because of the hotel environment. I didn't connect with anyone.

At about ten, I started making an effort to communicate. All the kids gravitated towards me because of the US accent. When I went to secondary school, my sister, who was four years older, was there. She had a reputation for being fierce and I thought she'd look after me, but I hardly saw her. I was in the first year and she was in the fifth year. But people gravitated towards me because of her reputation. I was her little brother. I didn't react well to other kids and it turned into me being aggressive.

Because I was Black, people didn't see the autism. I was a joker. Teachers didn't expect much of me and I was labelled a 'Jack the Lad'. I don't think my white teachers expected much of me. I thought they were on my side! Teaching assistants and teachers have to be very caring, but if I had had support in school, things would have been better.

I don't think anything was going wrong. I think I was particularly good at being bad. I had a thick skin. I wasn't bothered by insults. If I did feel insulted, I would just take the opportunity to be aggressive. I didn't get diagnosed until I was 38 years old. Loads of times I felt not quite right. Teachers said I was in a bit of a shell. My parents just said I was shy. I was learning a lot at home, but I wouldn't articulate it at school.

By the time I was 14, I was in lots of gangs all over London. People asked me to join their gang because I was ferocious, not because I was particularly charming. I was a well-known little guy. But, again, I was more of a loner. I didn't want to join everybody's gang. I was known by all of them and I was involved. The knowledge of that made me into a stronger person on the streets.

My parents sent me back to the US to live with my sisters because I was getting into trouble on the streets. The education system was different and I regressed a little. I lashed out. I could learn by listening and I remembered everything: theories, formulas. I didn't revise or study. I got into trouble with the police because I had taken a gun to school. I was popular with the ladies and somebody's girlfriend was writing me love letters, so her boyfriend said 'I'm going to shoot this new kid.' I went home and I knew where my brother-in-law kept his pistol so I took it to school every morning for months. Eventually, somebody called the police and they came and arrested me in a maths lesson. I went straight to the police station. I was given bail and awaited my court date. I was confident that I wouldn't get a long sentence as it was a first offence. It was an anxious time. At first, they tried me as a juvenile and I was put in a juvenile detention centre. I didn't get along well there and had a lot of fights so I was taken back to court and tried as an adult. I had to do the rest of my time in a proper high security state penitentiary, and that was a scary experience. The rats were massive, like little dogs. Everyone in there was pretty savage. I was overwhelmed. All sorts of people with mental health issues. Being the type of person who likes their own company, I was happy to do my whole time in my cell. I was on 23-hour lock-up. All you can hear is the screams of the other inmates.

I was interested in music and that kind of thing. My brother-in-law's friend Clarence was a DJ and he came to me with a sampling machine and encouraged me to write some songs. The challenge of writing songs made me concentrate so much that the rest of the world didn't really matter. That's when I started trying to change my life around.

I have two sons from different relationships, both on the autism spectrum, which must say something about the genetic component. I knew when I became a dad that I needed to be the best that I could possibly be.

My son was diagnosed in 2010 between the ages of 18 months and two years. Going through the diagnostic process with him, it sounded like me: the hypermobility, the hypersensitivity, the lack of connection, the lack of eye contact. I've always avoided looking into people's eyes because it makes me anxious. I was so surprised when they confirmed it was autism, as I didn't know any different. I was relieved at first. I always knew I was a little bit weird. It made me look deeper and try to perfect the bits that weren't quite right. Recently, I've decided to shake that off. It's tedious to think of every move.

The diagnosis made me think more about why I like a fight. It's like chess to me. I like to challenge myself against people who are much bigger than me. I'm not a bully and I like to protect people. The autism has made me understand why I love numbers so much, and also routine and repetition.

Recently, I've been working in Croydon with children who have different abilities, autism spectrum, and difficult behaviours, and who look like they are heading towards the crime route. We watch videos and we discuss what they could do in those circumstances.

I use my own life experience and talk through what they could do to get out of these situations. I'm not proud of what happened to me. For me, I wanted to belong and be considered as family. A lot of these children on the autism spectrum are easy targets and that's scary to see. I try to make sure that other children understand more about autism and treat them with respect.

I am now moving into a career with the NHS as an activities practitioner, working with autistic adults with additional conditions such as bipolar. They are in need of additional help with life in general and I work with them on activities to improve health and well-being and also improve their fitness levels.

The key thing to remember when working with autistic youngsters is flexibility – not being stuck in one way. You need to explore different avenues with individuals. You need to have a personable attitude. It helps to bring them out of themselves. I would certainly use my own experience and ask how they want to belong, and I tell them that they can belong with me in the music studio and develop skills elsewhere. We have a good network so that anybody at risk can be offered help to become a better person. I've had success on many levels. I've worked with children at risk of permanent exclusion and I have turned the situation around for them. I like to get the children as early as possible to work with them and help them to grow in confidence.

The warning signs are pretty clear. It's a change in behaviour: maybe more moody, not communicating, a change in style of clothes. You need to keep your eyes open and intervene in a gentle way. It's easy to push away an autistic teenager because it sounds as if you're preaching, but be a big brother, not a dad. You need to get on their wavelength.

Chapter conclusion

This chapter has covered an area of immense concern among professionals and parents alike. The media regularly depicts stories of autistic youngsters in trouble with the law and it is clear that the consequences can be grave. However, there is much to be positive about. Collaborative work between researchers such as Katie Maras, professionals such as Alexandra Lewis and Clare Hughes, and specialist police services such as those provided by Adam O'Loughlin provides evidence of a developing awareness of the needs and vulnerabilities of autistic individuals. Even Juliet Gittens's description of her family's experiences demonstrates a supportive and constructive response from the prison governor. Finally, it is indeed heartening to learn about JP Horsley's trajectory from being imprisoned in early adolescence to becoming a responsible father and a mentor for autistic youngsters at risk.

POINTS FOR REFLECTION

☞ Early identification and appropriate intervention and support may help to prevent later involvement with the CJS.

☞ Teaching autistic youngsters about when and how to disclose information about their diagnosis if they come into contact with the CJS may be extremely helpful.

☞ Providing autistic young people with the knowledge about when and how to ask for appropriate support is also vital.

Resources

Autism: A Guide for Police Officers and Staff (2020) The National Autistic Society. https://s3.chorus-mk.thirdlight.com/file/1573224908/63296026948/width=-1/height=-1/format=-1/fit=scale/t=446220/e=never/k=420e7a4a/NAS_Police_Guide_2020_17092020.pdf.

The Box – Communication Help for the Justice System (2015) A free e-learning tool designed for professionals working in the justice sector. Royal College of Speech and Language Therapists. www.rcslt.org/learning/the-box-training.

Equal Treatment Bench Book (2021) Courts and Tribunals Judiciary. www.judiciary.uk/announcements/equal-treatment-bench-book-new-edition.

Guidance for parents, carers and untrained Appropriate Adults. National Adult Appropriate Network. www.appropriateadult.org.uk/information/guidance-aa.

Mental Health, Autism and Learning Disability in the Criminal Courts. Prison Reform Trust and Rethink Mental Illness. www.mhldcc.org.uk.

Toolkit 3: Planning to Question Someone with Autism (2016) The Advocate's Gateway Lexicon Limited. www.theadvocatesgateway.org/toolkits.

What is an Appropriate Adult? National Adult Appropriate Network. www.appropriateadult.org.uk/information/what-is-an-appropriate-adult.

Youth Defendants in the Crown Court (2021) Judicial College, London. www.judiciary.uk/wp-content/uploads/2021/03/Youth-Defendants-in-the-Crown-Court-March-2021.pdf.

References

Allen, D., Evans, C., Hider, A., Hawkins, S., Peckett, H. & Morgan, H. (2008) 'Offending behaviour in adults with Asperger syndrome.' *Journal of Autism and Developmental Disorders, 38*(4), 748–758. https://doi.org/10.1007/s10803-007-0442-9.

Baron-Cohen, S. (2000) 'Theory of Mind and Autism: A Fifteen-Year Review.' In S. Baron-Cohen, H. Tager-Flusberg & D.J. Cohen (eds) *Understanding Other Minds: Perspectives from Developmental Cognitive Neuroscience* (pp.3–20). Oxford: Oxford University Press.

Ben-Sasson, A., Hen, L., Fluss, R., Cermak, S.A., Engel-Yeger, B. & Gal, E. (2009) 'A meta-analysis of sensory modulation symptoms in individuals with autism spectrum disorders.' *Journal of Autism and Developmental Disorders, 39*(1), 1–11. https://doi.org/10.1007/s10803-008-0593-3.

Blakemore, S. (2008) 'The social brain in adolescence.' *Nature Reviews Neuroscience, 9*(4), 267–277.

Bowler, D.M., Gaigg, S.B. & Gardiner, J.M. (2008) 'Effects of related and unrelated context on recall and recognition by adults with high-functioning autism spectrum disorder.' *Neuropsychologia, 46*(4), 993–999. doi: 10.1016/j.neuropsychologia.2007.12.004.

Bowler, D.M., Gardiner, J.M. & Berthollier, N. (2004) 'Source memory in adolescents and adults with Asperger's syndrome.' *Journal of Autism and Developmental Disorders, 34*(5), 533–542. https://doi.org/10.1007/s10803-004-2548-7.

Branston, G. & Norton, H. (2021) *Youth Defendants in the Crown Court.* London: Judicial College. Accessed 08/04/2021 at www.judiciary.uk/wp-content/uploads/2021/03/Youth-Defendants-in-the-Crown-Court-March-2021.pdf.

Brown-Lavoie, S.M., Viecili, M.A. & Weiss, J.A. (2014) 'Sexual knowledge and victimization in adults with autism spectrum disorders.' *Journal of Autism and Developmental Disorders, 4*(9), 2185–2196. https://doi.org/10.1007/s10803-014-2093-y.

Bruck, M., London, K., Landa, R. & Goodman, J. (2007) 'Autobiographical memory and suggestibility in children with autism spectrum disorder.' *Development and Psychopathology, 19*(1), 73–95. https://doi.org/10.1017/s0954579407070058.

Bull, R. (2010) 'The investigative interviewing of children and other vulnerable witnesses: Psychological research and working/professional practice.' *Legal and Criminological Psychology, 15*(1), 5–23. https://doi.org/10.1348/014466509X440160.

Bull, R. (2014) 'When in Interviews to Disclose Information to Suspects and to Challenge Them?' In R. Bull (ed.) *Investigative Interviewing* (pp.167–181). https://doi.org/10.1007/978-1-4614-9642-7_9.

Chandler, R.J., Russell, A. & Maras, K.L. (2019) 'Compliance in autism: Self-report in action.' *Autism, 23*(4), 1005–1017. https://doi.org/10.1177/1362361318795479.

Collins, K., Harker, N. & Antonopoulos, G.A. (2017) 'The impact of the registered intermediary on adults' perceptions of child witnesses: Evidence from a mock cross examination.' *European Journal on Criminal Policy and Research, 23*(2), 211–225. https://doi.org/10.1007/s10610-016-9314-1.

Cooke, J. (2018) *We Need an Education.* Ambitious About Autism. Accessed 24/08/2021 at www.ambitiousaboutautism.org.uk/sites/default/files/resources-and-downloads/files/we-need-an-education-exclusions-report.pdf.

Crane, L. & Maras, K.L. (2020) 'Autism in the Courtroom.' In *Encyclopedia of Autism Spectrum Disorders* (pp.1–2). https://doi.org/10.1007/978-1-4614-6435-8_102373-1.

Crane, L., Maras, K.L., Hawken, T., Mulcahy, S. & Memon, A. (2016) 'Experiences of autism spectrum disorder and policing in England and Wales: Surveying police and the autism community.' *Journal of Autism and Developmental Disorders, 46*(6), 2028–2041. https://doi.org/10.1007/s10803-016-2729-1.

Crane, L., Wilcock, R., Maras, K.L., Chui, W., Marti-Sanchez, C. & Henry, L.A. (2018) 'Mock juror perceptions of child witnesses on the autism spectrum: The impact of providing diagnostic labels and information about autism.' *Journal of Autism and Developmental Disorders, 50*(5), 1509–1519. https://doi.org/10.1007/s10803-018-3700-0.

Criminal Justice (Scotland) Act 2016. London: HMSO.

Criminal Justice (Scotland) Act 2016 (Support for Vulnerable Persons) Regulations 2019. London: HMSO.

Critchley, S.J. (2019) *Autistic Pupils and Exclusions*. Network Autism, National Autistic Society. Accessed 24/08/2021 at www.autism.org.uk/advice-and-guidance/professional-practice/autism-exclusion.

Department of Justice (2015) *Northern Ireland Registered Intermediaries Schemes, Pilot Project: Post-Project Review*. Accessed 03/04/2021 at www.justice-ni.gov.uk/sites/default/files/publications/doj/registered-intermediaries-post-project-review-feb15.pdf.

Devine, D. (2019) *'Countless' SEND children groomed by drug trafficking gangs*. Learning Disability Today. Accessed 19/08/2021 at www.learningdisabilitytoday.co.uk/2019/countless-send-groomed-by-drug-trafficking-gangs.

Dixon, D., Bottomley, K., Coleman, C., Gill, M. & Wall, D. (1990) 'Safeguarding the rights of suspects in police custody.' *Policing and Society, 1*(2), 115–140.

Ellison, L. & Wheatcroft, J. (2010) '"Could you ask me that in a different way please?" Exploring the impact of courtroom questioning and witness familiarisation on adult witness accuracy.' *Criminal Law Review, 1*, 823–839.

Geiselman, R.E., Fisher, R.P., Firstenberg, I., Hutton, L. *et al.* (1984) 'Enhancement of eyewitness memory: An empirical evaluation of the cognitive interview.' *Journal of Police Science & Administration, 12*(1), 74–80.

Gibbs, V. & Haas, K. (2020) 'Interactions between the police and the autistic community in Australia: Experiences and perspectives of autistic adults and parents/carers.' *Journal of Autism and Developmental Disorders, 50*, 4513–4526. https://doi.org/10.1007/s10803-020-04510-7.

Haines, A., Lane, S., McGuire, J., Perkins, E. & Whittington, R. (2015) 'Offending outcomes of a mental health youth diversion pilot scheme in England.' *Criminal Behaviour and Mental Health, 25*(2), 126–140.

Helverschou, S.B., Rasmussen, K., Steindal, K., Søndanaa, E., Nilsson, B. & Nøttestad, J.A. (2015) 'Offending profiles of individuals with autism spectrum disorder: A study of all individuals with autism spectrum disorder examined by the forensic psychiatric service in Norway between 2000 and 2010.' *Autism, 19*(7), 850–858. https://doi.org/10.1177/1362361315584571.

Holloway, C.A., Munro, N., Jackson, J., Phillips, S. & Ropar, D. (2020) 'Exploring the autistic and police perspectives of the custody process through a participative walk-through.' *Research in Developmental Disabilities, 97*, 103545. https://doi.org/10.1016/j.ridd.2019.103545.

Home Office (2017) *Interviewing Suspects*. London: HMSO.

Hughes, N., Williams, P., Chitsabesan, P., Davies, R. & Mounce, L. (2012) *Nobody Made the Connection: The Prevalence of Neurodisability in Young People who Offend*. London: Office for the Children's Commissioner.

Jacobson, J. (2008) *No One Knows; Police Responses to Suspects with Learning Disabilities and Learning Difficulties: A Review of Policy and Practice*. London: Prison Reform Trust.

Kebbell, M.R., Evans, L. & Johnson, S.D. (2010) 'The influence of lawyers' questions on witness accuracy, confidence, and reaction times and on mock jurors' interpretation of witness accuracy.' *Journal of Investigative Psychology and Offender Profiling, 7*(3), 262–272. https://doi.org/10.1002/jip.125.

Lennox, C. (2014) 'The health needs of young people in prisons.' *British Medical Bulletin, 112*(1), 17–25. https://doi.org/10.1093/bmb/ldu028.

Lewis, A., Pritchett, R., Hughes, C. & Turner, K. (2015) 'Development of autism standards for prisons.' *Journal of Intellectual Disabilities & Offending Behaviour, 6*(2), 68–80.

Lewis, A., Foster, M., Hughes, C. & Turner, K. (2016) 'Improving the management of prisoners with autistic spectrum disorders.' *Prison Service Journal, 22*(6), 21–26.

Liss, M., Saulnier, C., Fein, D. & Kinsbourne, M. (2006) 'Sensory and attention abnormalities in autistic spectrum disorders.' *Autism, 10*(2), 155–172. https://doi.org/10.1177/1362361306062021.

Maras, K. (in press) 'Obtaining Testimony from People with ASD.' In F. Volkmar, R. Loftin, L. Westphal & M. Woodbury-Smith (eds) *Handbook of Autism and the Law.* New York, NY: Springer.

Maras, K. & Bowler, D.M. (2011) 'Brief report: Schema consistent misinformation effects in eyewitnesses with autism spectrum disorder.' *Journal of Autism and Developmental Disorders, 41*(6), 815–820. https://doi.org/10.1007/s10803-010-1089-5.

Maras, K.L. & Bowler, D.M. (2012) 'Brief report: Suggestibility, compliance and psychological traits in high-functioning adults with autism spectrum disorder.' *Research in Autism Spectrum Disorders, 6*(3), 1168–1175. https://doi.org/10.1016/j.rasd.2012.03.013.

Maras, K.L., Crane, L., Mulcahy, S., Hawken, T. *et al.* (2017) 'Brief report: Autism in the courtroom: Experiences of legal professionals and the autism community.' *Journal of Autism and Developmental Disorders, 47*(8), 2610–2620. https://doi.org/10.1007/s10803-017-3162-9.

Maras, K.L., Crane, L., Walker, I. & Memon, A. (2019a) 'Brief report: Perceived credibility of autistic witnesses and the effect of diagnostic information on credibility ratings.' *Research in Autism Spectrum Disorders, 68*, 101442. https://doi.org/10.1016/j.rasd.2019.101442.

Maras, K.L., Marshall, I. & Sands, C. (2019b) 'Mock juror perceptions of credibility and culpability in an autistic defendant.' *Journal of Autism and Developmental Disorders, 49*(3), 996–1010. https://doi.org/10.1007/s10803-018-3803-7.

McCrory, E., Henry, L. & Happé, F. (2007) 'Eye-witness memory and suggestibility in children with Asperger syndrome.' *Journal of Child Psychology and Psychiatry, 48*(5), 482–489. https://doi.org/10.1111/j.1469-7610.2006.01715.x.

Milne, R. & Bull, R. (1999) *Investigative Interviewing: Psychology and Practice.* Chichester: Wiley.

Mouridsen, S.E., Rich, B., Isager, T. & Nedergaard, N.J. (2008) 'Pervasive developmental disorders and criminal behaviour: A case control study.' *International Journal of Offender Therapy and Comparative Criminology, 52*(2), 196–205. https://doi.org/10.1177/0306624X07302056.

Neil, L., Olsson, N.C. & Pellicano, E. (2016) 'The relationship between intolerance of uncertainty, sensory sensitivities, and anxiety in autistic and typically developing children.' *Journal of Autism and Developmental Disorders, 46*(6), 1962–1973. https://doi.org/10.1007/s10803-016-2721-9.

O'Mahony, B.M. (2010) 'The emerging role of the registered intermediary with the vulnerable witness and offender: Facilitating communication with the police and members of the judiciary.' *British Journal of Learning Disabilities, 38* (3), 232–237. https://doi.org/10.1111/j.1468-3156.2009.00600.x.

O'Mahony, B.M., Milne, B. & Grant, T. (2012) 'To challenge, or not to challenge? Best practice when interviewing vulnerable suspects.' *Policing, 6*(3), 301–313. https://doi.org/10.1093/police/pas027.

Pierpoint, H. (2006) 'Reconstructing the role of the appropriate adult in England and Wales.' *Criminology and Criminal Justice, 6*(2), 219–237.

Rava, J., Shattuck, P., Rast, J. & Roux, A. (2017) 'The prevalence and correlates of involvement in the criminal justice system among youth on the autism spectrum.' *Journal of Autism and Developmental Disorders, 47*(2), 340–346. https://doi.org/10.1007/s10803-016-2958-3.

Restorative Justice Council (2015) *Restorative Justice in Youth Offending Teams: Information Pack.* Accessed 04/04/2021 at https://restorativejustice.org.uk/sites/default/files/news/files/dpn8_yot_infopack.pdf.

Ridley, A.M., van Rheede, V. & Wilcock, R. (2015) 'Interviews, intermediaries and inter-ventions: mock jurors', police officers' and barristers' perceptions of a child witness interview.' *Investigative Interviewing: Research and Practice, 7*(1), 21–35.

Rogers, C. (2019) *Too Many Children with Autism Are Let Down by Schools and End up in Prison.* The Conversation. Accessed on 20/12/21 at https://theconversation.com/too-many-children-with-autism-are-let-down-by-schools-and-end-up-in-prison-107376.

Rogers, S.J. & Ozonoff, S. (2005) 'Annotation: What do we know about sensory dysfunc-tion in autism? A critical review of the empirical evidence.' *Journal of Child Psychology and Psychiatry, 46*(12), 1255–1268.

Salerno-Ferraro, A.C. & Schuller, R.A. (2020) 'Perspectives from the ASD community on police interactions: Challenges & recommendations.' *Research in Developmental Disabilities, 105,* 103732. https://doi.org/10.1016/j.ridd.2020.103732.

Shannon, B.J., Raichlea, M.A., Snydera, A.Z., Faiet, D.A. *et al.* (2011) 'Premotor functional connectivity predicts impulsivity in juvenile offenders.' *Proceedings of National Acad-emy of Sciences of USA, 108*(27), 11241–11245. https://doi.org/10.1073/pnas.1108241108.

Smethurst, A. & Collins, K. (2019) 'Mock Jury Perceptions of Vulnerable Defendants Assisted in Court by Intermedaries–Are Juror's Expectations Violated?' *Applied Psychology in Criminal Justice, 15*(1), 23–40.

Special Educational Needs (SEN) Code of Practice (2015) London: HMSO.

Special Educational Needs and Disability (Detained Persons) Regulations (2015). London: HMSO.

Stone, M. (1988) *Cross-Examination in Criminal Trials.* London: Butterworths.

Tager-Flusberg, H., Paul, R. & Lord, C. (2005) 'Language and Communication in Autism.' In F.R. Volkmar, A. Klein & D. Cohen (eds) *Handbook of Autism and Pervasive Devel-opmental Disorders,* vol. 1 (pp.335–364). New York, NY: Wiley.

Tint, A., Palucka, A.M., Bradley, E., Weiss, J.A. & Lunsky, Y. (2017) *Correlates of Police Involvement Among Adolescents and Adults with Autism Spectrum Disorder, 47.* https://doi.org/10.1007/s10803-017-3182-5.

United Nations Committee on the Rights of the Child (2016) *Concluding Observations on the Fifth Periodic Report of the United Kingdom of Great Britain and Northern Ireland,* CRC/C/GBR/CO/5. Accessed 04/04/2021 at https://tbinternet.ohchr.org/Treaties/CRC/Shared Documents/GBR/CRC_C_GBR_CO_5_4195_E.docx.

United Nations Committee on the Rights of the Child (2019) *General Comment No. 24 On Children's Rights in the Child Justice System,* CRC/C/GC/24. Accessed 20/08/2021 at www.ohchr.org/Documents/HRBodies/CRC/GC24/GeneralComment24.pdf.

Valentine, T. & Maras, K.L. (2011) 'The effect of cross-examination on the accuracy of adult eyewitness testimony.' *Applied Cognitive Psychology, 25*(4), 554–561. https://doi.org/10.1002/acp.1768.

Vrij, A., Fisher, R.P. & Blank, H. (2017) 'A cognitive approach to lie detection: A meta-analysis.' *Legal and Criminological Psychology, 22*(1), 1–21. https://doi.org/10.1111/lcrp.12088.

Weiss, J.A. & Fardella, M.A. (2018) 'Victimization and perpetration experiences of adults with autism.' *Frontiers in Psychiatry, 9,* 203. https://doi.org/10.3389/fpsyt.2018.00203.

Wheatcroft, J.M. & Ellison, L.E. (2012) 'Evidence in court: Witness preparation and cross-examination style effects on adult witness accuracy.' *Behavioral Sciences & the Law, 30*(6), 821–840. https://doi.org/10.1002/bsl.2031.

Woodbury-Smith, M.R., Clare, I.C.H., Holland, A.J., Kearns, A., Staufenberg, E. & Watson, P. (2005) 'A case-control study of offenders with high-functioning autistic spectrum disorders.' *Journal of Forensic Psychiatry & Psychology, 16*(4), 747–763. https://doi.org/10.1080/14789940500302554.

Youth Custody Service (2017) *The Youth Custody Service Placement Team: Overview of Operational Procedures.* Accessed 04/04/2021 at www.gov.uk/guidance/youth-custody-service-placement-team.

CHAPTER 8

Autism, Sexuality and Relationships

Editors: Judith Gainsborough and Ursula Cornish

Introduction

Some years ago, a colleague of Judith's, who was providing employment and life skills support and advice for an autistic man in his early 20s, was concerned that this young man was particularly worried about how to develop relationships with other young people. He was asking many questions, particularly about the physical aspect of relationships. Aware of the difficulties for autistic people in making sense of sexuality and relationships, this colleague opened a dialogue, providing clear information and advice. Judith and her colleague applauded the young person who had openly asked questions to which so many of his peers secretly wanted to know the answers. It is essential that those of us who work with young autistic people acknowledge our responsibilities to be clear and open in helping them to develop their understanding of relationships and sexuality. This, in turn, will help to keep young people safe and prevent misunderstandings, as well as giving them a better chance of experiencing healthy relationships. Lynne Moxon's contribution to this chapter provides a clear, comprehensive and frank approach, packed full of immensely useful facts and advice for parents/carers and for teachers on providing such an education for autistic young people.

This is followed by a case study of Zaffy Simone which represents the personal narrative of an extraordinarily resilient young person who found his own path to self-expression with very little access to information about sexuality. The interplay between autism and transgender issues is an area of much debate currently and further research is required to determine how best we can support autistic people who are gender diverse. What is clear, at this point in time, is that providing support on relationships and sexuality is vital for ensuring the overall well-being of neurodiverse people, just as it is for the neurotypical.

HELPING YOUNG AUTISTIC PEOPLE INTERPRET RELATIONSHIPS AND BEHAVIOURS

Lynne Moxon

Introduction

There are many challenges that face young autistic people and their parents. Families and carers are often concerned about the growing sexual behaviour in autistic young people because it is generally not accompanied by a corresponding growth in the field of social understanding, which can lead to socially embarrassing behaviour.

Hannah and Stagg (2016) suggest that it is difficult and confusing for an autistic young person to experience and learn about sex and relationships. Furthermore, avenues of potential knowledge, such as peer groups, tend to be an inaccessible option for autistic young people without support. The participants in the study presented as vulnerable to the manipulation of others and in danger of breaking the law due to inappropriate behaviour.

In addressing social issues, we must not forget that sexual curiosity is a normal feature of childhood and therefore we need to provide young people with the information and tools that will enable them to deal with sexual content and behaviour safely and successfully. This includes children with a learning disability as well as autism. Providing young people with a set of realistic, non-exploitative representations of gender and sexuality would go a long way towards ensuring their healthy emotional and sexual development and to promoting gender equality.

This contribution will provide guidance on what autistic individuals need to know and how to teach it, and will also describe the complexity of challenges in this area for parents, carers and all those working with autistic individuals.

Why do we need education for sex and relationships?

There are building blocks to being able to have relationships, and without them as a foundation for adult life, relationships do not happen or they falter. Hatton and Tector (2010) interviewed young people at school when devising a Sex and Relationships Education (SRE) curriculum. All of the autistic children wished they had understood themselves better when they were younger; they wished they had known about their autism and learned about its implications and how people without autism are different. They particularly would like to have been taught something about relationships and how they worked.

- 'I thought to get a boyfriend you had to agree to have sex with them and so I told the first boyfriend I had that I knew about this and would have sex.'

- 'I like things to be my way: I am not able to know what someone else is going to do so it seems better if I just masturbate on my own.'

- 'I wish I had learned to keep myself safe and what is meant if someone asks you to go for a walk and then they want to touch you – I did not understand.'

The legal context

The Department for Education introduced compulsory Relationships Education and SRE for secondary school pupils from September 2020. Relationships Education is to be introduced at primary level, 'to put in place the building blocks needed for positive and safe relationships of all kinds' (Department for Education 2020). This will start with family and friends, how to treat each other with kindness, and recognizing the difference between online and offline friendships.

Many primary schools choose to teach sex education (going beyond the existing national curriculum for science, and supported by the government) tailored to the age and physical and emotional maturity of their pupils. Parents who may worry about the young age need to be aware that the average age for girls to start their periods is ten. I have always taught mixed-sex groups as they learn from each other with very little embarrassment.

What needs to be taught and understood

For effective sex education, we are not talking about sexuality as a defining and human characteristic of all of us. You do not need to teach how to have sex. What needs to be taught are the rules around sex and the law for the most able groups. Sexuality and sexual feelings are very basic, so important, and yet there is only very recent literature and research to enable the teaching of autistic people on how to behave appropriately in terms of their own bodies and how to respect other people's needs (Jackson 2016; Reynolds 2014; Steward 2019). Those written by autistic adults can be very useful. This is not a discussion on how to or whether to, but rather what every human being, autistic or not, should know about safe sexual and consensual behaviour.

The content of SRE changes with age.[1] Knowledge of age-appropriate sexual behaviours that vary with situational and environmental factors can assist in differentiating sexual behaviours from sexual behaviour problems. Sexuality of individuals with ASD has been little studied. Human sexuality can be described as a developmental process showing different characteristics throughout the human lifespan, resulting in stages and milestones consisting of biological and behavioural components. These are some of the key sexual developmental milestones throughout an individual's lifespan:

- Early childhood and gender identity

- Puberty

- Menstruation

- Masturbation

- Awareness of sexual orientation

- First sexual experience with another person

- Ongoing sexual relationship

- Pregnancy and becoming a parent

- Marriage and civil partnership

- Menopause.

Most SRE curricula cover the early years but there is little information on menopause.[2] There is increasing information on marriage and long-term relationships (Hendrickx 2008).

---

1   www.bigtalkeducation.co.uk/parents
2   https://megsmenopause.com

Gender

How someone feels about their gender is known as gender identity. Some people identify as the gender they were assigned with at birth, others do not. Recent research has suggested that gender identity and sexuality are more varied among autistic individuals than in the general population (George 2018). One study, for instance, reported that 15 per cent of autistic adults in the Netherlands identify as transgender or non-binary (Walsh, Krabbendam & Begeer 2018). It is important that sex education with autistic individuals normalizes attraction to both sexes.

Ten years ago, children with gender dysphoria were treated with watchful waiting and I always recommended this alongside counselling and helping the young autistic person to enjoy their current life to the full. I suggest encouraging exploration of gender roles with a view to keeping options open and not having any preconceived ideas of the longer-term outcome. This was more easily achieved in a specialist setting where all staff understood and supported autism, and peer support was fantastic. One young man I worked with wanted to change gender because he believed that women were better communicators and so changing gender would help his communication. Arranging for him to have additional speech and language therapy helped to improve his all-round skills, including learning to drive, and he subsequently changed his mind about the gender reassignment. An autistic child or adolescent in distress is not reducible to one problem.

Many autistic girls have a difficult puberty (periods, body changes, hormones) and they need to be supported through this. Wild (2019) describes her impressions as headteacher at a special school for girls, and notes that puberty and the changes in the body can be a huge source of anxiety. She describes how girls often do not understand that puberty lasts for a few years and is irreversible, which can lead to controlling behaviours in an attempt to stop the process. Zaffy Simone, later in this chapter, talks about his horror when he realized his body was changing, and how his anorexia started at this time.

Relationships

Building social relationships by developing the ability of first making friends, which later result sometimes in becoming intimate partners, is a key developmental life stage for young adults. How can you move to a more intimate relationship if you have never had a friend? Social challenge does not mean no socializing. There is no known link between knowledge obtained from the SRE curriculum about sexuality and (inappropriate) interest or behaviours, including those of young people with autism (Henault 2006). We must teach that sex is not compulsory. I have found that some autistic students are very relieved by this and we must also remember that some young autistic people are not interested in sex at all and regard themselves as asexual.

Although many autistic people report a desire for relationships, they may tend either to approach others in an inappropriate physical or verbal manner or to misread subtle social cues or body language. Furthermore, sometimes their actions are misread as sexual overtures, when that may not have been the intent. They may insist on imposing their views on a group which can lead to rejection (Hellemans *et al.* 2007).

Teaching the 'hidden curriculum'

The 'hidden curriculum' (Alsubaie 2015) is the set of unwritten rules that no one has been directly taught, but everyone knows. Violations of these rules can make an individual a social outcast and increases vulnerability. Jackson (2016) reports that he did not recognize the need for social rules and wishes now he had been taught them at a younger age. In his early teenage book (Jackson 2002), he frequently rejects the need to follow social mores.

Phrases associated with the hidden curriculum:

- 'I shouldn't have to tell you but...'

- 'But it's common sense...'

This is the area that autistic students find the most difficult. Break down abstract concepts, avoid euphemisms, but teach them too. Live 'out loud': describe what you and others are doing and why. Provide observational opportunities. Teach how to lie and pretend (e.g., 'Do you like this dress?'). I have taught academic, autistic young men who were not aware that females have periods every month. We cannot assume that autistic people intuitively understand anything unless they have experienced it, read about it or been taught it; hence universities are using increasingly explicit preparation for even the most able group of students, such as the University of Newcastle (2020). Most students attend university for the social life and to make new friends as well as to study, but some autistic students become upset if others do not follow the rules (e.g., cheating in a French oral test, which the tutor did not mind as long as it was in French).

Useful strategies

I have found that exercises which can lead to a discussion and a concrete answer work well.

- What age is the youngest person you can date? A student told me he was taught that you can date someone who is half your age plus seven years. This worked well to help avoid underage partners but also led to querying the motives of much older people targeting you.

- How many times can you shake the drops from your penis before it is judged as masturbation? This query came from a doctor in a court case when an autistic person had been charged with masturbating in public toilets. The answer is three times.

- How many times can you ask someone for a date before it is harassment? This is important as these days many businesses discourage colleagues dating and you need to know the rules. The answer is three times.

A parent explained that she and the school nurse had prepared her autistic daughter well for the start of her periods. The first one started and her daughter was happy, but they had not told her that periods would happen every month from now on; they assumed she knew. She was devastated.

If you have a person who is a concrete learner, a black-and-white thinker, or thinks in pictures, then you need to be visual, clear and literal. Do not put a condom on a banana and expect someone to be able to generalize that to their own bodies. Use realistic photos and literal words (Attwood & Powell 2008; Davies & Dubie 2012). Keep the message simple and repetitive. Because of inappropriate behaviours, the deficit in social skills is even more evident and isolating for the autistic person. Start early.

Social life

It is vital to try to encourage friendship skills at a young age. There have to be realistic expectations of acquaintances and friends. Later in this chapter, Zaffy Simone recalls, 'I had no friendships and spent most of my time following around a boy who was a friend of the family. I attached myself to him. I don't think he enjoyed that.'

What works is joining groups related to special interest (trains, astronomy, geocaching, Lego therapy). Support groups for other autistic children are vital, particularly for girls who may feel very alone in mainstream school. Mentoring, befriending and counselling should be available from a young age. Social skills training is important, including joining supportive groups like the Scouts or Air Cadets, and Internet chatrooms and internet contacts – but it is essential to monitor these and know the rules.

What is normal in a relationship?

With the opening up of the internet, nothing is 'normal' but my autistic students liked some facts. They could not tune in to 'What would other people think if you did that?' Social facts, such as that the average age to lose your virginity in England is 16, were welcomed. Healthy, long-lasting relationships are based on trust and kindness, not just sex and physical activity, and it is fine not to have sex in a relationship. Relationships are private, and the intimacy of a relationship should not be shared with mates or on phones or networking sites.

For the question 'What does a "normal" body look like?', it is useful to use pictures of both sexes, including many examples of the variety of bodies and genitals. Ideas will be distorted by pornography.

Sexualization

Sexual content in mainstream media has increased, and become more explicit in recent years, and sexual imagery has become more widely circulated within society more broadly. Different people have different views on what counts as sexualized. UK children encounter some very diverse messages about sex, including advertising (Buckingham *et al.* 2010). Most parents surveyed in this study talked about childhood in terms of 'innocence'; but interpretations of this varied. Some saw experimenting with make-up and imitating 'sexy' dance styles (and similar behaviour) as innocuous, natural, fun and devoid of adult sexual connotations. For others, innocence meant play, untroubled by concerns about the adult world, which made the same activities distasteful.

There is pressure to imitate gender stereotypes from a younger and younger age, although many autistic children do not notice. Statistics obtained from research (Martellozzo *et al.* 2016; NSPCC 2021) indicate some startling facts about the general population. For instance, 70 per cent of all 12–15-year-olds report that they have had unintended access to websites containing pornography. Furthermore, 58 per cent of the entire teenage population view pornography on a regular basis, with 10 per cent viewing it daily. Sixty per cent of 13–17-year-olds attending mainstream schools would like SRE to start from eight years of age. Additionally, knowledge about sexually transmitted infections (STIs) among young adults is dangerously lacking.

It is important to keep a check on what an autistic child has tuned into on their mobile phone or laptop. They may tell you it's only 'Thomas the Tank Engine,' but it might be the pornographic version. It seems that there are pornographic versions of many children's TV characters.

Parents and carers can lay the basic building blocks for a child's online life really early, such as the fact that what we see on screen is not real. A non-autistic five-year-old knows that Maggie Smith is a witch in the Harry Potter films and a nun in *Sister Act*, and in the real world, she is neither of those people. The distinction between reality and fantasy can be blurred in autism. Computer games and films can be thought of as real and the news as unreal. Some primary schools are now using activities like photo manipulation to change pictures and to show how to evaluate digital content.

Although, for example, there is a correlation between aggression and playing violent computer games for autistic children (Mazurek & Engelhardt 2013), there is also a benefit from playing social cooperative games.

Behaviour towards other people

Many of my autistic students never thought about how other people saw them and what effect their behaviour had on others. One activity I used to start a group SRE session was to have the students describe themselves and their interests. At the end of the session, the students had to feed information back about their peers. Many students found this quite emotional: no one had listened to them before or remembered what they said. There are a number of books on behaviour which help autistic students look at and rate what they are doing (e.g., Buron & Curtis 2003).

Sexual behaviour

SRE allows socio-sexual behaviours to develop in the areas of communication, emotions and interpersonal relationships by giving access to the sexual knowledge that autistic young people can manage. In the long-term, young people will understand interpersonal relationships better and be able to engage in appropriate behaviours. There is no doubt that sex and sexuality are areas of concern for parents and carers and all those who come into contact with young people in professional capacities. The problems of violence, harassment and coercion many young people will meet in their lives, as well as their sexual relationships, need to be rigorously addressed.

What constitutes 'risky' sexual behaviour?

Some sexual behaviour displays more risk to a person than others. Certain sexual behaviours expose individuals to higher risk of pregnancy and STIs, such as not using condoms. Some of my students could not touch condoms because of sensory issues but they needed direct instruction and practice in how to use them. Polyurethane condoms are a type of male condom that is made from a type of thin, clear plastic, instead of rubber, which may be more tolerable for them. Vulnerability, especially in young autistic women who can become desperate for friendship, can be a real cause for concern as they might have difficulty understanding social cues and not recognize the difference between good attention and bad attention. Autistic girls may need explicit instruction and guidelines to ensure safe dating. They are at special risk of being taken advantage of because they may not understand when someone is harassing them or even abusing them (Steward 2013). Social Stories can be written, or concrete examples broken into small parts or stories from TV 'soaps', so as to be sure girls understand the concepts you are trying to present. Again, because of a lack of sex education, some may be coerced into early sexual intercourse. Some autistic women have written about becoming pregnant before they understood about sex.

Vaginal, anal or oral sex without a condom, or with a condom that is not used correctly, or having multiple sexual partners can lead to STIs. Many young autistic people will have heard about a 'blow job' but not understand what it is. One young autistic man was raped in his mainstream school lavatory but as he did not know that males can be raped did not immediately report it. The Brook Traffic Light Tool (2014) contains helpful information on these issues and outlines warning signs for problems developing.[3] Behaviours identified in the tool are examples used to show the differences between healthy and unhealthy sexual development. SRE is not a one-off experience: it needs repeating as the young person gets older and is ready for more information.

An autistic young person's psychological and social maturity does not keep pace with their physical maturity, irrespective of ability, and many do not receive the right teaching of boundaries on social and sexual behaviours. It is vital to keep thinking ahead to what needs to be in place five years from now. It may be acceptable for a three-year-old to run around on a beach naked, but one needs to ensure that the same child is not doing that at ten. If an eight-year-old is touching himself in the classroom, he needs to be taught to understand that he cannot do that in public. Thus the rules on acceptable behaviour as a child grows older need to be updated constantly. Does the young person have a private place to masturbate? Once a young person reaches 14 years of age, masturbation in public is a criminal offence. Parents and carers may need to start teaching him or her relatively early about the appropriate time and place because the longer that difficult behaviours go on, the harder they are to redirect.

Communication and consent

Consent is active and willing participation in sexual activity. It means that both parties have the freedom and capacity to make a choice.[4]

You can talk to very young children about consent. Just because your daughter likes being tickled one day does not mean she will like it today. She can say 'no'. A child is allowed to say 'no' if they do not want to be kissed by a grandparent. There are many occasions in a young disabled child's life when 'no' is not an option because they are

---

3   Sexual Behaviours Traffic Light Tool (adapted with permission): https://www.brook. org.uk/training/wider-professional-training/sexual-behaviours-traffic-light-tool

4   www.schoolsconsentproject.com

constantly reminded that they are supposed to do what a grown-up tells them to do. However, they need to understand when saying 'no' is the right thing to do.

While autism affects every person differently, difficulty with communication is one of the most unifying characteristics. Many able autistic people are anxious about whether they read body language, facial expressions and those subtle nuanced changes correctly, as Luke Jackson (2016) recalls about his own experiences. He needed clarity and has had to practise flirting, and an expectation to read body language is more likely to make him anxious. I had a student who understood the rule of consent but could not always interpret consent or understand people's intentions, so he decided to let women make the first moves. There is also the whole area of theory of mind (Baron-Cohen, Leslie & Frith 1985) – the ability to put yourself in someone else's place. I have had young autistic adults tell me there are no victims in child pornography.

Unwanted touch

It is important to teach young people about unwanted touch. There are all kinds of reasons that friends sometimes do not want to be touched in various ways, and physical touch can be a sensory difficulty in autism. If you do not want someone touching your leg or holding your hand, it is absolutely your right to have it stop. Friends do sometimes inadvertently violate the boundaries of friendship, and if they respect their friends, they stop when they find out it is not welcome.

When two people are having an argument, often the first thing one of them will do is move in close, invading the other person's personal space. This is interpreted by that other person as aggression. A popular term for this, in fact, is 'getting in someone's face'.

Personal space

Young autistic people need to learn that certain behaviours that were acceptable at an earlier age, like hugging everyone and anyone, or sitting in people's laps, may be inappropriate and send out the wrong messages as they become older. We need to teach appropriate social distancing and where to stand/sit in public. For academic young people, it may be useful to study proxemics, the branch of knowledge that deals with the amount of space that people feel it necessary to set between themselves and others.[5]

Eye contact is important, although it can be difficult (Jackson 2016). Teaching young people to look at a person's forehead instead of the eyes can be effective. Staring can be more of a problem and often makes other people feel uncomfortable, so it needs to be discouraged.

Stalking can lead to imprisonment (Stokes, Newton & Kaur 2007). Using examples of behaviour reported in the local press to emphasize the reality of the law can be helpful. This can be used in many social circumstances which lead to criminal charges. For instance, an autistic young person may read too much into a friendly smile and follow a young woman home, thinking she wants to have a relationship with him. Furthermore, it is crucial to discuss a wide range of examples as differential responses may be required for even slightly different situations and, therefore, a young person may get into trouble for making a taught response if the situation is different.

Although there are many behaviours that can be considered inappropriate, none upset people quite like those behaviours that are sexual in nature. Because of inappropriate behaviours, the deficit in social skills can be even more evident and isolating for the autistic person. Children become aware at very young ages that it is inappropriate to touch other people in certain places; an autistic child does not have that built-in control and 'if curious' may try to touch a person's body out of curiosity. This is particularly common in adolescent boys attempting to touch a woman's breast. Dealing with these behaviours when a child is young is important so that they are not a problem when a child becomes an adult. Sexual offences tend to be associated with obsessions or lack of social understanding, and the young person may be prosecuted as it is the victim that the law protects. Having a diagnosis of autism is not an excuse (Dubin 2014).

Sexual assault

The criminal law does apply to autistic people and other disabled people (although some parents think otherwise), and a young person who attacks their parents or carers or members of the public can be charged

---

5   For practical strategies and ideas to support young people with understanding personal space in social situations see https://twinkl.co.uk.

with assault. Sexual assault is a crime; it includes unwanted touching, kissing, grabbing and rape. It is important to teach young people that they need to exit from any situation where they, themselves, are being treated badly.[6]

Warning signs that someone may become abusive within a relationship

The abusive person attempts to cut the other person off from friends and family, including stopping the person from calling them or meeting them, or from attending events when they are present. The abusive person also attempts to control lots of tiny details about the other person's actions and appearance, such as what they wear or eat. When they make a mistake, the abusive person is quick to criticize the partner rather than apologizing themselves. They handle stress badly; the other person often feels like they are 'walking on eggshells' (having to be very careful about everything said or done to avoid reactions) as they never know what will make the person angry. An autistic person can be considered to be abusive in a relationship by insisting on control.

What skills do we need to teach?

The more an autistic person wants to be independent, the more social rules we need to make them aware of. Many parents have suggested that using public toilets can be problematic. There are a number of examples of urinal etiquette on the internet and it is important for parents to provide information about appropriate behaviour when using a urinal.[7]

Actual skills needed

It is important to teach both the correct names for private body parts and, as children get older, the meaning of common slang terms so that they do not get bullied for not knowing. We must remember that actions have consequences, and we do our sons and daughters no favours by pretending that they can behave inappropriately without facing them. In particular, teach:

---

6   www.childline.org.uk/info-advice/bullying-abuse-safety
7   www.bigtalkeducation.co.uk/parents/parents-of-children-with-autism-your-questions-answered

- 'No, not now'/'Later', 'Stop'

- What is public?

- What is private?

There are many things that are acceptable in private but not in public and it is important they know the difference. Quizzes with pictures are useful, for example, illustrating taking clothes off in various appropriate and inappropriate circumstances.

One young man I worked with wanted to be a prostitute so he could have a lot of sex with women and be paid for it. When the reality was explained to him that it would likely be men who wanted sex, he reconsidered his idea. In many cases, it can be a basic lack of knowledge of the world that can lead to difficulties.

Masturbation

This is the most frequent form of sex for autistic people and, for some, the only form.

Strong and colleagues (2005) note that masturbation can teach people about their bodies and what is sexually pleasing to them. It can teach people how to move their bodies to become aroused and it has no harmful physical effects. It is a form of safer sex (as no body fluids are exchanged that could carry STIs), and as long as the person is not harming him/herself, it may be one of the few examples of physical pleasure the autistic person experiences. Occasionally it can be a form of obsessive or compulsive behaviour.

There are powerful hormones at work, so while a parent's response needs to be measured, calm and consistent, they need to be aware that they are also overriding some strong sensory feelings. It is always a good idea to rule out any medical issues. Some medication can dampen the ability to orgasm and therefore can cause excessive masturbation. Reynolds (2015) has written two books on addressing masturbation in autistic boys and girls.

The internet and the social network

It has not been established that any children under nine years old have the capacity to engage with the internet in a safe and beneficial manner in all circumstances (Department for Children, Schools and Families 2008), especially when it comes to children socializing online, either within age-appropriate virtual worlds or as underage participants in sites intended for teenagers and adults, such as Facebook or YouTube.[8]

It is vital to ensure that autistic children can understand how to access the internet safely and independently, and that they understand the difference between appropriate and inappropriate sites, and appropriate and inappropriate images on the internet. They need to know the law (Dubin 2014). It is crucial to teach age rules and the ability to recognize when children are featured online, and that even if they are at the same emotional level, it may not be appropriate to engage with them. For example, it is illegal to download or own pornography showing children (age 17 and under) or take or make any indecent photograph of a child. Owning pornography of adults who look like children is illegal. It is illegal for an adult to contact children on the internet and pretend they are a child, as this is what a paedophile would do.

Mobile phone cameras

What are the pictures they are taking? Have they asked permission? Sexting is sending sexually explicit text or photographs from mobile devices. Sexting can lead to embarrassment and can also be a crime. It has become an increasingly popular and concerning pastime among young people. Autistic young people may be particularly vulnerable in this area as they may not be aware of the rules and the consequences.

Pornography

The NSPCC reports that mainstream secondary school pupils, especially boys, are viewing porn to learn about sex, and they are developing very skewed views (Martellozzo et al. 2016). The average age for first viewing porn for mainstream boys is seven years (NSPCC 2021). We can offset this by conveying to young people early on that porn is fantasy. Pornography shapes young people's sexual knowledge but does so by portraying sex in unrealistic ways. The nature of online pornography is changing. It is increasingly dominated by themes of aggression, power

---

8   For more practical resources to help you protect children from abuse and neglect see https://learning.nspcc.org.uk

and control, blurring the lines between consent, pleasure and violence (Haggstrom-Nordin, Hanson & Tydén 2005). There are non-confrontational ways of opening a dialogue on porn. For instance, 'Have your friends started to look at this sort of thing?' 'Have you got any questions?' 'What things do you think people will worry about?', or 'Do you think that's what normal people do?' For an adolescent, talk about how the body reacts to certain pictures: a certain excitement is normal. Talk about how the body works. Discuss what they've seen, without making the young person feel uncomfortable, sinful, dirty or ashamed.

Conclusion

Autistic children grow up to become autistic adults. As Gabriels and Van Bourgondien (2007, p.59) state:

> It is imperative that professionals working with school-age children and adolescents with autism be alert to sexuality issues in this population so preparations to address and teach appropriate social boundaries and personal self-care can be made long before the child with autism enters puberty.

It is important to provide knowledge that autistic adults need even if you do not like discussing it. Sexual awareness is normal. Sexual feelings are normal, and there are many ways of expressing them. If a person has a disability, it does not change any of this. What often changes is the different socialization that provides the foundation for sexual identity.

All autistic individuals need to learn, as a minimum, the basics of body parts, how they work and how to keep safe (Gill & Hough 2007). If their learning disability or autism is severe, the content may need to centre on masturbation and establishing a sexual identity in a solo manner (Cambridge & Forrester-Jones 2003).

Autistic people need a completely different and individual approach, including extra clarification. As an example, they need a specific set of rules for each type of risk. Otherwise they often do not have the social interpretation skills to deal with slightly different situations. This explains why you may have repeat instances of concerning behaviour with different media, such as mobile phones, Skype and Facebook, as well as with direct physical contact, despite the many hours of counselling and support received (Steward 2013). Adults with autism report starkly higher rates of sexual victimization than do other adults, and the risk appears to rise with lack of sexual knowledge.

For autistic young people, the most important thing to remember about sexuality is to provide an open, respectful environment where they feel comfortable asking questions. Autistic people should have the right to fulfil their sexual needs and to express sexual impulses in a socially acceptable way. They need to receive training in socio-sexual behaviour and to have access to sexual knowledge they can understand and manage.

We must also acknowledge that we have a lot to learn from autistic individuals themselves and the problems and differences experienced by them. It is crucial that we respect individuals who develop their own values which may be different from ours.

CASE STUDY OF ZAFFY SIMONE

Judith Gainsborough and Zaffy Simone

Introduction

Zaffy has talked in detail about the long transformational journey to find a way to understand himself and to try to match his internal feelings to his physical appearance and self. Zaffy's recollections describe his experiences and the struggles that led him finally to understand his gender identity as well as his needs as a person on the autism spectrum. This lengthy and uncertain journey into new territory provides us with some opportunities to gain further insight into gender dysphoria. It offers an examination of the arduous process Zaffy underwent to find out not only about his physical self but also his psychological self. The description of Zaffy's journey has profound implications for professionals and families in terms of identifying precursors or indicators of hugely complex and lifelong issues, and offering appropriate and timely support.

Early years

Zaffy was raised in a remote coastal town in Australia. His family were part of a sheltered and relatively isolated Jehovah's Witness community. He was the youngest girl of three children. He describes his family as having a 'volatile family dynamic', with his elder sister leaving the family when Zaffy was ten years old.

Zaffy says: 'I do remember that my brother and sister used to talk about me as being odd, but I was accepted in the family even though they thought I was odd.' Zaffy remembers that there were three children in another family who lived across the road and he used to play with the youngest boy, and that there was a connection between them.

School experiences

When he started school, 'that's when it became more evident,' Zaffy recalls. 'Being at school was not something I wanted to do any day. I had no friendships and spent most of my time following around a boy who was a friend of the family. If he moved, I moved. It was the same in the playground. He was the only thing I could make sense of.' Zaffy comments that with hindsight and the understanding he now has about his social difficulties in childhood, he understands that this wasn't a friendship on equal terms. 'I attached myself to him. I don't think he enjoyed that.'

As Zaffy grew older he began to enjoy all kinds of sports and found that this was the only way he could connect with other children. During his primary years, Zaffy (still recognized as a girl) only interacted with his peers outside the classroom during breaks. He enjoyed rigorous physical activity, perhaps affording him opportunities to feel calm and reduce his unease in the school environment. He had a great deal of energy and chose games such as chasing, cricket, football, soccer and handball with the boys. Zaffy is tremendously insightful now about his social communication difficulties and the challenges that he experienced with team sports. He says, 'I was very poor at team dynamics and working out how to fit in, so I didn't really play team sports, and surfing became my focus and passion.'

At secondary school, there was a tendency for girls and boys to separate off into same-sex groups and there were fewer opportunities for physical play at break times. Thus, Zaffy became even more socially isolated and bewildered.

'I remember just standing and watching girls talking and feeling completely lost, wondering what they were talking about. There were a couple of girls who as a group I would sometimes spend time with, but this was mostly me just sitting and listening. I never felt a connection or really fitted in with the conversation. I was very different from them.'

Zaffy remembers that he was often in trouble for bad behaviour and was regularly made to sit outside the principal's office as punishment. He says: 'Most of my behaviour was the result of not understanding what I was meant to be doing or not wanting to do what I was asked. School for me was an over-stimulating chaotic sea of confusion.'

It seems there was little help or understanding for Zaffy's situation. Zaffy recalls: 'There was no help at school. A letter did go home to Mum with concerns that I wasn't engaging in activities with other children. Nothing was done throughout the entirety of my school life. I missed out a lot because I wasn't able to keep up.'

This was 30 years ago in a remote part of Australia, and Zaffy's teachers probably had no knowledge of autism spectrum conditions and thus interpreted his reactions (to finding himself in an intolerable and incomprehensible environment) as bad behaviour. Sadly, this situation continued throughout his primary and secondary years. Zaffy makes mention of the impact of his community and family culture on his social skills, describing them as 'robotic and formed by the cult I was raised in'. Perhaps his teachers also interpreted his behaviour in terms of the isolated nature of his home environment.

Adolescence

Zaffy remembers his unhappiness about the dresses and skirts he was expected to wear and the physical changes he was undergoing during adolescence. At that time and in his community, there was no forum for open discussions about his feelings and confusion.

'I was always called a tomboy and wanted to wear trousers. I never felt comfortable in a dress or skirt. I would change as soon as I could. Midway through high school, there was an awakening that my body was a female body. There was a realization that I wasn't going to develop the way I wanted to develop. My chest developed very quickly and it was big and I couldn't hide it. I certainly was unhappy, uncomfortable, horrified. Nothing inside felt instinctive about being female; male things felt more instinctive and I was attracted to females sexually from as early as primary school. There was no open discussion about sex, sexuality or gender in my religious culture, and only some basics of these things were taught in school.'

Health issues

'The more my mum was delighted about the physical changes, the more I withdrew into myself. This is when I believe my undiagnosed eating disorder started. It wasn't a conscious decision, but I realize now that I kept my body underweight, which meant my menstrual cycle stopped and my body had an androgynous shape (apart from the chest). In a nutshell, I was uncomfortable and confused, with no one to talk to, and my alcohol intake increased.'

Zaffy describes a number of health issues in early adolescence. Alcohol abuse began at around ten years old. This may have been a way of reducing feelings of anxiety and depression. Around this time, Zaffy developed an eating disorder. It is now well known that autistic girls are more likely than boys to internalize their problems, leading to the development of emotional or mental health difficulties such as an eating disorder (Happé, 2019). All this, and the added impact of a young girl desperate to resist the physical changes she was experiencing. Zaffy was then diagnosed with multiple sclerosis. He describes himself as being as low and unhappy as a person could get.

Socio-cultural influences

Zaffy remained in the community as a young woman and was married to a man at the age of 23. He says, 'It was just part of the culture. The game you were playing, that was what your life was all about. I believed that if I followed the rules then God would make things better, but He didn't and that was when I needed to break free from it all. It wasn't just about going to church. That whole life could no longer be my life... It was difficult to leave the only life you knew of, but the drive was so powerful, I had to do it. I was stepping out into nothingness.'

As Zaffy broke away from his family and community, he began to make links within the gay community, where he discovered a tolerant approach to individuality. Zaffy remembers, 'I wasn't being judged by these people.' He recalls that he struggled with the social dynamic and there was a 'lot of clashing' but, he says, 'Two people from the early stages – they did connect: they were rare and looked beyond the weird aspects and got to know me. My health was a mess; alcohol didn't help. I wasn't taking care of myself and this impacted on my MS.'

New experiences

With support from new friends, Zaffy began not only to find ways to improve his physical health, but also developed greater self-awareness. Zaffy says, 'At the age of 26 I started exploring alternative therapies and this had a massive impact on my entire well-being. I was really fortunate and blessed in meeting some extraordinary people – in the gay scene, therapists, people at university (when I finally went in my 30s). They have a piece of my path in my growth. I'm still connected to them now. They enabled my self-reflective path.'

Autism diagnosis

Zaffy recalls, 'It was later on, when I began consciously improving my health, that I became aware of sensory issues and that I was processing things differently. Other people noticed things and autism was mentioned. I struggled at university; I could understand and talk about things, but got low marks for essays and tests. It was suggested that I be assessed to see if I had a learning disability, but the tests I had at that time just highlighted what we would now refer to as a spiky profile. Years later, by chance, I happened to hear Tony Attwood speaking at a conference, and his descriptions about sound sensitivities and unusual processing resonated with me. I looked at the book displays at the conference and picked up *Thinking in Pictures* by Temple Grandin (2006 [first published 1995]) and I started crying. It was exactly how I think, in pictures.'

Zaffy was eventually diagnosed with an autism spectrum condition. When asked about his initial reaction to the diagnosis, Zaffy says, 'Initially, it was a relief. Then I slipped into a mild depression. If I'd known sooner, then I wouldn't have been pushing myself so hard to fit in. I understood about my limitations and stopped pushing myself to fit in, and started to challenge myself differently. Then I started drawing my cartoons and that pulled me out of it.'

Gender dysphoria

'I didn't know much about gender dysphoria, having come from such a sheltered community. I had kept my head buried in the sand and this continued. My girlfriend would throw words at me. Then, one day, I picked up a psychology book and came across a chapter on gender variances. It was the same experience as when I picked up Temple Grandin's book. I didn't know this existed in people. There was a nice sequence to my diagnostic, healing process. My diagnosis of MS led me into alternative therapies, which helped heal childhood trauma and made it easy for both my autism and gender diagnosis. It was like each layer of me being revealed and I was now ready to deal with this bit of myself. The process started in Australia and then continued in the UK. I was in my early 40s when the process started – the therapy, the hormone treatment and then the surgery. I was in a good place to deal with it.'

Relationships

Zaffy reports that he has had no contact with his father for decades. Zaffy and his mother, who is still part of the Jehovah's Witness community, have been in contact intermittently for some time. Zaffy reports, 'I stayed in contact with my mum. We had a relationship of sorts, but there were lots of things we couldn't talk about. Communication between us has been off and on. There's no real connection. She doesn't know about my life, my beliefs, my relationships. It tends to be a bland conversation with no depth to it. However, Zaffy reports, 'I am back in contact with my sister and that has been really lovely. A genuine connection. Our separate journeys have taken us to the same place. We are matching rather than clashing.' Both Zaffy and his sister felt compelled to leave the family as young adults, both rejecting the culture they were born into and trying to find a different way to live. Their experiences have helped to establish the sibling bond again.

Zaffy reports that the relationship with his girlfriend ended, not long before he spoke at the EP-ASIG study day. 'In 2016, the relationship that I moved to the UK for had ended. I was devastated and terrified. But it was another blessing in disguise. I'd moved to a male body and my girlfriend couldn't cope with what had become a heterosexual relationship. I was then a single person, no longer being viewed as a female. Other people identified me as male and that felt incredible. I enjoyed exploring the dating scene until eventually I met my current partner and that was amazing from the get-go.'

The present

Zaffy reports that he is now happily involved in a heterosexual relationship and is back in contact with his sister. He still struggles with aspects of learning. 'Even now, in my job there are things which I really struggle with and I rely on one my colleagues, one in particular, to help me understand. She is brilliant at breaking things down and explaining them to me and I can grasp it after she explains it. There is an element in my philosophy that says the journey that you're on is yours: it's the deck of cards you have been given to play in this life; how you play them is up to you.'

Conclusions

When asked what might have been helpful to him, Zaffy responds, 'I'm not sure what might have helped. I feel this was the journey I had to go on. There could have been interventions with my education. I struggle with that learning journey even now. The whole school environment didn't work for my learning needs. Now, there's more in place, more aids, more one-to-one, more explanations.'

Zaffy experienced much unhappiness and inner torment in his childhood and young adulthood. The process he underwent – to come to an awareness and understanding of his needs as both an autistic person and a person with gender dysphoria – took many years. It would appear that, in Zaffy's community 30 years ago, there was little awareness and even less support for a socially isolated child, struggling with social communication, the demands of the school curriculum and, additionally and crucially, with gender identity. Zaffy's instinct and tremendous drive to find peace forced him to leave his family and community in search of answers and understanding. In time, he found both, largely due to his own intelligence, curiosity and determination.

The last 30 years have seen a revolution in terms of knowledge and attitudes about autism and gender dysphoria. Nevertheless, there are important messages here for today's schools and practitioners in terms of making holistic assessments of children's needs, considering all factors including cultural and family circumstances, ensuring effective communication between schools and families, and collecting as much information as possible from observations, assessments and interviews to try to get a meaningful picture of a child or young person.

Zaffy emphasizes that 'Doing *to* or *for* someone is not right; it is the equivalent of someone else deciding or telling you how to play your deck of cards. You have to 'do *with*' the person: work out what cards they have and most importantly how they like to play them. Once you work these things out you will have formed a connection, which will enable you to show them how to play other games. Ask questions about what motivates us. Are you trying to help the person for what they want or what, you *think* they want? You need to connect to get a sense of what they are wanting help with. Even with a very young child, it's still the same. You need to tune in and connect with that person.'

Chapter conclusion

This chapter has afforded the opportunity for us all, as parents, educators and those professionals who support parents and educators, to reflect on whether we are providing our autistic youngsters with appropriate support as they begin to explore their sexuality. There continues to be a need for comprehensive training and support for educators and for parents and carers to ensure that they can encourage their autistic young people to have a safe, healthy and appropriate sexual life.

POINTS FOR REFLECTION

☞ What training and advice are available for parents on supporting their autistic youngsters on issues around sexuality?

☞ Are educators and parents recognizing precursors and indicators of complex issues of sexual identity and providing appropriate support?

☞ Are we providing an open and respectful environment where youngsters feel comfortable to ask questions and develop an understanding of what is and what is not socially and sexually acceptable in different contexts?

Further reading

Dean, E. & Garling, H. (2010) *Fantasy vs Reality: A Sex and Relationship Education Resource for Key Stages 3 and 4*. Brighton: NHS Brighton and Hove City Council.

Hannah, L.A. & Stagg, S.D. (2016) 'Experiences of sex education and sexual awareness in young adults with autism spectrum disorder.' *Journal of Autism and Developmental Disorders, 46*(12), 3678–3687.

Lawson, W. (2005) *Sex, Sexuality and the Autistic Spectrum.* London: Jessica Kingsley Publishers.

Ripley, K. (2014) *Exploring Friendships, Puberty and Relationships: A Programme to Help Children and Young People on the Autism Spectrum Cope with the Challenges of Adolescence.* London: Jessica Kingsley Publishers.

References

Alsubaie, M.A. (2015) 'Hidden curriculum as one of current issue of curriculum.' *Journal of Education and Practice, 6*(33), 125–128.

Attwood, S. & Powell, J. (2008) *Making Sense of Sex.* London: Jessica Kingsley Publishers.

Baron-Cohen, S., Leslie, A.M. & Frith, U. (1985) 'Does the autistic child have a "Theory of mind?"' *Cognition, 21*(1), 37–46.

Brook Sexual Behaviours Traffic Light Tool (2012) *True Relationships and Reproductive Health: Traffic Lights Guide to Sexual Behaviours in Children and young People: Identify, Understand and Respond.* Brisbane: True Relationships and Reproductive Health.

Buckingham, D., Willett, R., Bragg, S. & Russell, R. (2010) *Sexualised Goods Aimed at Children: A Report to the Scottish Parliament Equal Opportunities Committee.* Edinburgh: Scottish Parliament Equal Opportunities Committee.

Buron, K.D. & Curtis, M. (2003) *The Incredible 5-Point Scale.* Shawnee, KS: AAPC Publishing.

Cambridge, P. & Forrester-Jones, R. (2003) 'Using individualised communication for interviewing people with intellectual disability: A case study of user-centred research.' *Journal of Intellectual and Developmental Disability, 28* (1), 5–23.

Davies, C. & Dubie, M. (2012) *Intimate Relationships and Sexual Health: A Curriculum for Teaching Adolescents/Adults with High Functioning ASD and Other Social Challenges.* Shawnee, KS: AAPC Publishing.

Department for Children, Schools and Families (2008) *The Byron Report: Safer Children in a Digital World.* London: HMSO.

Department for Education (2020) *Relationships Education, Relationships and Sex Education (RSE) and Health Education: FAQs.* London: HMSO.

Dubin, L. (2014) 'A Father's Journey to Protect his Son: A Legal Perspective.' In T. Attwood, I. Henault & N. Dubin (eds) *The Autism Spectrum, Sexuality and the Law: What Every Parent and Professional Needs to Know.* London and Philadelphia, PA: Jessica Kingsley Publishers.

Gabriels, R.L. & Van Bourgondien, M.E. (2007) 'Sexuality and autism: Individual, Family, and Community Perspectives and Interventions.' In R. Gabriels & D. Hill (eds) *Growing up with Autism.* New York, NY: Guilford Press.

George, R. (2018) 'Gender identity and sexual orientation in autism spectrum disorder.' *Autism, 22*(8), 970–998.

Gill, K.M. & Hough, S. (2007) 'Sexuality training, education and therapy in the healthcare environment: Taboo, avoidance, discomfort or ignorance?' *Sexuality and Disability, 25*(2), 73–76.

Grandin, T. (2006) *Thinking in Pictures.* London: Bloomsbury.

Haggstrom-Nordin, E., Hanson, U. & Tydén, T. (2005) '"It's everywhere!" Thoughts and reflections about pornography among young people in Sweden.' *Scandinavian Journal of Caring Sciences, 20*(4), 386–393.

Hannah, L.A. & Stagg, S.D. (2016) 'Experiences of Sex Education and Sexual Awareness in Young Adults with Autism Spectrum Disorder.' *Journal of Autism and Developmental Disorders, 46*(12), 3678–3687.

Happé, F. (2019) 'What does research tell us about girls on the autism spectrum?' In B. Carpenter, F. Happé & J. Egerton (eds) *Girls and Autism: Educational, Family and Personal Perspectives*. London: Routledge.

Hatton, S. & Tector, A. (2010) 'The building blocks to social competency for an effective SRE curriculum for pupils with ASD.' *British Journal of Special Education, 37*(2), 69–76.

Hellemans, H. Colson, K., Verbracken, C., Vermeiren, R. & Deboutte, D. (2007) 'Sexual behaviour in high-functioning male adolescents and young people with Autism Spectrum Disorder.' *Journal of Autism and Developmental Disorders, 37*(2), 260–269.

Henault, I., (2006) *Asperger's Syndrome and Sexuality: From Adolescence through Adulthood*. London: Jessica Kingsley Publishers.

Hendrickx, S. (2008) *Love, Sex and Long-Term Relationships: What People with Asperger Syndrome Really Want*. London: Jessica Kingsley Publishers.

Jackson, L. (2002) *Freaks, Geeks, and Asperger Syndrome*. London: Jessica Kingsley Publishers.

Jackson, L. (2016) *Sex, Drugs and Asperger's Syndrome (ASD): A User Guide to Adulthood*. London: Jessica Kingsley Publishers.

Martellozzo, E., Monaghan, A., Adler, J.R., Davidson, J., Leyva, R. & Horvath, M.A.H. (2016) *'"I Wasn't Sure it Was Normal to Watch it": A Quantitative and Qualitative Examination of the Impact of Online Pornography on the Values, Attitudes, Beliefs and Behaviours of Children and Young People.'* Middlesex University, London.

Mazurek, M.O. & Engelhardt, C.R. (2013) 'Video game use and problem behaviours in boys with autism spectrum disorders.' *Research in Autism Spectrum Disorders, 7*(2), 316–324.

NSPCC (2021) *Online Safety*. www.nspcc.org.uk.

Reynolds, K. (2014) *Sexuality and Severe Autism: A Practical Guide for Parents, Caregivers and Health Educators*. London and Philadelphia, PA: Jessica Kingsley Publishers.

Reynolds, K.E. (2015) *Things Tom Likes and Things Ellis Likes*. London: Jessica Kingsley Publishers.

Steward, R. (2013) *The Independent Woman's Handbook for Super Safe Living on the Autistic Spectrum*. London: Jessica Kingsley Publishers.

Steward, R. (2019) *The Autism-Friendly Guide to Periods*. London: Jessica Kingsley Publishers.

Stokes, M., Newton, N. & Kaur, A. (2007) 'Stalking and social and romantic functioning among adolescents and adults with autism spectrum disorder.' *Journal of Autism and Developmental Disorders, 37*(10), 1969–1986.

Strong, B., DeVault, C., Sayad, B.W. & Yarber, W.L. (2005) *Human Sexuality: Diversity in Contemporary America* (fifth edition). New York, NY: McGraw Hill.

University of Newcastle (2020) *Guide to Independent Living in University-owned Accommodation*. Accommodation Services Access for All Guide. Newcastle: University of Newcastle.

Walsh, R.J., Krabbendam, L. & Begeer, S. (2018) 'Brief report: Gender identity differences in autistic adults: Associations with perceptual and socio-cognitive profiles.' *Journal of Autism and Developmental Disorders, 48*(12), 4070–4078.

Wild, S. (2019) 'Building a Specialist Curriculum for Autistic Girls.' In B. Carpenter, F. Happé & J. Egerton *Girls and Autism: Educational, Family and Personal Perspectives*. London: Routledge.

CHAPTER 9

Autism, Ethnicity and Culture: Developing Culturally Responsive Practice

Editor: Ken Greaves

Introduction

There is an increase in the number of students within our education system who come from a cultural background which is different from the majority white British background. However, the proportion of children identified with autism within our school systems does not always match the overall proportion of children from minority ethnic communities in the population. Statistics from the school population (Department for Education 2019) and research studies highlight that the prevalence of autism varies across ethnic groups (Tromans *et al.* 2020) with both over- and under-representation of children with different ethnicity. This chapter explores the potential reasons for this with a specific focus on the role of educational psychologists in the process. It will also consider issues to be aware of while supporting students with autism from minority cultural groups and working with their families. In this chapter, Prithvi Perepa will draw from existing research on the subject to provide an overview of some of the key issues. Venessa Bobb will then describe her personal experience as a Black parent, while Ken Greaves will give a personal account of his life as a Black EP, both providing an insight into the impact of culture on individual lives, at personal and professional levels.

AN OVERVIEW OF RESEARCH INTO AUTISM, CULTURE AND ETHNICITY

Prithvi Perepa

Before we move further it is important to clarify the concepts of ethnicity and culture. In the Western world, ethnicity is often used to describe place of origin, either a specific country (e.g., Chinese) or sometimes a whole region, such as South Asian. Official systems in the UK also use skin colour as a description of ethnicity by using categories such as White other, or Black African. We prefer using the word 'culture', although we have also used the term 'ethnicity' in this chapter. Culture can be defined as a set of values, traditions, knowledge and beliefs which influence the worldview of a specific community. This can be influenced by the place of origin and immigration history, but also other factors such as religion, language, gender, sexual orientation, socio-economic status and disability. This could mean that the official classification of ethnicity could include a range of different cultures. Similarly, people coming from different parts of the world could share similar cultural experiences, such as familiarity with religious norms and beliefs.

The above definition highlights the intersectionality of identity. This could mean that for some individuals with autism, different aspects of their cultural identity are perhaps more important than their autism identity, whereas for others their autism identity could be more important. In recognition of this, we have decided to use a mixture of person-first (e.g., 'person with autism') and identity-first (e.g., 'autistic person') language in this chapter.

Assessment issues

As an EP, it is likely that you will be involved in a range of assessments, starting from contributing to diagnostic assessments of autism, to identifying whether a child's needs qualify them for special educational support, to more general educational assessments. Staff from schools and early years centres are usually the people responsible for engaging EPs in this process. Based on the findings from his study of EPs' involvement in the process of assessment, Rupasinha (2015) argues that wider contextual factors such as the nature of schooling can impact on whether a child's differences are noted or not. If the behaviour of the child with autism is not dissimilar to that of the other children within a setting, then the staff are unlikely to identify the difference. This could mean that staff's knowledge and understanding of typical child development and their cultural variations, and norms of the children within the setting, could contribute to which children are referred for an autism diagnosis.

Identifying differences could be challenging for staff and indeed for EPs as most behaviours which are used to identify autism are based on cultural norms. Since the diagnostic criteria for autism and the assessment tools were developed in Western countries and are based on norms from a Western perspective, it can cause difficulties in identifying autism in children from minority cultural groups. For example, it has been reported that non-verbal behaviours such as eye contact and pointing are culturally specific and may not be encouraged in many non-Western cultures such as Chinese, Indian and Nigerian (Norbury & Sparks 2013; Perepa 2014, 2019). Similarly, Rupasinha (2015) argues that different language and play skills may be encouraged in different cultural groups. Since all these areas are an important part of identifying autism in children, it is understandable that these cultural differences could be misinterpreted whereby children from some ethnic groups could be over-identified with autism by the professionals. Using an assessment tool which is not standardized on specific cultural groups of children could lead to false positive or false negatives. It is important when EPs are involved in any assessment process that they check their interpretation of the behaviour with people from the similar cultural group to that of the child (Perepa 2019).

Parents are often important participants in the assessment process. In a comparative study on parent reports of children with autism without intellectual disabilities, Ratto and colleagues (2016) found that parents of Black children reported fewer difficulties in the areas of executive functioning and social and emotional behaviour and better adaptive skills, compared to parents of white children. This suggests that children from certain cultural backgrounds are less likely to receive a diagnosis if the assessment process is heavily based on parental reports. In their study of parental concerns of children's behaviour among Anglo-American and Latino parents, Blacher, Stavropoulos and Bolourian (2019) also found that the behaviour which parents reported as cause for concern varied based on their cultural and social norms. Therefore, understanding social and cultural norms of the family is important before providing a diagnosis of autism, or identifying challenging behaviour. Asking parents clear questions to understand the functioning levels of the child is also needed.

Professionals involved in the assessment are not immune to their own unconscious bias. Based on their research, Lindsay, Pather and Strand (2006) and Reijneveld *et al.* (2005) suggest that even when professionals are presented with children with similar behaviour patterns, the diagnostic label which the professional gives to a child seems to vary. Similarly, Sullivan, Sadeh and Houri (2019) found that school psychologists in the USA were more likely to identify Black students with autism compared to white students. Ironically, even though Black students were identified with autism, they were often considered as ineligible for state special education support. They also found that school psychologists were reluctant to give a dual diagnosis of autism and intellectual disabilities even when this might be appropriate.

There can be many reasons why this could be the case, including cognitive bias of the professionals involved. This could mean that the preconceived notions of these professionals regarding a specific cultural group influence the type of information that they seek during the assessment process, and how they interpret this information. Since cognitive bias is often unconscious, one of the main ways to address this would be to be conscious of your own values and beliefs and consider these when assessing children's behaviour. If you are working in a team, where appropriate, challenge colleagues' decisions and interpretations in a supportive way.

Child development and supporting students

Cultural factors not only influence assessment process but also could impact the thinking and learning process of children from different cultural groups. Over the years, many theories have been developed in the field of autism to explain cognitive differences seen in individuals with autism, such as theory of mind, weak central coherence, and executive functioning difficulties (see Chapter 1 for further explanation). However, the limited cross-cultural studies that are emerging in the field of child development and autism are beginning to question the universality of these theories for individuals with autism across the world.

For example Goetz (2003) found, in her research with monolingual English-speaking children, monolingual Mandarin-speaking children, and children who were bilingual in English and Mandarin, that bilingual children exhibited better inhibitory control and theory of mind. It could be speculated that this is because bilingual children need to develop flexible thinking in terms of understanding that the same object could be called different names based on the language they use. They also need to understand which language to use based on the person they are speaking to, which involves theory of mind. Although Goetz's study was not focused on children with autism, it does highlight how some of the factors associated with cultural and linguistic diversity can actually be beneficial. Similarly, Bialystok (2009) argues that bilingual individuals tend to be better at executive functioning tasks than monolinguals.

Along with language abilities, parenting styles could also influence executive functioning and inhibitory behaviour. According to a study conducted by Oh and Lewis (2008), three- to four-year-old South Korean children perform better in these areas compared to Western children. They suggest that this could be a result of the strict rules of social interaction which are part of the Korean culture and therefore are developed by parents in children from a young age. Oh and Lewis did not include children with autism in their study, but their findings draw attention to the cultural factors which can contribute to cognitive development.

The only study which we are aware of that did include students with autism was conducted by Koh and Milne (2012), where they compared the cognitive styles of UK students with and without autism with students from Singapore. They found that while students with autism in the UK were more likely to show a detailed focused thinking style, this was not the case with those from Singapore. Students with autism in Singapore were just as likely to look at the broader context as neurotypical students from the UK and Singapore. This could be because in a context-dependent culture, where it is important to understand the situation to communicate and learn, children may develop better central coherence compared to non-context-dependent cultures.

All these studies highlight that we should not be accepting as universally applicable the cognitive theories developed in the West to explain the learning styles of students with autism. This would also mean that we need to be careful about using autism strategies based on these theories with students coming from different cultural backgrounds. Even though most of these studies are based in a different country, multilingualism, different parenting style, and different communication and interaction style could well be characteristic of the experiences of the children with autism from minority ethnic communities living in the West, and therefore just as relevant.

Tensions can arise when selecting educational goals to be set for students from culturally diverse backgrounds, as parents and school staff may have different views about the skills and needs of the child. For example, Thompson and Winsler (2018) found in their study that parents of children with autism and their preschool teachers disagreed on how they perceived social skills and behaviour difficulties in the children. Parents on the whole considered their children had better social skills and fewer behaviour problems compared to the views of the teachers. It is possible that both parents and teachers were assessing these skills based on their own cultural norms. Because of these differences in perceptions of children's skills, it is also likely that parents have different expectations of the skills and knowledge their child needs to develop (Perepa 2014).

Even when targets have been agreed, how the skill needs to be developed may vary based on the cultural background of the family. For example, it is recognized that people from South-East Asia tend to look at the middle of an individual's face to recognize their face. People who are exposed to more than one ethnic group, such as the Malaysian Chinese, are more likely to use a mixed approach where they look at the eyes of the individual as well as the nose, rather than mouth, as most Westerners would do (Tan *et al.* 2012). Tan *et al.* (*ibid.*) suggest that this adaption enables them to recognize South-East Asian as well as Western faces. Unless teachers are aware of the skills that people from a specific community use in their day-to-day living, it could prove to be difficult to provide strategies which would be useful for the student. It is important to understand from family members what skills are important for a child from a minority culture to ensure that these are part of the child's curriculum. Along with this, discussions are also needed to understand how these skills are developed typically in the cultural group the child belongs to so that there is some consistency in the strategies.

Questions are raised about the relevance of evidence-based autism strategies for students from culturally diverse backgrounds as very few of the research studies conducted to evaluate these approaches included non-White participants (West *et al.* 2016). This means that even when using autism-specific strategies, we need to be aware that their efficacy has not been proven with children from culturally diverse groups. There might also be cultural differences with some of the popular approaches in the field of autism. For example, use of visuals or singing songs for developing communication skills may not be acceptable for some families due to their cultural values (Norbury & Sparks 2013). Therefore, decisions about appropriate strategies will have to be made based on your assessment as an EP, the skills of the school staff and the preferences of the family.

Working with families

Working with parents is often an integral part of an EP's role. However, based on their previous experiences and perceptions of the professionals, parents could be wary of interacting with them. In their work with Latino parents in the USA, Estrada and Deris (2014) found that parents often reported negative interactions while working with professionals, where they felt that their voice was not being heard and their concerns were not taken on board. Similarly, Jegatheesan, Miller and Fowler (2010) found in their research with South-Asian Muslim families in the USA that there was a difference in parental and professional perceptions of the abilities of the child. Parents reported that professionals underestimated their child's skills, which the parents resented. Parents in this study also felt that the importance they placed in rearing their children in a multilingual community and aiming for fuller inclusion was not shared by professionals.

Parents who have limited literacy skills or had poor education themselves or experienced racism may be apprehensive of seeking support or interacting with professionals (Gray & Donnelly 2013). To develop good collaborative partnership with parents from diverse cultural groups, it is important that time is spent to understand parental concerns and priorities, and to learn about their culture and style of communication (Estrada & Deris 2014). Many cultures also place importance on developing personal relationships to build trust, which may be contrary to Western norms.

Parental level of acceptance of their child's autism and their desire to seek support from professionals are influenced by the way autism or any other disability is perceived within their community. For example, Qi, Zaroff and Bernardo (2016) suggest that in the Chinese community, where parents are held responsible for the values and behaviour of the child, autism is often understood as a result of poor parenting by lay Chinese people. Some families may also be ostracized by people from their community because of their child's autism (Hussein, Pellicano & Crane 2019). This would mean that parents from such communities could be sensitive to any criticism of their parenting style or comments which question their values. Social stigma attached to disabilities such as autism in some communities can lead to families hiding the full details of their child's difficulties from professionals or not seeking any professional support at all (Fox *et al.* 2017). Understanding cultural perceptions about causation of autism and how this can influence the experiences of the family within that community can help professionals in approaching the family in a more sensitive way. It also needs to be remembered that differences in parenting style do not necessarily mean wrong parenting, as discussed above; some styles of parenting may actually develop better executive functioning and adaptive skills (Ratto *et al.* 2016).

Some parents may not be aware of the education or support systems available in the UK. Finding out about appropriate services can be particularly difficult if the parents have limited English proficiency (Fox *et al.* 2017). Even parents who are fluent in English may find technical terms used in reports difficult to understand or interpret (Papoudi *et al.* 2020). Therefore, considering the language that is used in reports and signposting families to appropriate local services can be an important role for an EP. However, not all parents from minority ethnic communities will have similar views. For example, in their research with immigrant families, Rivard and colleagues (2019) found that the social class of the parents also influenced their understanding of autism and their experiences with seeking support. Similarly, the role that culture and religion play for individual members from any given community may vary (Papoudi *et al.* 2020). Therefore, assumptions should not be made based on an individual's ethnicity as this can create stereotypes and could create a different set of barriers and issues.

A BLACK PARENT'S PERSPECTIVE

Venessa Bobb

My background

I was born in Lambeth, South London, and grew up with my mum. She was from Guyana and my dad was born in Aruba. Mum worked hard, and people at school saw me as privileged. I was called a coconut (because some of my peers thought I behaved like a white person) and I was bullied. I found it hard to hold on to friendships. After school, I had a successful career in television as a technician.

I have three children: two daughters aged 20 and 15 and a son of 18.

My son and one of my daughters have a diagnosis of autism and ADHD as well as a severe receptive expressive language disorder; my younger daughter has benign Rolandic epilepsy (BRE), while the older one has moderate learning difficulties.

Experiences with my son and working with professionals

My son was a very quiet baby and I used to have to wake him to feed. From two to three years of age, he was non-verbal and there was a lot of hitting, pinching and pushing. He used to suck his finger a lot and when a family member tried to get rid of that, other things took its place like kicking, rocking, swinging his legs and flapping his hands. I was told it was my parenting skills. When I attended the National Autistic Society's EarlyBird course, I realized that I was literally on my own when it came to talking about cultural perspectives.

My son was seen as the class clown when he was in the nursery school. Since then, he has attended two nursery schools, three primaries, one independent paid school, one day special school for autism, a residential school and an independent autism sixth form. There were lots of difficulties. He was bullied in primary school and had some very unhappy experiences which he does not like talking about, even now. He was clearly misunderstood and forced to fit into a mainstream school. I feel guilty at times that I let him go to places thinking it would be good for him. Instead, I had a very over-stressed and confused child. Even when he got a diagnosis, he was denied a lot of services and that continues to this day. As he got older, I had the support and advice from staff at two specialist schools and gained a better insight into his difficulties. I learned to recognize his triggers and how to support him more effectively.

It seems that a lot of professionals questioned my home life and the reason for my son's behaviour. As I was spending too much time with their brother, my daughters struggled and were seen as having social, emotional and mental health (SEMH) difficulties. I requested help from social services in 2007 and gave up my career to focus on the children and put into practice what I had learned from the EarlyBird courses.

I believe that my son's needs were never seen as complex. At school, when he was younger, he had the routine. But he still struggled within classroom settings and in the playground. He may have done the flapping, the running around, but I used to hear, 'He seemed to be naughty today. He's very disobedient. Are you giving him firm boundaries? Maybe you need to go to a parenting workshop.' I have been on lots of parenting workshops, but they did not help. Even though he had a diagnosis of autism spectrum condition (ASC), I felt that mainstream school staff would not listen to me. One of the special educational needs coordinators blamed my behaviour, parenting skills and my childhood trauma.

The problem really started with the first assessment by the local authority EP. It is very sad how reports can be a false, misleading account of your child. I was honest about my experiences with my son, but it seemed that their dad, who had no relationship with him, was able to have input that changed the report. Most of the EPs' reports seemed to focus on my home life and not school. Apparently, the school appeared to have no problems with my son, and my children were thought to have an attachment disorder. Third parties seemed to have the upper hand and yet again my voice was ignored. I would say my experiences with professionals has not been good and I am petrified and do not really trust them due to what I have experienced. It is the same experience for many other families I work with.

There is one EP who took account of my son's cultural needs when looking at his transition package. This was overlooked and social services continued to assign child protection social workers. Social services denied my son many of the services as he did not meet the criteria and threshold. My question is, how can he be attending residential school but not be thought to require a specialist disability social worker?

My son has progressed so well. He has said, 'Mum, thank you for being there for me.' This means a lot to me. There was a time, between the ages of 12 and 14, when I would question if I had made the right decision to send him to a residential school. I know now that I did. If you have the right family support, the right professionals around you, the right school, and the right teachers and specialist after-school provision, your autistic child/young person can excel. My son is a success story as he has proved many wrong. Currently, my only issue is his social care, which has been refused, and this is an area that needs to be challenged when it comes to autistic people who do not have a learning disability. To be honest, I am scared for him. I am scared that if I die tomorrow, how will he cope? It is not just me who thinks this way; it is any parent who has an autistic child.

He now feels sad that society, especially during the pandemic, is still not including autistic people and making reasonable adjustments.

He is not ready to travel alone on public transport; he still wants to have a mentor. Social services have a neurotypical approach that has clearly failed my son. He does not see the importance of sixth form because he feels that he does not want to work with people. He is happy with making gaming his career. He wants to be happy and be part of the community but can see that mainstream provision is not for him. Being at residential school has made friendship an issue, although he has got virtual friends. I have talked a great deal about my son. My daughters also have significant needs. I think too many girls are sadly getting diagnosed late, after years of suffering in silence.

Why I set up A2ndVoice

I set up A2ndVoice in May 2012 as a voluntary group because of the lack of provision for my son. The local special educational needs and disability groups did not seem to understand the cultural perspectives, and my son's autism and ADHD caused confusion when I attended some groups. My church pastor suggested I set up a support group and put me in touch with several people who were very helpful. The support group was started in recognition of the challenges autistic people and their families have in terms of childhood trauma and domestic abuse, and to engage Black and Asian communities. I realized that our upbringing was different, with a different kind of discipline and child-rearing practice. When I used to go to ASC groups, I was the only Black person and if I did see a parent, they were African and not from my cultural background. The focus of my support group was a holistic approach that would include the entire family and those involved with the person on the autism spectrum.

At the beginning, the majority of my members were white families and I was fine with that, but eventually I realized that Black families were not attending even though I was advertising the group. I was criticized for only having white speakers and asked how they could possibly support Black families. Eventually, I started to find more Black speakers. A2ndVoice was more about who to go to. Many families refused to tap into the system. So, my bad experience with professionals and my frustrations at the lack of local provision for my son made me set up A2ndVoice. I have never felt appreciated by my local authority and can get frustrated when professionals talk to me like I do not know anything.

I had so much anger towards EPs for how they all portrayed me but once I started speaking at events and working with EPs who were passionate about autism, I realized it was about educating. What we need are EPs, health professionals and social workers specializing in autism. Autistic people and their families will easily lose trust if professionals are neither knowledgeable nor dependable.

My perspective on autism, ethnicity and culture

When it comes to autism and my journey with my son, I did not see the problem with him being a Black boy. My experience was that everyone around me made things hard for me and confused me. The majority of the professionals I put my trust in, because I thought they had my son's interest at heart, made me believe they understood. Those who had a lot of influence during my son's early years, from the headteacher, special educational needs coordinator and the social workers, were Black. I thought they knew best. Later, I realized that they had no expertise in autism, even though they had a lot to say about the diagnosis. They would question the diagnosis, and tell me to get a second opinion and that white people love to label Black boys with ADHD. I found it difficult to hold conversations with Black professionals because I could tell from the tone of their voices that they looked down on me. I did not have any support and felt trapped and lonely.

I was invited by the National Autistic Society to be involved in compiling the *Diverse Perspectives* report in 2014 and things began to change for the better. I started to see more Black people and professionals moving forward. A2ndVoice attracted a very diverse audience but the key families were white families, and especially those from dual heritage. These members and well-wishers were the ones who supported, advised and helped me. Autism can be a struggle for all communities. If a Black professional with little knowledge of autism sees a Black boy acting inappropriately or a Black girl being loud and feisty, they will see the colour of the individual's skin first. Even if there is already a diagnosis, it would not make a difference. Stigma, taboo and prejudice can cloud their vision so that they refuse to accept autism.

I believe that it is an understanding of the cultural elements that is missing from all establishments, so training is essential. Statutory agencies such as social services, local authorities and the child and adolescent mental health services need to have a deep understanding of ethnicity and culture and the interplay with autism. We are told that professionals know everything. If they are assigned to help our family, we are trusting and will disclose much to help our case. Instead, we get something else. It is much worse for families with additional languages, where they may be denied access to services and blamed for the problems. Autism can be the most overlooked and over-used condition for many reasons.

Being in diverse groups we can be open about ethnicity because everybody is able to experience it, but if one is in a predominantly white group, it is much more difficult to talk about these issues. For instance, if a family joined a local autism support group and then disclosed that their child has sickle cell anaemia, how could the group assist them? Would they know who to connect with? Such issues may be of no interest to one group, but of paramount importance to another, depending on cultural awareness.

During the Covid-19 lockdowns, when travel was not possible, I began attending Team Around The Child meetings outside London online. This meant that Black families had support from a Black representative when everyone else in the meeting was white. Parents will feel, at times, happier if they see someone who looks like them. Racism is a major issue right now and if professionals have little comprehension of the interplay between autism, culture and ethnicity, this will cause more grief for the families involved.

My personal experiences have shown me that it is very important for any professional working with a child who has a behaviour problem, especially a very young child, to explore all avenues and ask the right questions. It is important not to make quick assumptions. It was the numerous professionals who made their own assumptions and made comparisons between my child and somebody else's who caused damage to my family. If you are a professional who thinks autism is over-rated, then maybe you are in the wrong job.

Looking back now, I can see that it is not just about getting a diagnosis: it is a lifelong journey. I have learned so much over the years. Going to events and meeting so many people have made a difference. My life has been a 'rollercoaster', but I am grateful to those people who have stood by me and helped me.

PERSPECTIVE OF A BLACK
EDUCATIONAL PSYCHOLOGIST

Ken Greaves

My background

When I think back to my childhood, I realize that my life could have so easily gone in a very different direction. My parents were part of the Windrush Generation and I was born into a culturally diverse area. When I was eight, my family moved to a predominantly white working-class area. It was there that I started to experience racism. My siblings and I were singled out because we were the only Black family going to our local school. There was bullying and I learned that we had to look after ourselves. What that meant was that I ended up getting myself into difficulties with my peers. They were physically aggressive towards me and I fought back. Looking back, I understand now that going to primary school was not an education for me; it felt very much like a war zone. The teachers were not protective of me. They saw me as an instigator of trouble, a bit of a behaviour problem, and I was assessed by someone (an EP I think) at the school. The school gave me a letter to take home, but I hid it. However, my mother found it. The report said that I was potentially bright, but I had significant behaviour problems and recommended that I be placed in a special school for children who had emotional and behavioural difficulties.

Recently I watched Steve McQueen's film *Education*, released in 2020 as part of the BBC's *Small Axe* series, which explores a period in the 1960s and 1970s when a significant number of working-class, often Black boys were considered to be failing in mainstream schools and were sent to special schools. The story of 12-year-old Kingsley in this film had much resonance with my own experiences. In 1971, Coard, a Grenadian writer who had been a teacher in the UK, published his book entitled *How the West Indian Child is Made Educationally Sub-normal in the British School System* (Coard 1971). This book gave voice to a huge level of concern among Black communities and led to the founding of many groups for Black parents and supplementary schooling. Eventually, this led to government reviews such as the *Swann Report* (Department for Education and Science 1985) and a series of legislative changes. It also triggered a period of profound challenge and change for the profession of educational psychology and the acknowledgement among many EPs of the need for more comprehensive assessment practices which took account of culture, language and experience and included parental views from the outset.

Unpicking these events now, it seems incredible that my school had referred me for an assessment without discussing this with my parents and that no parental permission was obtained. The first they knew of it was a letter sent to home suggesting a move to a special school. My salvation was my father's reaction. He was livid when he read the letter and made an appointment to speak to the headteacher. He insisted on taking responsibility for me and told him, 'I will discipline my son.' Basically, he stopped me participating in activities that I was interested in, such as football, and encouraged me to do well at school, saying often that, 'In order to get on in this world, you must have letters after your name.'

Later, the headteacher at my secondary school told me that I had talent which could be nurtured if I stayed away from trouble and focused more on studying and sports. I listened to him and, to cut a long story short, became head boy and did well in my A-levels. I applied to university and got a place to study psychology. There were no other Black young men from the East End of London at my university. I was acutely aware that there was no one like me there. I decided to train as an EP after being advised by my course tutor that there was a great need for Black people due to the lack of diversity in the profession, which was not something I had seriously thought about due to my negative experiences in primary school.

In order to pursue this, I needed to qualify and obtain relevant experience as a teacher in the first instance. I was successful in obtaining a place to train as a teacher in London. When I started my career as a teacher, my overriding impressions were that many of the parents of my students and my colleagues had negative assumptions. They made me feel very uncomfortable. I recollect parents withdrawing their children from my class after being told by the headteacher of my colour. My colleagues were also negative about my pedagogic style which promoted the ethic of working as a team and promoting self-esteem. Fortunately, I was very successful in changing perceptions over time.

My experiences as a Black EP
In spite of these difficult experiences, I progressed well to become a teacher in charge of a speech and language unit which first introduced

me to children who I now realize were on the autism spectrum. When I became an EP, I obtained a job in a local authority which I believed had a poor track record in terms of equality of opportunity. I was passionate about doing something to challenge racism in education and allow Black children to have a more positive school experience. My experience of working with culturally diverse families was quite limited at the beginning, as I was working within a culture where I was the minority.

I remember being perceived by professionals in a very stereotypical way. For example, when first appointed I was given a patch within the borough which was very white and intolerant of different cultures. When I queried why this was so, I was advised that it would not look good to place a Black EP with minority ethnic people as this could be seen as stereotypical. I have found that professional perceptions and preconceived notions can have a huge impact. For instance, one of my cases was a child with a single African mother who had a number of children, and who, I believe, was judged by professionals as having children in order to get benefits from the state. I found myself having to defend this mother and challenge those professionals. Then, of course, I was acutely aware that I was a Black professional defending a Black mother and that others may have believed that I had a vested interest in defending this person. I have found myself in some very uncomfortable situations over the years.

I worked for the same local authority for nearly 30 years during which time the demographic changed markedly, becoming much more culturally diverse, with families moving in from West Africa, Asia and Eastern Europe. While building effective working partnerships with a large group of schools, I tried to work with them to understand their practices with regard to ensuring equality of opportunity for their students. With my EP colleagues, we looked at the accessibility of our referral systems and re-evaluated our assessment processes. An emphasis was placed particularly on empowering parents as partners and eliciting the voice and views of children and young people. We also developed a holistic approach to assessment over time, taking on board the differing contexts to understand the child, family, school and community.

I have no doubt that things have improved and I saw some very encouraging developments in terms of equality of opportunity and support for different communities. There was a clear and focused over arching strategy which proposed data collection, an audit of community resources, and partnership working with communities, community leaders, religious organizations and so on. I feel strongly that a local authority's local offer must provide cross-referenced information about autism support within different communities.

Issues for minority ethnic families

The concept of autism can vary greatly among different cultures. In fact, autism does not exist as a word in certain languages and is often perceived as a condition that affects only white people (Perepa, 2019). Autism may be misunderstood or misinterpreted in a very negative way and perhaps linked to bad behaviour and intellectual impairment. In some cultures, there may be some stigma attached to having the label of autism, and families might feel uncomfortable with a label which might be perceived to ostracize them from the rest of their family and community. Therefore, they do not mention that the child might have autism.

There is much to do in promoting awareness within communities by providing clear information about autism, answering questions and dispelling myths. There is a great deal more to do in terms of working with communities and showing community leaders what they can do to support families. This will help to increase the chances that a child on the autism spectrum and their family are able to access the resources and opportunities to which they are entitled.

I believe there continues to be a lack of commitment from some professionals to learn about the communities they are working in. It is vital that they understand something of a community's practices and beliefs, and also the impact, for instance, of fleeing a war-torn country and experiences of persecution, violence, loss and grief. Professionals must appear accessible, respectful and interested in the family's culture and past experiences, which may have had an effect on the child's development. A professional who shows little interest in these factors may alienate a family or, at the very least, make them feel uncomfortable and undervalued. I am additionally concerned that some families may perceive professionals as authority figures who cannot be challenged. Therefore, empowering families to perceive themselves as partners and be confident about challenging and advocating for themselves is very important.

Moving forward

As the above discussion and personal experiences highlight, there are clearly some key issues such as fair assessments, culturally biased systems, lack of supportive professionals or organizations, and lack of cultural awareness among professionals. As an EP working in a multi-cultural society, it can feel daunting to work out how you will be able to provide culturally sensitive support to individuals on the autism spectrum and their family members. This final section highlights some practical suggestions for moving forward, along with research and planning priorities.

Culturally appropriate assessments

There is a need to conduct research on culture-fair assessment tools and carefully examine the standardization procedures in the tests we use. Standardized tests are not always appropriate and EPs must continue to broaden their practices to include observational assessments, assessment through teaching approaches, and dynamic assessment approaches. It is also important to be aware of one's own judgements, and engage in developing new practices and gathering a range of appropriate assessment tools. An EP who is making use of psychometric materials must be cognizant of the implications of their design as a Euro centric measure, which can be completely inappropriate for a child who is coming from any other cultural background. When planning an assessment, we need to question why we are using our chosen tools. Ask yourself:

- Can I justify to the family that this is in the best interest of their child?

- Can I justify myself to an adult I am assessing?

However, professional reports which do not include psychometric scores may not be accepted by some funding authorities – the decision-makers with regard to additional resources. I believe that part of the EP's role is to challenge that perception and find alternative ways of providing the evidence.

It is vital that assessment procedures include a consideration of environmental factors, the ethos and the context. How do these factors impact on the child and family? What are the reasonable adjustments that can be made? Working collaboratively with other professionals is a significant part of supporting a child and their family effectively. In order to provide the high-quality and coherent support that is due to all families, there needs to be a holistic, whole-team approach. It is not helpful for professionals from different disciplines to be arguing among themselves while a parent is fighting separately for the rights of their child.

Professionals working within minority ethnic communities

All professionals, even those who are from a minority ethnic community themselves, need to question their attitudes and practices and where and how these have developed. Their training may have been Euro centric, and they may have become comfortable with these and failed to broaden their knowledge and skills. Similarly, professionals coming from a specific minority ethnic community may use their cultural values as the norms. Therefore, it is important to question your own assumptions and have a broader view when working with children from minority ethnic communities and their families. Engaging with the child and the family to understand their views, concerns and strategies is the first step to move in this direction.

Diagnosis may well be a first step for some, but it is crucial to consider the pathways. What have we got out there to help these people? Diagnosis might help those who have already got the strategies to deal with their world. But what about the ones who are even more vulnerable and in need of direction? Our role must involve developing support resources and providing families with ongoing support as required.

I believe that a considered use of language is an important part of establishing trust and good partnership working with someone from an ethnic minority group. Building knowledge of their culture is very much part of this. My experiences have shown us that it is much more difficult to understand the impact of cultural and environmental factors if one is a decision-maker, with little or no contact with the local community on a day-to-day basis. It is crucial that EPs and other practitioners clarify these issues for the readers of their reports. It is also hugely important to try to comprehend the complexity of and interaction between culture and a diagnosis of autism within a family.

Issues facing children on the autism spectrum from minority ethnic communities

All EPs need to develop their knowledge and understanding of the interaction between cultural factors and autism. This needs to feature on all EP training courses and in continuing professional development opportunities. What is clear is that there is a dearth of research data about the experiences of autistic individuals from minority ethnic communities. As a result, the services and support systems which are available may not consider their cultural appropriateness for different communities, nor reflect on factors which may put up barriers in accessing these services for people from different cultural communities. This means that it can be much more difficult for people with autism and their families to access the right kind of support.

Venessa Bobb and I have been working with the National Autistic Society since 2014 to gather information from autistic people from minority ethnic communities and their families about their needs and experiences. So far, the following themes have emerged from the discussions:

- There are more barriers to getting an autism diagnosis for a number of reasons, including a lack of information about autism in some community groups. Additionally, some individuals and their families feel that professionals consider their autism to be behavioural problems or language difficulties.

- There are more challenges for minority ethnic parents because additional difficulties understanding autism, and reduced accessibility because of language differences.

- There are communication difficulties between minority ethnic communities and professionals, and concerns about difficulties in forming mutually trusting relationships.

- Due to a lack of awareness and understanding of autism within communities some parents may feel stigmatized or blamed.

- Some families may struggle to accept a diagnosis or feel ashamed and remain secretive, leading to isolation and further difficulties in accessing support.

Chapter conclusion

EPs have a key role in challenging barriers, prejudices and misconceptions. There also must be an acknowledgement of the need to act as an advocate, at times, to support the family to negotiate systems and processes; and, crucially, there must be consideration of the impact of complex environmental factors on the child's development. With reflective practice and a sensitive approach, EPs can contribute to making their services culturally inclusive for people from all communities.

POINTS FOR REFLECTION

☞ To what extent do you consider the cultural and linguistic background when you are working with an individual or their family?

☞ Do you reflect on how your own cultural background could influence your practice and your choice of appropriate intervention?

☞ Think of the assessment tools you use and the range of strategies you draw on in your recommendations to support children and young people on the autism spectrum. How culturally neutral are these?

References

BBC One (2020) *Small Axe*. Accessed 08/04/2021 at www.bbc.co.uk/programmes/m000qfb1.

Bialystok, E. (2009) 'Bilingualism: The good, the bad, and the indifferent.' *Bilingualism: Language and Cognition, 12*(1), 3–11.

Blacher, J., Stavropoulos, K. & Bolourian, Y. (2019) 'Anglo-Latino differences in parental concerns and service inequities for children at risk of autism spectrum disorder.' *Autism, 23*(6), 1554–1562.

Coard, B. (1971) *How the West Indian Child is Made Educationally Sub-Normal in the British School System*. London: New Beacon Books.

Department for Education (2019) *Special Educational Needs in England*. Accessed 15/12/2020 at www.gov.uk/government/statistics/special-educational-needs-in-england-january-2019.

Department for Education and Science (1985) *The Swann Report: 'Education for All' Report of the Committee of Enquiry into the Education of Children from Ethnic Minority Groups*. London: HMSO.

Estrada, L. & Deris, A. (2014) 'A phenomenological examination of the influence of culture on treating and caring for Hispanic children with autism.' *International Journal of Special Education, 29*(3), 4–15.

Fox, F., Aabe, N., Turner, K., Redwood, S. & Rai, D. (2017) '"It was like walking without knowing where I was going": A qualitative study of autism in a UK Somali migrant community.' *Journal of Autism and Developmental Disorders, 47*(2), 305–315.

Goetz, P.J. (2003) 'The effects of bilingualism on theory of mind development.' *Bilingualism: Language and Cognition, 6*(1), 1–16.

Gray, C. & Donnelly, J. (2013) 'Unheard voices: the views of traveller and non-traveller mothers and children with ASD.' *International Journal of Early Years Education, 21*(4), 268–285.

Hussein, A., Pellicano, E. & Crane, L. (2019) 'Understanding and awareness of autism among Somali parents living in the United Kingdom.' *Autism, 23*(6), 1408–1418.

Jegatheesan, B., Miller, P. & Fowler, S. (2010) 'Autism from a religious perspective: A study of parental beliefs in South Asian Muslim immigrant families.' *Focus on Autism and Other Developmental Disabilities, 25*(2), 98–109.

Koh, H. & Milne, E. (2012) 'Evidence for a cultural influence on field-independence in autism spectrum disorder.' *Journal of Autism and Developmental Disorders, 42*(2), 181–190.

Lindsay, G., Pather, S. & Strand, S. (2006) *Special Educational Needs and Ethnicity: Issues of Over- and Under-Representation.* DfES Research Report 757. Nottingham: Department for Education and Skills.

National Autistic Society (2014) *Diverse Perspectives – The Challenges for Families Affected by Autism from Black, Asian and Minority Ethnic Communities.* London: National Autistic Society.

Norbury, C. & Sparks, A. (2013) 'Difference or disorder? Cultural issues in understanding neurodevelopmental disorders.' *Developmental Psychology, 49*(1), 45–58.

Oh, S. & Lewis, C. (2008) 'Korean preschoolers' advanced inhibitory control and its relation to other executive skills and mental state understanding.' *Child Development, 79*(1), 80–99.

Papoudi, D., Jørgensen, C., Guldberg, K. & Meadan, H. (2020) 'Perceptions, experiences, and needs of parents of culturally and linguistically diverse children with autism: A scoping review.' *Review Journal of Autism and Developmental Disorders, 8*, 195–212. https://doi.org/10.1007/s40489-020-00210-1.

Perepa, P. (2014) 'Cultural basis of social "deficits" in autism spectrum disorders.' *European Journal of Special Needs Education, 29*(3), 313–326.

Perepa, P. (2019) *Autism, Ethnicity and Culture.* London: Jessica Kingsley Publishers.

Qi, X., Zaroff, C. & Bernardo, A. (2016) 'Autism spectrum disorder etiology: Lay beliefs and the role of cultural values and social axioms.' *Autism, 20*(6), 673–686.

Ratto, A., Anthony, B., Kenworthy, L., Armour, A., Dudley, K. & Anthony, L. (2016) 'Are non-intellectually disabled black youth with ASD less impaired on parent report than their white peers?' *Journal of Autism and Developmental Disorders, 46*(3), 773–781.

Reijneveld, S., Harland, P., Brugman, E., Verhulst, F. & Verloove-Vanhorick, S. (2005) 'Psychosocial problems among immigrant and non-immigrant children – Ethnicity plays a role in their occurrence and identification.' *European Child and Adolescent Psychiatry, 14*(3), 145–152.

Rivard, M., Millau, M., Magnan, C., Mello, C. & Boulé, M. (2019) 'Snakes and ladders: Barriers and facilitators experienced by immigrant families when accessing an autism spectrum disorder diagnosis.' *Journal of Developmental and Physical Disabilities, 31*(4), 519–539.

Rupasinha, J. (2015) 'Addressing an imbalance? Educational psychologists' considerations of ethnic minority cultural factors in assessments for autistic spectrum condition.' *Educational & Child Psychology, 32*(2), 77–88.

Sullivan, A., Sadeh, S. & Houri, A. (2019) 'Are school psychologists' special education eligibility decisions reliable and unbiased? A multi-study experimental investigation.' *Journal of School Psychology, 77*, 90–109.

Tan, C.B.Y., Stephen, I. D., Whitehead, R. & Sheppard, E. (2012) 'You look familiar: How Malaysian Chinese recognize faces.' *PLoS ONE, 7*(1), e29714.

Thompson, B. & Winsler, A. (2018) 'Parent–teacher agreement on social skills and behavior problems among ethnically diverse preschoolers with autism spectrum disorder.' *Journal of Autism and Developmental Disorders, 48*, 3163–3175.

Tromans, S., Chester, V., Gemegah, E., Roberts, K. *et al.* (2020) 'Autism identification across ethnic groups: A narrative review.' *Advances in Autism, 7*(3), 241–255. https://doi.org/10.1108/AIA-03-2020-0017.

West, E., Travers, J., Kemper, T., Liberty, L. *et al.* (2016) 'Racial and ethnic diversity of participants in research supporting evidence-based practices for learners with autism spectrum disorder.' *Journal of Special Education, 50*(3), 151–163.

CHAPTER 10

Information Technology and Autism

Editor: Laurence Hime

The use of information technology (IT) has become an integral part of our daily lives and, similarly, computers and smart devices are now common in educational settings to enhance the learning of all young people. To help those autistic individuals, innovative program and applications have been developed to improve their access to learning and to bridge the gap to the neurotypical world. The use of technology dedicated to supporting the differences within autism has now gone considerably beyond simple desktop computers (Grynszpan *et al.* 2013). It has been noted that during the periods of lockdown and the recourse to online learning, familiarity with IT was accelerated for all children. For autistic children, they were often able do this with a level of independence, particularly when they understood the activities and found them motivating. Some caution is needed with this. While many autistic children enjoy using smart devices to look at their favourite videos, listen to music, game or research their special interests, the development of IT skills is not true for all and (contrary to popular perception) not all autistic children can navigate the IT world with equal ease or become technological geniuses.

Improving communication, the provision of an immediate visual tool, support for decision-making, motivation, modelling through videos, vocational assistance and emotional regulation are all important ways in which technology can be used to support autistic individuals (Autism Speaks 2021). The advantages of IT, with respect to the core differences found in autism, include the consistency of a clearly defined task, visual input and a better focus of attention, with reduced distractions from unnecessary sensory stimuli (Murray 1997). Valencia and colleagues (2019) also identify how IT activities can be planned to occur in a safe and trustworthy environment.

Educational psychologists have applied IT in their practice, such as Video Interactive Guidance (VIG), to obtain data to work in partnership with parents/carers of autistic individuals at home (see Chapter 3). Other educational psychologists, such as Houghton (2020), developed IT approaches to motivate learning through the creation of animated videos, which was especially helpful for online learning during the Covid-19 lockdown. Outreach services often use tablets as a convenient library of resources and as a modelling tool for school staff to see in practice the recommended methods of support.

The increasing range of innovations for autistic individuals include social robots, video modelling of verbal behaviour, video game programs targeting face-processing skills, and the educational aspects of virtual reality, all of which have now appeared in educational settings (Shic & Goodwin 2015). Effectiveness for the use of IT for autistic children, using specific interventions such as desktop computers, interactive DVD with shared active surface, and virtual reality, was found by Grynszpan and colleagues (2013).

The emphasis on goal-first planning when considering the choice and use of appropriate digital technologies for autistic children and young people, in order to make a meaningful difference in their lives, is made by Alyssa Alcorn and Sue Fletcher-Watson in the first contribution in this chapter. The view of IT as isolating is addressed in Nicola Yuill's contribution, where she proposes that differences with social behaviour can be addressed through online collaborative approaches and shared engagement within IT.

The reviews and feedback of online learning during the Covid-19 lockdowns in 2020 have revealed how access to IT activities was not always easy for autistic children. The Autism Centre for Education and Research (ACER) at Birmingham University surveyed parents of autistic children during the summer of 2020, who reported that it could be tiring to motivate them and that they missed their teacher and the classroom, where they felt 'real learning' took place. An advantage was that some children liked to spread out tasks over the day, such as writing, so they became less of a challenge (ACER 2020).

Adams and colleagues (2019) found similar results with further education students on the autism spectrum in their review of the online environment. Although the online environment provided flexibility for learning, such as being able to pause videos or rewatch videos while taking notes, and to work at times convenient to them, the online delivery may unintentionally create barriers to the learning experience, such as tutors not being visible, not gaining immediate feedback to answers, and the disconnection between the description that online learning is 'flexible', the high amounts of work required, and the firm deadlines for assignments.

Parents have explained how their children's difficulties with executive functioning (first described by Luria in 1966 as using a problem-solving approach to achieve an outcome), required increased adult moderation of the activities, with clear and explicit explanations of the steps and what was being achieved at the end. The role of the experienced adult was found to be essential and one that parents/carers at home found to be hard.

The importance of autism-skilled teachers delivering and moderating IT-based interventions (e.g., being able to make adjustments to increase effectiveness) was reported by Shurr and colleagues (2021) in their study of using IT to build conceptual understanding of basic computation and word problem-solving through visualization.

Another area of difficulty for individuals with autism is generalizing the skills that have been learned through computer-assisted instruction (Whyte, Smyth & Scherf 2015). This is also reported by Rao, Beidel and Murray (2008), with social skills-training programmes failing to generalize beyond the teaching setting into real-life contexts. Owen Rhys Barry's contribution to this chapter investigates this, through his pioneering research, which examines the application of empathizing–systematizing theory, where autistic individuals are taught to understand social systems and to predict behaviours, so helping the generalization of social skills.

Finally, when considering the use of IT, Lorah and colleagues (2015) warn against making the device the focus rather than the process. They state that simply using a technology does not automatically mean understanding or analysing. Other researchers address this same issue and how to fulfil the promise of increasing sophistication of technology for autistic individuals. Shic and Goodwin (2015) also emphasize the necessity to focus on process and outcomes and how IT can be realistically used in practice.

CHOOSING AND USING TECHNOLOGIES TO SUPPORT AUTISTIC CHILDREN AND YOUNG PEOPLE

Alyssa Alcorn and Sue Fletcher-Watson

In this contribution, we hope to provide a practical guide to choosing and using technology to support autistic children and young people. By 'technology', we mean digital technologies, and use this term to refer to hardware (i.e., physical devices), software (e.g., apps), and internet content. We've largely focused on the most widespread consumer technologies at the time of writing, such as smartphones, desktop computers, tablets, apps and websites. We briefly discuss emerging technologies, such as social robotics and virtual reality (VR).

Through questions and answers, we will consider whether you need a technology specifically designed for autistic users, and what technology can be used to achieve. We will also consider the evidence base and how to determine whether a technology works, not only to achieve your goal, but also whether it is functional on a day-to-day basis. The contribution ends by reviewing the responsibilities that practitioners and parents have as gatekeepers for young people's use of technology.

Do I need a technology 'for autism'?

In a nutshell, the answer is no. A recent survey found that the technologies most commonly used by autistic children and young people (according to their parents) were 'mainstream' technologies such as social media apps and popular games like Candy Crush™ (Laurie *et al.* 2019). There are multiple reasons to endorse what these parents reported, not least the fact that access to best-selling video games and apps connect autistic children to the stories and characters known by their non-autistic classmates.

There are technologies specifically made for autistic users, but it is important to be aware of the absence of any quality-control mechanism for websites, apps and so on which are marketed 'for autism' (see Fletcher-Watson 2015). There is no regulatory body with oversight that checks the evidence for claims made, and it is incredibly rare for any technology to have been evaluated formally. It is important to be sceptical about radical claims of benefit.

That said, there are cases in which a mainstream technology will not be appropriate. A good example is in the domain of augmentative and alternative communication support (AAC), where visual symbol systems (e.g., Boardmaker, PECS) and voice-output communication aids (VOCAs) (e.g., Proloquo2Go, Widgit Go) can both provide concrete benefits for autistic young people (Aydin & Diken 2020; Logan, Iacono & Trembath 2017). In the case of the former, a range of low-cost options are available for smartphones and tablets, all benefitting from far greater flexibility and portability than a ring-binder full of laminated symbol cards and Velcro strips. VOCAs require more careful consideration, however; these technologies are often high cost in terms of both initial expenditure and investment of time and effort when integrating the communication aid into the individual's life and helping them become a confident user. We would always recommend working with a specialist such as an educational psychologist or speech and language therapist when selecting and deploying a communication aid for an autistic user.

Swathes of content are released or updated every day, even in a single marketplace such as the Apple App Store. If we accept that technologies for autistic users don't have to be autism specific, then no one can tell you which technology to pick because there are too many potentially relevant ones to choose from. These factors partially explain why we, or any experts, cannot recommend 'the best' devices or apps for autistic users. Another reason is that a key factor in the selection of a technology is 'user fit', and each person is unique. Therefore, instead of making specific recommendations for this or that app, the most helpful thing we can do is provide a framework for making choices between the relevant options available.

What is the technology for?

Before you can select a device or app, you need to determine what you are trying to achieve by asking, 'What does this young person want to accomplish?', rather than 'What can we do with this laptop?' There may be a new goal, or a well-established one which might benefit from a technological tool to achieve it. If you're interested in using technologies with a particular autistic person but *don't* have an exact goal in mind, you should consider the following:

- *Goals don't have to be 'educational' or 'therapeutic' to be meaningful.* You could also have goals about connecting people, creativity and expression, showing ownership and responsibility, or having fun.

- *Your new goals don't exist in a vacuum.* Most autistic children will already use technologies of some kind, and they may have strong, specific ideas about these: that they belong at home or in school; they are for fun or work; 'mine' or shared. For example, autism educators reported introducing iPads with little planning and mostly for leisure, 'creating knock-on problems' in which autistic learners might 'see an iPad or a technological device as something that is mainly a toy' and resist using it for other purposes (Alcorn *et al.* 2019, p.6). Your goals will be more feasible if they don't contradict ways the child already uses a technology, or if you carefully manage expectations about the purpose and ownership of *new* technologies.

- *Avoid 'interventionizing' leisure and chill-out time.* Where someone has a go-to technology as their fun reward, personal interest or stress release, it's easy to conclude that you could *also* leverage it towards an education or therapy goal. Please don't. That specific app, website or other technology is already playing an important role for them, so choose another. For example, if playing *Minecraft* or video calling grandma are someone's fun time, don't try to use them as the basis of a social skills intervention. This issue can intersect with the one above, where a *device* associated with leisure may also be needed for 'work'. Strategies like switching between different-coloured cases on the same phone or tablet can help signal the difference.

- *Technology skills are daily living skills.* People of all ages increasingly require technologies to engage with daily living and may incur costs if they can't do so – from electronic transport tickets to googling life's questions. Treat technology skills as meaningful and important, and help children recognize them as part of their knowledge and strengths.

- *Would you know if you met the goal?* Consider whether and how your goals are measurable. Is there any way to evaluate whether that technology is 'doing its job'?

Identifying a clear goal doesn't automatically make it a goal to address with technology. If you think a technology is the right tool, challenge yourself by asking: 'Is this better than paper?' For example, would a visual schedule app or social story app meet your needs any *better* than the paper versions? Are there *drawbacks* compared to paper? The 'paper question' matters most when you are considering digital technologies to replace things that you or the child already uses. Will a technology be sufficiently better than your current practice to be worth the initial cost, the set-up for you and the user, and any ongoing 'maintenance'? Even a free app still costs your time!

Relatedly, you may seek a technological solution to enable a child to become more independent, perhaps in their learning, daily living or leisure time. This is a reasonable goal and sometimes a plausible one but, as above, it is essential to reflect on the role that an adult plays in that activity and whether it can be reasonably substituted by a technology. The transition from adult support to tech-enabled activity will almost certainly need to be carefully managed and may take some time.

If you find yourself unsure about possible benefits, you may want to think more about what's truly needed in your situation or seek more details about the features of a technology. Keep in mind that digital technologies *aren't* automatically the best tools for every goal, and won't always offer benefits over current practice, no matter what the marketing says!

Does it work?

In order to critically consider your goal – including how you will know when it has been achieved, and the question of sufficient benefit over existing tools – you will also need to ask, 'Does the technology work?' This question means several different things.

The simplest type of working is usability: Are children and young people able to understand and engage with a technology? Can *you* do it without tearing your hair out? Labels like 'age five to eight' may not be helpful for autistic children with spiky profiles or strong sensory sensitivities. If you're trying something out yourself to estimate suitability, you might want to consider the look, feel and sensory aspects of the technology, the demands it makes on the user, and its options and other design choices (see Table 10.1).

Table 10.1: Factors to consider when estimating technology usability for autistic children and young people

Categories	Usability factors
Look, feel and sensory aspects	• **Apparent target age group:** Labelled age group aside, do language or graphics seem 'babyish' (a big deterrent for some children) or overly mature? • **Sounds and music:** Might they distress the user? Might they distress or annoy *others* when the app is used? Can they be turned off or turned down? • **Colours and visual busyness:** Some designs for children can be luridly coloured with many moving items – great for some, overwhelming for others.
Demands on the user	• What is the **level of literacy** needed to use the item, and the requirements for typing or reading on-screen instructions? • What are the **motor demands**, such as size of buttons or sliders, need to press multiple buttons/keys, or requirement to drag items on a touchscreen? • **Time pressure:** Are there timers or countdowns forcing a user to process information or make decisions quickly (e.g., in an app with a quiz component)? This could be very stressful for some. Don't forget to check for things that may time out due to inactivity.
Other options and design choices	• **Menus and personalizability options:** Can you find them? Are they helpful? How hard or easy would it be for a child to open and change them – by accident or on purpose? • **Visible points, scores or ranking:** These may highly motivate some users, but be a significant source of anxiety for others. • **Errors:** For educational or puzzle apps, what happens if you don't know what to do, or your answers are wrong? Might you get stuck somewhere in the app? Conversely, is it possible to complete activities by giving random answers – e.g., will it *give* you the right answer or automatically advance after an error?

Especially if choosing for younger children, make sure to 'test like a child'. Tap and swipe everywhere, press all the buttons at once – does it freeze or shut down? Is it easy to close by accident, lose progress, or produce other effects that can be frustrating or distressing? For options too costly to buy and try (like some VOCA apps), parent reviews, blog posts, and user-created demo videos might help you to get beyond the marketing hype. It is always worth reaching out to the developers and asking if a free test copy can be made available for a limited time: you might be surprised how often the answer is yes.

Then there is reliability. It's working now but will it *keep* working?

This is another key place to check reviews, just as you might when purchasing for yourself. With time and system updates, chunks of content may become incompatible or obsolete – sometimes unexpectedly. Products from larger companies might be most likely to be *kept* up to date and get their bugs patched. Autism apps from parents, charities or universities may lack the long-term resources required to do so. Don't forget to consider internet or data access as a reliability ingredient: Can something be accessed offline, or does it require an active connection? If the latter, how will that affect its deployment in the user's daily life?

A third type of 'working' question is about effectiveness. Does a technology have the effects it is advertised to have, such as improving numeracy? The most rigorous way to secure an answer is by conducting an independent research evaluation – a study by a team not involved in the app's development, not profiting from its sales, and with expertise in relevant research methods. However, when it comes to technology, the number of digital tools that have been evaluated in this way is a minuscule fraction of what's available commercially (Fletcher-Watson 2014, 2015).

In the absence of a research evidence base, you can *gather your own evidence* to try to determine whether technology 'works', for the same reasons as you would evaluate other strategies in your setting, and often in the same ways. This may mean you need to get more specific about your initial goal. With a numeracy skills app, it may be easy to keep track of a child's in-app scores or content progress. With something like a visual schedule app, you may need to look externally at things like task-completion or recording how well the user is coping with transitions. For goals that are about socializing, fun or creativity, the amount of time engaging with the technology may be relevant, as well as observed increases in signs of well-being and decreases in signs of distress.

'Working' questions are trickier for novel or experimental technologies that combine hardware and platform-specific content, such as social robots, virtual reality headsets, and biofeedback sensors. Being an early adopter can be risky. There may be no real evidence-base yet, from research or other users. Specialized hardware may be physically fragile (especially with child users!), but also fragile in the sense of relying on scarce, specialized knowledge and equipment to set it up, run it and repair it. There is unlikely to be an 'ecosystem' of readily available support locally or online, as exists for computers or smartphones. Be realistic: is a broken device likely to gather dust somewhere? Content availability is also an issue. What's available for a given platform may be proprietary, limited in scope, or may not fit your goals. Currently, there is no App Store for robots!

If you're concerned about getting technologies working in your setting and keeping them working, the best advice is to assume everything will break at least once and to plan accordingly, starting before you buy. Read the warranty. Ask about tech support from the maker/seller, or locally in your setting. As far as you can, work out possible future costs like additional content, software subscriptions, import costs and repairs. Can your setting afford to *keep* this technology running? Don't forget about the humans, either. Document your technology practices carefully, especially if you've gathered evidence and found that they work!. Share practice and troubleshooting skills within your professional community, particularly if formal technical training and support are limited. Have a back-up plan for how to support children if there are problems with a device or digital service that they rely on – especially if they are using it to communicate, self-regulate or manage daily tasks.

What are my responsibilities?

In our experience, many problems with applying technology to support autistic children and young people result from barriers to *adults* playing an informed and effective role in the deployment. Such barriers include: lack of time to review options or get to know the selected device/software, local (e.g., within school) policies preventing administrative rights over device settings, or lack of suitable training. Adults have crucial roles to play, in partnership with the user, in selection and ongoing use. Your first step must be to work with the user to identify goals for the technology – what do they want to achieve? If this is about socializing with other people, there's no point in selecting a game for a solo player or that no one else at school plays. If this is about independence or creative self-expression, the technology should have a completely accessible interface. If the young person just needs more ways to relax and unwind, the technology has to appeal to them.

Having selected the device, website or app you want to use, it's very important that you take the time to get to know the range of settings and permissions available on that platform. Tablets and smartphones now offer an exceptional range of accessibility options, as well as the ability for a parent or teacher to impose restrictions to prevent access to unsuitable content. Some entertainment apps have specific versions for children (such as *YouTube Kids* or *Kids iPlayer* from the BBC). Within each app, you may be able to select whether the app delivers notifications, accesses the camera, plays sound effects and so on. Getting to grips with these is an essential part of getting the most from a new piece of technology as well as keeping a young person safe. Especially for people with an intellectual disability as well as autism, a tablet can provide a rare opportunity for self-determination, choosing what to do and when, following their own selections all the way. Making the underlying settings secure can give them the freedom to explore without supervision. However, don't forget to check how easy it would be for young users to accidentally (or purposely) access and change the security settings or in-app purchases. Easily altered settings may *not* be secure!

As users grow up it is also important to make sure the technology grows with them. You will want to talk to them about online safety. This includes the possibility of cyber-bullying and grooming, but also more mundane risks like password security or inadvertently sharing personal information. Digital etiquette too is something which is worth discussing explicitly. How many text messages is it appropriate to send in a row without receiving a reply? Does it matter if not everyone 'likes' the latest picture you posted? The online social world is an essential part of our lives, and keeping young people safe online means giving them skills to navigate it, not denying them access altogether.

Conclusions

Choosing and utilizing technologies with autistic children and young people will be most successful when you set clear goals, and critically reflect on whether you need *a technology* to meet them. Be specific: how will you know that something is 'working' and the goals are being met? If you do go forward with technology, it may not need to be an autism-specific one. Mainstream, off-the-shelf options can be useful and are easily available. Among specialist technologies, not all will have a good evidence base nor make realistic claims about their effectiveness. Trying things out yourself is essential – consider usability issues, settings and possible sources of stress for the user (or others!). We recommend the BETA Project site as a way to help you during this process and to share what you learn with the autism community[1] (Zervogianni *et al.* 2020). Remember that throughout a process of technology choice and

---

1   www.beta-project.org

use, the most important ingredient is often *you, the adult.* With your supportive involvement, technologies can be incredibly rewarding for autistic children and young people as opportunities for independence, choice, play and fun, as well as for daily living or academic needs.

TECHNOLOGY AND AUTISM! A DIGITAL BUBBLE?

Nicola Yuill

This quote encapsulates well some deep contradictions in attitudes to technology in the classroom: 'Technology is neither good nor bad; neither is it neutral' (Kranzberg 1986, p.547). Difference in social behaviour is a core feature of autism, and support for social interaction will often be a key goal in autistic children's support plans, both for the benefits it can bring for well-being and for the learning opportunities provided through peer collaboration. Technology, and in particular the bogeyman of 'screen time', are very often pictured as isolating children in a 'digital bubble' that robs them of the opportunities needed for social interaction and learning. This perceived danger sits alongside the affinity that some autistic people commonly feel with technology, an affinity associated with the opportunity to withdraw from others, and with highly predictable, systematic structures. This stereotype of technology as isolating does not fit with its role as a powerful social and communicative lifeline, with tools such as Picture Exchange Communication Systems (PECS) apps providing highly adaptable communication support, and touchscreen technologies opening up new powers of action to children who have learning, communication and motor difficulties that could otherwise limit their opportunities. In this contribution, I focus on how we can use technology to support autistic children's learning in ways that don't lead to isolation, and especially those that can support collaborative learning.

Any discussion of autism needs to acknowledge the breadth of the autism spectrum, and in particular the wide range of communicative needs. The underlying approach in this contribution involves:

- Thinking of technology as a tool that 're-creates and shapes the whole structure of behaviour' (Vygotsky 1930–1934/1978). Even something as simple as using a tablet rather than a paper book for shared reading can alter the ways that people interact (Yuill & Martin 2016)

- Seeing interaction as involving bodies as much as minds: children learning together do so through physical action

- Considering the classroom technology that is available to most children, generally touchscreens: large shared surfaces such as whiteboards and smaller screens such as tablets or phones.

Part 1 defines collaboration and why it is so important in development. Technology gives us particularly flexible ways to design collaborative environments, just as teachers might plan the layout of their physical classroom environment or playground to be autism-friendly (e.g., Yuill *et al.* 2007). Part 2 describes how we can use technology to support behaviour needed for collaboration. I discuss three aspects of behaviour to consider: sharing awareness, managing control and supporting shared understanding.

Part 1: Understanding collaboration

Evolutionary theorists argue that sociability, notably the capacity to cooperate with each other, was an important factor in the reproductive success of humans. Early humans were adept at social learning and building on each other's knowledge to develop increasingly complex tools. The invention of culturally transmitted cognitive aids such as writing systems made it much easier to save and share knowledge, so as to build on the work of others, creating intricate artefacts such as economies, political systems and religions that are part of modern cumulative cultures. Looking at individual development, Moll and Tomasello (2007) proposed the Vygotskyan intelligence hypothesis, that cooperation is a crucial means of boosting how young children learn from others. From the earliest interactions with caregivers, through shared attention and coordinated action, infants learn socially. When children enter formal education, peer interaction boosts this learning through peer interactions, and in particular through *collaborative interaction*. I use Roschelle and Teasley's (1995, p.70) definition of collaboration as 'coordinated, synchronous activity that is the result of a continued attempt to construct and maintain a shared conception of a problem'.

On the face of it, the role of collaboration should pose a particular disadvantage for young autistic people in school. Social differences, and difficulty in engaging in social interactions, are two of the main diagnostic characterizations of autism. This does not mean that sociability is necessarily absent, but it is markedly atypical. The barriers to collaboration seem particularly acute for children with minimal or no spoken language: the educational literature rests heavily on the role of spoken dialogue as a crucial medium for collaboration (Mercer & Littleton 2010). Without access to collaboration, children can lose out not just on the intrinsic benefits of shared experience but also on the benefits it brings in learning through others.

Fortunately, technology can provide ways to support collaboration. Educational psychologists have long had a role in guiding teachers and parents in how to arrange the child's environment to support learning, with social interaction as part of this. Some (but not all) the technologies I mention are available in schools. Where this is unlikely to be the case, I use the research to illuminate what it is about the technology that supports interaction, to enable ways we might replicate it by other means.

Collaboration can be defined as involving three aspects of behaviour: sharing *awareness* (how to capture children's attention to support their joint engagement in activity), sharing *control* of actions to support reciprocal interaction, and constructing shared *meaning* to enable the co-construction of knowledge. In keeping with the Vygotskyan approach, this entails knowledge that is first interpsychological (e.g., between peers) and then intrapsychological, appropriated by individual children for themselves. Each of these aspects can be a challenge in autism. How can technology be used to support each of these?

Part 2: Using technology to support collaboration through sharing awareness, control and meaning
SHARING MEANING

Shared awareness involves children attending to the actions of others, as a step towards being engaged in joint activity, anticipating and acting contingently on others' actions. Some autistic children can find it difficult to have their attention captured, and to shift away once attention is engaged, which can make shared awareness difficult to achieve and maintain fluidly. Technology design allows many ways to capture attention initially, through salient 'hooks' in different sensory modalities such as sound or vision. A striking example of this is provided by the example of the Augmented Knights' Castle (AKC) (Hinske *et al.* 2009), an augmented Playmobil castle set that uses radio frequency identity tags (RFID) on the feet of the characters to enable them to make specific sounds and speeches when placed in particular locations in the playset. Yuill and colleagues (2014) showed that typically developing children engaged in double the amount of cooperative play using the augmented set compared to a traditional non-augmented set, and this effect seemed to occur because children were better able to get others' attention successfully. Holding up a toy or vocalizing while placing the toy to make a particular sound effect, such as making the ghost moan when standing in the dungeon, gets peers' attention and seems to help children to stitch together a more connected play sequence. The same playset was also used to stimulate increased social engagement in small groups of autistic children in special education (Farr, Yuill & Hinske 2012).

While this specific set is not commercially available, the point is that providing children with tools that enable them to create controllable attention-grabbing effects through sound or vision helps them share engaging experiences with others. For example, having children take turns to play a favourite video on a tablet while their peers round the table wait for their turn can enable sharing interests through the shared sound and vision that the group experience together. Lechelt and colleagues (2018) evaluated how programmable cubes could be used to support collaborative learning in a special needs classroom. Children working in pairs or small groups shared attention and enjoyment, as they could create interesting effects, such as creating a coloured light display that then engaged others in the classroom to look, learn, and replicate with their own kit.

For autistic children with learning difficulties, little or no spoken language, and possibly other sensory and motor disabilities, sharing attention to interesting sensory effects has also been a feature of the many sensory environments provided, with devices such as ReacTickles (Keay-Bright & Howarth 2012) supporting children to notice interesting cause-and-effect relations and to share those experiences with peers or support workers. Research with more structured bespoke systems, such as the collaborative virtual/mixed-reality game *Lands of Fog* (Mora Guiard *et al.* 2016; further details in Yuill 2021), also illustrates how providing both effects that draw children in, and tasks that require more than one person to achieve, support sharing experience which can be a first step to closer collaboration.

SHARING CONTROL

Getting attention is a stepping-stone for watching and learning from others, but acting together, in coordination, is also a crucial part of the benefits of collaboration. The tangible technologies just mentioned support widely accessible means of control, where cause-and-effect relations can become manifest, for example in the ways that sounds and visual effects are contingent on children's own movements. Interacting with others requires *sharing* control, whether that is co-creating audio-visual effects, as part of a conversation or game, or working together to construct a story or solve a problem. Turn-taking is commonly taught as a social skill, and technology can be used to support this. For example, Piper, O'Brien, Morris and Winograd (2006) used a large multi-touch surface that could identify each user, so that turn-taking could be regulated through the technology. Children in a special education class found this technology-imposed constraint more acceptable than when managed by a teacher. Turn-taking is clearly useful but can lead to children tuning out while waiting their turn, and not engaging fully with what their peers are doing. This can reduce the chances of peer learning, sharing experiences, imitating or otherwise acting contingently.

The question is therefore how to support more fluid sharing of control beyond the acquisition of turn-taking behaviours. Most research into how technology supports equitable shared control involves typically developing children, and using large multi-touch table surfaces with user ID, which are unfortunately not commercially widely available (Yuill 2021). Most classrooms have large touch surfaces but these are vertically mounted interactive whiteboards rather than tables. Such whiteboards can be used for peer collaboration, but create some barriers, not least their mounted height (Mercer *et al.* 2010) and their tendency to be treated as teachers' rather than children's space. Large surfaces seem to promote easier collaboration when oriented horizontally rather than vertically (Rogers & Lindley 2004), so it is worth considering changing the orientation of surfaces large enough for easy use by several children.

Tablets are usually widely available, but a psychological barrier is that users and organizations often treat them as personal devices for one individual. Moreover, many design features (login access, personal ownership) work against them being used as shared spaces. Of course, in many classrooms, tablets are used for collaborative working, but sometimes the nature of this co-working is more like cooperation (each person completing a sub-task independently) than the constant to-and-fro of collaboration as defined here. However, the research findings with large horizontal multi-touch surfaces can provide some guidance for using smaller touch surfaces collaboratively. Surfaces readily support shared awareness and shared control. Further, combining different tools and media, such as cameras, captured drawings, creation of physical models and audio recording, can support children to co-create shared narratives; these tools could be implemented to create enduring and cumulative story-creation cultures in school, in the inspiring way that the *TellTable* tabletop app was used in a school library over several weeks (Cao *et al.* 2010).

Because of the lack of availability of large shared surfaces with touch identification as used by Piper *et al.* (2006), we developed an app, *ChatLabConnect*, which instead uses two tablets, wi-fi-connected, side by side, in a design illustrating how shared control can benefit autistic children's collaboration. In a recent evaluation of its daily use over six weeks in special schools, with teaching staff paired with minimally verbal autistic children, we found increases in children's attention to and awareness of the other person, as well as significant increases in children's performance on the Early Social Communication Scales and in their language, compared with a waiting-list control (Holt, Viner & Yuill, in preparation); see also (Holt & Yuill 2014, 2017).

Figure 10.1: ChatLabConnect dual-tablet communication activity

The app (Figure 10.1) has three features that we designed to support this closer social interaction and communication. The task involves simply sorting pictures into categories, such as play equipment vs.

buses. Before starting, each child individually can choose the pictures for sorting, as supported by the teacher. The ease of uploading pictures of the child's favoured objects means that they can be tailored to the intense, very particular, and sometimes fluctuating interests experienced by many autistic children, as well as supporting the teacher to engage with the child's specific interests. This feature can be replicated with many different tablet apps. Second, each player has their own space (tablet), so has freedom to sort each picture in whichever box they choose. However, there are also constraints on control, which involve tying the actions of the two players together. This means the child necessarily faces the dependency of their own actions on the actions of the teacher. Thus, players can sort pictures as they choose, but only up to a point. Once each person has chosen a picture, they can only progress to get the next picture once they have agreed on positioning. Each person controls their own space, but the two have to reach agreement to move on, by each one pressing a 'we agree' button. This agreement isn't reached just by one player forcing their choice on the other – each player has to choose freely how to sort, but in negotiation with the other. Negotiation can be helped by verbal communication, for example saying 'bus' to indicate what the grouping category is, but there is also a rich set of non-verbal social gestures, such as pointing, looking and waiting for the other to place a picture correctly before moving on, that support the pair to be aware of the other and to act contingently. Teaching staff can be supported to focus on scaffolding these collaborative skills, rather than the individual skill of correct sorting.

Commercially available and open-source software also provides apps and games that can support some sharing behaviours on single tablets, such as *Zody* (Boyd *et al.* 2015), *Open Autism Software* (Hourcade *et al.* 2013) and *Incloodle* (Sobel *et al.* 2016). Inevitably, the availability of these changes over the years, so professional network recommendations are useful to keep up to date. However, even basic apps such as story creators and drawing tools can readily be used collaboratively. Laurie and colleagues (2019) found that parents of autistic children reported that YouTube and video games were their most popular uses of technology. Gaming communities, such as those with *Minecraft*, can provide potential for collaborative action and a social community (Ringland *et al.* 2016). Some authors have suggested that autistic people may naturally interact with lower levels of contingency; for example, Heasman and

Gillespie (2018) reported that autistic adults playing a computer game showed looser connections in their conversations and were tolerant of non-sequiturs. Loosely connected interactions can be valuable in themselves, but technology supporting closer contingent interactions does seem to have some follow-on benefits, with the Holt *et al.* (n.d.) study finding benefits maintained after several weeks.

SHARING MEANING

One of the earliest signs of sharing meaning involves infant and carer mutually attending to an object that the carer might bring into view. Both are aware of the object, and also of the other's awareness (cf. Trevarthen's (1998) primary and secondary intersubjectivity). Much more complex shared meanings are developed in early childhood through sharing activities such as art, games and narrative creation. For many autistic children, the world may be full of meanings they struggle to construe, but technology design that engages children in shared awareness and enables shared control can produce shared meaning, even if this is not always verbalised explicitly. For example, Frauenberger, Spiel and Makhaeva (2019) describe ways of supporting participatory design with autistic children to create their own artefacts. Children can express shared meaning not just through creation of products, but also through simple movement. Psychologists have shown that movement synchrony plays a role in cooperation and positive social contact, and that this synchrony may be different when one of the partners is autistic (Glass & Yuill, under review). Movement synchrony is involved in many forms of music and movement therapies used with autistic children, such as Intensive Interaction; contingency of one movement on another, often by the therapist following the child's movements, supports the child to recognize contingency and connection with other people. Technology is well suited to capture and reflect such synchrony. For example, Villafuerte, Markova and Jorda (2012) created the *Reactable* multi-user tabletop instrument to support social interaction involving autistic children. Shared sound composition can be enabled through other digital music technologies that may be more readily available in schools. Ragone, Good and Howland (2020) described software for use with a Microsoft Kinect to convert child's and therapist's body movements into sound, as a way of supporting the creation of shared meaning.

Technology can also be a powerful tool to capture, present and share the perspectives of autistic children who may not use spoken language, so as to express their interests, experiences and ways of creating meaning in the world. Parsons, Kovshoff and Ivil (2020) describe the use of Digital Stories in a nursery as a means of capturing autistic pupils' voices, as part of their Education Health and Care Plan, and especially to support transitions between nursery and school.[2] Children and professionals used video and wearable cameras collaboratively in and around the classroom to produce short films with images, sound and narrative, creating a child's eye view of experiencing the world. Work on the Our Stories project is ongoing to develop and use this method more widely, using technology widely available in schools.

Conclusion

Technology can be highly motivating for autistic learners and this can provide both a respite from busy group activity and a means of supporting shared engagement, contingent interaction and sharing meanings. Covid-19 restrictions on school attendance have revealed how school environments might better support autistic learners (Shepherd and Hancock 2020), and have also stimulated creative consideration of online collaboration through technology. For in-person settings, touchscreens are widely available and offer opportunities for collaborative use, supporting social interaction and its associated benefits for learning and well-being.

USING VIRTUAL ENVIRONMENTS TO SUPPORT THE DEVELOPMENT AND GENERALIZATION OF SOCIAL SKILLS

Owen Rhys Barry

Introduction

This contribution to the chapter aims to provide an overview of the current research on using virtual environments (VEs) as a tool in social skills training (SST) programmes for children and young people who are autistic and who experience social communication needs. The aim

---

2   https://autismtransitions.org

is to provide the reader with some implications for practice relating to recommending and delivering SST programmes in schools.

Social skills training programmes and autism

SST programmes are common group-based interventions that educational psychologists, specialist teachers and local authorities refer to when supporting teachers in meeting the social communication needs of autistic children and young people. In general, SST programmes aim to provide learning experiences that support the development of social skills or abilities that can be used in a range of situations to support the child, young person or adult to engage with the social world and achieve their own social goals. This can include a number of communication skills such as how we use our voice (e.g., volume or intonation), our non-verbal responses (e.g., facial expression or gestures), the social use of language and social problem-solving.

'Traditional' and early SST programmes focused on behaviourist teaching approaches, including behaviour modelling and rule-based direct teaching (Cappadocia & Weiss 2011). However, more recent programmes attempt to employ peer and adult mediation approaches, modelling, cognitive behaviour therapy techniques and social problem-solving (Bauminger-Zviely *et al.* 2013). As research and practice have developed over time, it is widely agreed that group facilitators must avoid ableist ideas or teaching that suggests to the pupil that there is a 'normal' or correct way of being, but rather help the child or young person to navigate a social world that can often be complex and confusing to them. The goals of social skills programmes are to help young people engage in whatever functional social experiences they need to or would like to engage with throughout their life.

There is a modest evidence-base for using SST programmes with autistic children, adolescents and adults, with many studies describing some level of functional improvement on the basis of skills developed within the programmes themselves (Hotton & Coles 2016). However, past research has focused too heavily on measuring the frequency of behaviours learned in SST rather than considering measurement of the participants' quality of life following an SST programme or intervention (Sabey, Ross & Goodman 2020).

Despite the positive evidence of the efficacy of SST programmes, one of the most common limitations reported in research is that those skills taught in school or clinic-based SST programmes are not generalized or transferred to real-life contexts by the participants (Bellini *et al.* 2007). This is often the case for the traditional rule-based teaching programmes that are likely to be used in schools. One of the ideas as to why these skills do not transfer to novel contexts following SST is that the classroom-based programmes can only recreate the real-world context or social scenario to a certain extent (Barry *et al.* 2003). As the participant would not be practising the skills in the natural environment in which they would need to be applied, it seems that they are less likely to transfer their learning to novel and real-life contexts. This is often described as the programme's ability to facilitate an accurate 'representation' of the real-life context.

Virtual environments for learning

How can we identify what a learning environment would need to include in order to promote the transfer of skills learned in an SST programme to appropriate circumstances beyond that teaching environment? Kozlowski and DeShon (2004) describe these factors as the 'physical' and 'psychological' fidelity of the learning environment. The physical fidelity is concerned with how the environment replicates the target context, including the realism of objects and characters, how natural the responses are of the simulation, and how 'real' the environment is perceived to be by the pupil. The psychological fidelity relates to how well the simulation causes the psychological responses, including cognitive, affective, perceptive processes and so on, relevant to using that skill in a real-world context.

One way of creating an accurate representation of the psychological and physical fidelity of a social context could be through the use of a virtual environment (VE). VEs are created through the use of virtual reality; Virtual reality is generally achieved through three dimensional computer-generated images (as in Figure 10.2), but also through video-based approaches and augmented reality. A pupil or user can access this software through screens, or by using virtual reality headsets and motion sensors for a more immersive experience (Lorenzo, Pomares & Lledo 2013). A VE can be described as an interactive representation of an environment which can simulate real-life scenarios in real time (Mitchell, Parsons & Leonard 2007). Within a VE, the user is able to explore or move in the environment and may be able to interact with a number of objects, rooms, items and characters. This can be arranged to be viewed from a first-person perspective or it can be achieved through an on-screen avatar.

Figure 10.2: Example of a computer-generated virtual environment

One of the biggest benefits of VEs is that a teacher has the tools to create a unique environment that is designed to develop a specific skill or individualized learning goal. It can be seen as akin to creating a role play in a classroom but also simulating everything you might see and hear in that role play in real life. The flexibility of a VE allows for the environment to be programmed so that it can represent natural contexts, tasks, activities, scenes and 'presentational features', which can allow for a wide range of learning experiences over time (Ke, Moon & Sokolikj 2020). This could include different scenarios such as job interviews, purchasing something from a shop or buying ticket at a cinema, paying a bill over the phone, and so on.

Further to this, Lorenzo and colleagues (2013) highlighted that VEs can be flexible so that the teacher can change the number of features of a simulation to suit the ability of the learner. This could allow them to adapt the difficulty of the training scenario or look to focus tasks or simulations on particular aspects of learning. For example, a teacher could remove background noise and make the characters in the simulation respond in a particular way for the benefit of teaching, such as adapting the avatars to speak at a slower speed, or they could change the complexity of the language used.

Virtual environments and SST programmes

Not only do VEs provide huge benefits for the teacher in terms of the adaptability of the environments that can be created; they also provide a number of positives for the participant as well. We could argue that the best way to develop social skills is to practise skills as often as possible in real-life situations. However, there are some problems with this idea. The pupil may make mistakes in real-life situations and may not realize it or may experience the negative consequences of a social mistake in person (for example, the experience of social embarrassment following a misunderstanding). VEs create role-play situations where the user feels safe to practise and try different responses, while not then experiencing the real-life consequences of the exchange (Parsons & Mitchell 2002). This is an important benefit as some autistic people report that they can find new social situations distressing and confusing (DeRosier *et al.* 2010). Some VEs also provide the option of recording an interaction and playing it back on screen, which allows for review, reflection and future planning. The use of a VE can also reduce the number of potentially worrying or negative social factors that are uniquely experienced by the individual, as many of these factors can be removed, added or manipulated by the facilitator (Parsons 2005). For example, if the pupil is worried that an avatar will use a loud voice the teacher can ensure the avatars chosen then speak in a quiet voice to help the pupil access the learning experiences.

A further benefit of a VE is that the programme can be used any-where, meaning that it could be used as a tool for teachers in school and this process can then be continued or supplemented with practice at home or in other environments from a suitable device (Ke, Moon & Sokoliki 2020). Tasks can be repeated and experienced at different times of day and in different places suited to the learner. There is also the ability to incorporate 'gamification' into the learning experience, which may lead to a greater motivation to engage and to more positive outcomes in social skills development (Craig 2016).

While research is still emerging, there are now numerous examples of studies that have successfully used VEs in SST programmes. There have been improvements observed in pupils' skills in ordering from a cafe and finding a seat at a venue (Mitchell *et al.* 2007); in executive functioning and planning ahead (Lorenzo *et al.* 2013); in pretend play in children (Herrera *et al.* 2008); and in conversational skills (Ke & Im 2013). Virtual environments have also been used to coach autistic adults to develop their job interview skills through the process of interacting with a virtual interviewer on screen (Burke *et al.* 2018).

Using a video-based virtual environment (VVE)

There has been some positive evidence for the use of video-based approaches for social skills training, for instance video modelling, self-modelling and video feedback (Shukla-Mehta, Miller & Callahan 2010). At this point in time, there are very few SST programmes that have used a video-based virtual environment and there is not an 'off the shelf' or 'ready to use' video-based system that could be used for such training.

In a study completed by Barry (2015), a novel video-based virtual environment was used for SST where participants stood in front of a monitor, and a depth camera captured a video representation of the participant which was then layered onto a background video on the monitor. To the participant, it looked as though they had been 'transported' into the live video feed. The facilitator then had a bank of pre-recorded video responses in which it appeared that the actor on the video layer was looking at the participant's on-screen representation (see Figure 10.3). The facilitator could change the responses of the video avatar based on the participant's responses in the interaction. This created a real-time, interactive experience for the participant where they could see both themselves and the response of the character who they were interacting with.

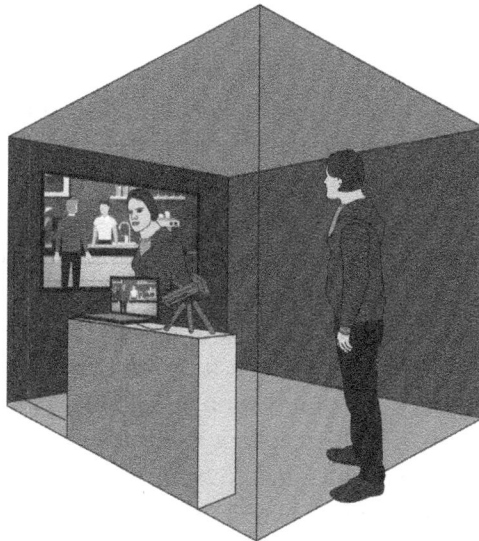

Figure 10.3: A video-based virtual environment teaching arrangement

The study was interested in developing the social skills needed to place an order with a server at a cafe counter (see Figure 10.4). A cafe counter interaction was chosen for the study as it is a common and often enjoyable social experience for many young people on school trips and in everyday life. Each participant experienced three interactions in each of the training sessions. Each interaction could have been used more than once for practice purposes, where the avatars could respond differently each time as they were controlled by the facilitator.

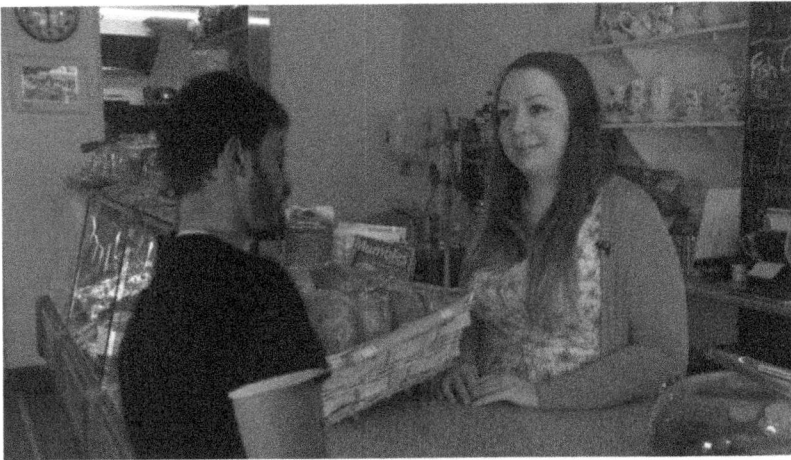

Figure 10.4: The learner's view of the video-based virtual environment

The VVE training consisted of three 50-minute sessions delivered on a weekly basis; the participants experienced the VVE training by themselves. The researcher and one member of school staff administered the training, teaching and learning. In each session, there was a teaching component, a practice phase in the VVE, and a review. The skills that were targeted included greeting the host, placing an order, paying for their order, and ending the exchange by saying thank you or goodbye.

The outcome of the intervention was that pupils who received the VVE training applied the skills that they learned in a real-life cafe as measured by structured observations over time. This learning was sustained a month after the teaching had finished. A pre- and post-intervention measure of the pupil's overall social skills completed by parents and teachers did not show an improvement in the pupil's overall general social functioning. A tentative conclusion of this finding was that skills need to be practised in a number of situations and social contexts to generalize to new interactions beyond the teaching context. The study's main finding was that the VVE appeared to support pupils to generalize skills to a targeted real-life context to a greater degree than just a classroom-based SST programme alone.

Conclusions

The evidence considered gives us an early indication that social skills can be developed with the use of virtual environments in SST programmes. There also seems to be some early support for the idea that the more practice a young person has in a learning environment that represents the social situation in which the targets skills need to be used, the more likely it is that the individual will be able to transfer and apply those skills to the real-life context.

It must be stressed that VEs should be seen as a teaching tool that can be employed in SST programmes but that VEs by themselves would not be a replacement for teaching and targeted support. An important mediator in the effectiveness of any type of SST is the teaching strategies and approaches employed (Ke & Lee 2016), and this is just as true with those who use VEs.

The evidence-base for virtual approaches is very much in its early stages and the area is only currently being considered by a small number of researchers who have generally completed studies with small sample sizes. Furthermore, from a practical perspective there is currently not an accessible, 'off the shelf' SST programme that uses a VE, but there have been some important implications generated from this body of work for supporting autistic individuals to transfer social learning from a teaching context to real life.

Some applications to professional practice

- Professionals need to reflect on what they are asking teaching staff to do when an SST programme is recommended for autistic children and young people:
  - What is the goal of the suggested programme and is this person-centred?

- Are we explicit enough in what skills have been identified to be taught and why?

- Is the teaching environment suited to developing the skills that we have identified?

- What does the pupil want to achieve and are we empowering them by using this approach?

- Are the staff who are delivering the programme confident with the type of teaching approaches that are appropriate to teach different skills?

- Are there naturalistic opportunities to practise the skills identified?

- SST programmes may be more effective if the teaching is focused on the context in which the skills need to occur. This may be more successful than training a set of non-specific broad skills that can be applied in multiple contexts.

- The skills should be practised in an environment as close as possible to the target environment, or using a VE that is as 'representative' of the target social context as feasible.

- If an SST programme is taught in a classroom or clinic, the programme will need to at least include teaching strategies that help the child or young person make links between the classroom learning and the target social context. This could include approaches such as discussion, visualization and/or role play.

Chapter conclusion

In conclusion, there are exciting developments in the use of information technology to improve the access to learning for autistic children. IT can be highly motivating for pupils and provide opportunities for independence, social awareness and fun.

The contributors have also raised issues and questioned commonly held beliefs concerning the use of IT. The evidence base and quality assurance for autism-specific IT are still at an early stage. The choice of device, program or app needs to be made carefully, with the intended goal in mind, and the role of the adult experienced in autism is essential.

With carefully planned programmes, social awareness and skills can in fact be improved through collaborative interventions and the use of virtual environments.

POINTS FOR REFLECTION

☞ What are the levels of understanding and engagement with technology?

☞ What are the specific intended goals to be achieved?

☞ Are there alternative, more effective methods to achieve the stated goals?

☞ What skills are required by the young person in order to use the IT?

☞ Is there a mainstream technology that can be used rather than autism-specific technology?

☞ Have we ensured the essential role of the adult in facilitating and evaluating progress?

☞ Are there opportunities built in for generalizing the skills being learned?

References

Adams, D., Simpson, K., Davies, L., Campbell, C. & MacDonald, L. (2019) 'Online learning for university students on the autism spectrum: A systematic review and question-naire study.' *Australasian Journal of Educational Technology, 35*(6), 111–131.

Alcorn, A.M., Ainger, E., Charisi, V., Mantinioti, S. *et al.* (2019) 'Educators' views on using humanoid robots with autistic learners in special education settings in England.' *Frontiers in Robotics and AI, 6,* 107.

Autism Centre for Education and Research (ACER) (2020) *Covid-19 and the Impact on Families with Autistic Children.* Birmingham: University of Birmingham.

Autism Speaks. Accessed March 2021 at www.autismspeaks.org/information-topic# technology.

Aydin, O. & Diken, I.H. (2020) 'Studies comparing Augmentative and Alternative Communication systems (AAC) applications for individuals with autism spectrum disorder: A systematic review and meta-analysis.' *Education and Training in Autism and Developmental Disabilities, 55*(2), 119–141.

Barry, O.R. (2015) *A Video-Based Virtual Environment for Teaching Social Skills to Adolescents with Autism: In Search of Generalisation.* DEdPsy thesis, Cardiff University.

Barry, T.D., Klinger, L.G., Lee, J.M., Palardy, N., Gilmore, T. & Bodin, S.D. (2003) 'Examining the effectiveness of an outpatient clinic-based social skills group for high functioning children with autism.' *Journal of Autism and Developmental Disorders, 3*(6), 685–701.

Bauminger-Zviely, N., Eden, S., Zancanaro, M., Weiss, P.L. & Gal, E. (2013) 'Increasing social engagement in children with high-functioning autism spectrum disorder using collaborative technologies in the school environment.' *Autism, 17*(3), 317–339.

Bellini, S., Peters, J.K., Benner, L. & Hopf, A. (2007) 'A meta-analysis of school-based social skills interventions for children with autism spectrum disorders.' *Remedial and Special Education, 28*(3), 153–162.

Boyd, L.E., Ringland, K.E., Haimson, O.L., Fernandez, H., Bistarkey, M. & Hayes, G.R. (2015) 'Evaluating a collaborative iPad game's impact on social relationships for children with autism spectrum disorder.' *ACM Transactions on Accessible Computing (TACCESS), 7*(1), 1–18.

Burke, L., Bresnahan, T., Li, T., Epnere, K. *et al.* (2018) 'Using Virtual Interactive Training Agents (ViTA) with adults with autism and other developmental disabilities.' *Journal of Autism and Developmental Disorders, 48*(3), 905–912.

Cao, X., Lindley, S.E., Helmes, J. & Sellen, A. (2010) 'Telling the Whole Story: Anticipation, Inspiration and Reputation in a Field Deployment of TellTable.' In *Proceedings of the 2010 ACM Conference on Computer Supported Cooperative Work* (pp.251–260). New York, NY: Association for Computing Machinery.

Cappadocia, M.C. & Weiss, J.A. (2011) 'Review of social skills training groups for youth with Asperger Syndrome and High Functioning Autism.' *Research in Autism Spectrum Disorders, 5*(1), 70–78.

Craig, A. (2016) 'Enhancing children's social emotional functioning through virtual game-based delivery of social skills training.' *Journal of Child & Family Studies, 25*(3), 959–968.

DeRosier, M.E., Swick, D.C., Davis, N.O., McMillen, J.S. & Matthews, R. (2010) 'The efficacy of a social skills group intervention for improving social behaviors in children with high-functioning autism spectrum disorders.' *Journal of Autism and Developmental Disorders, 43*(8), 1402–1403.

Farr, W., Yuill, N. & Hinske, S. (2012) 'An augmented toy and social interaction in children with autism.' *International Journal of Arts and Technology, 5*(2), 104–125.

Fletcher-Watson, S. (2014) 'A targeted review of computer-assisted learning for people with autism spectrum disorder: Towards a consistent methodology.' *Review Journal of Autism and Developmental Disorders, 1*(2), 87–100.

Fletcher-Watson, S. (2015) 'Evidence-based technology design and commercialisation: Recommendations derived from research in education and autism.' *TechTrends, 59*(1), 84–88.

Frauenberger, C., Spiel, K. & Makhaeva, J. (2019) 'Thinking OutsideTheBox: Designing smart things with autistic children.' *International Journal of Human–Computer Interaction, 35*(8), 666–678.

Glass, D. & Yuill, N. (under review) 'Social motor synchrony in autism spectrum conditions: A systematic review.' University of Sussex.

Grynszpan, O., Weiss, P.L., Perez-Diaz, F. & Gal, E. (2013) 'Innovative technology-based interventions for autism spectrum disorders: A meta-analysis.' *Autism, 18*(4), 346–361.

Heasman, B. & Gillespie, A. (2018) 'Neurodivergent intersubjectivity: Distinctive features of how autistic people create shared understanding.' *Autism.* https://doi.org/10.1177/1362361318785172.

Herrera, G., Alcantud, F., Jordan, R., Blanquer, A., Labajo, G. & De Pablo, C. (2008) 'Development of symbolic play through the use of virtual reality tools in children with autistic spectrum disorders: Two case studies.' *Autism, 12*(2), 143–157.

Hinske, S., Lampe, M., Yuill, N., Price, S. & Langheinrich, M. (2009) 'Kingdom of the Knights: Evaluation of a Seamlessly Augmented Toy Environment for Playful Learning.' In *Proceedings of the 8th International Conference on Interaction Design and Children* (pp.202–205). New York, NY: Association for Computing Machinery.

Holt, S. & Yuill, N. (2014) 'Facilitating other-awareness in low-functioning children with autism and typically-developing preschoolers using dual-control technology.' *Journal of Autism and Developmental Disorders, 44*(1), 1–13.

Holt, S. & Yuill, N. (2017) 'Tablets for two: How dual tablets can facilitate other-awareness and communication in learning-disabled children with autism.' *International Journal of Child–Computer Interaction, 11*, 72–82. https://doi.org/10.1016/j.ijcci.2016.10.005.

Holt, S., Viner, H. & Yuill, N. (in preparation) 'Controlled trial of an intervention to support collaboration in learning-disabled autistic children.' University of Sussex.

Hotton, M. & Coles, S. (2016) 'The effectiveness of social skills training groups for individuals with autism spectrum disorder.' *Review Journal of Autism and Developmental Disorders, 3*(1), 68–81.

Houghton, K. (2020) *Virtual Interventions: Using Technology to Engage and Motivate Children and Young People.* Educational Psychology Reach Out, YouTube. Accessed 06/02/2021 at www.youtube.com/watch?v=8k8ssnqGpos.

Hourcade, J.P., Williams, S.R., Miller, E.A., Huebner, K.E. & Liang, L.J. (2013) 'Evaluation of Tablet Apps to Encourage Social Interaction in Children with Autism Spectrum Disorders.' In *Proceedings of the SIGCHI Conference on Human Factors in Computing Systems* (pp.3197–3206). New York, NY: Association for Computing Machinery.

Ke, F. & Im, T. (2013) 'Virtual-reality-based social interaction training for children with high-functioning autism.' *Journal of Educational Research, 106*(6), 441–461.

Ke, F. & Lee, S. (2016) 'Virtual-reality-based collaborative design by children with high-functioning autism: Design-based flexibility, identity, and norm construction.' *Interactive Learning Environments, 24*(7), 1511–1533.

Ke, F., Moon, J. & Sokolikj, Z. (2020) 'Virtual reality-based social skills training for children with autism spectrum disorder.' *Journal of Special Education Technology*, 1–14. https://doi.org/10.1177/0162643420945603.

Keay-Bright, W. & Howarth, I. (2012) 'Is simplicity the key to engagement for children on the autism spectrum?' *Personal and Ubiquitous Computing, 16*(2), 129–141.

Kozlowski, S.W.J. & DeShon, R.P. (2004) 'A Psychological Fidelity Approach to Simulation-Based Training: Theory, Research, and Principles.' In E. Salas, L.R. Elliott, S.G. Schflett & M.D. Coovert (eds) *Scaled Worlds: Development, Validation, and Applications* (pp.75–99). Burlington, VT: Ashgate Publishing.

Kranzberg, M. (1986) 'Technology and history: "Kranzberg's Laws".' *Technology and Culture 27*(3), 544–560.

Laurie, M.H., Warreyn, P., Uriarte, B.V., Boonen, C. & Fletcher-Watson, S. (2019) 'An international survey of parental attitudes to technology use by their autistic children at home.' *Journal of Autism and Developmental Disorders, 49*(4), 1517–1530.

Lechelt, Z., Rogers, Y., Yuill, N., Nagl, L., Ragone, G. & Marquardt, N. (2018) 'Inclusive Computing in Special Needs Classrooms: Designing for All.' In *Conference on Human Factors in Computing Systems – Proceedings*. New York, NY: Association for Computing Machinery. https://doi.org/10.1145/3173574.3174091.

Logan, K., Iacono, T. & Trembath, D. (2017) 'A systematic review of research into aided AAC to increase social-communication functions in children with autism spectrum disorder.' *Augmentative and Alternative Communication, 33*(1), 51–64.

Lorah, E.R., Parnell, A., Whitby, P.S. & Hantula, D. (2015) 'A systematic review of tablet computers and portable media players as speech generating devices for individuals with autism spectrum disorder.' *Journal of Autism and Developmental Disorders, 45*(12), 3792–3804.

Lorenzo, G., Pomares, J. & Lledo, A. (2013) 'Inclusion of immersive virtual learning environments and visual control systems to support the learning of students with Asperger's Syndrome.' *Computers & Education, 62*, 88–101.

Luria, A.R. (1966) *The Higher Cortical Functions in Man.* New York, NY: Basic Books.

Mercer, N. & Littleton, K. (2010) 'The Significance of Educational Dialogues Between Primary School Children.' In K. Littleton & C. Howe (eds) *Educational Dialogues: Understanding and Promoting Productive Interaction* (pp. 271–288). London: Routledge.

Mercer, N., Warwick, P., Kershner, R. & Staarman, J.K. (2010) 'Can the interactive whiteboard help to provide "dialogic space" for children's collaborative activity?' *Language and Education, 24*(5), 367–384. https://doi.org/10.1080/09500781003642460.

Mitchell, P., Parsons, S. & Leonard, A. (2007) 'Using virtual environments for teaching social understanding to adolescents with autistic spectrum disorders.' *Journal of Autism and Developmental Disorders, 37*(3), 589–600.

Moll, H. & Tomasello, M. (2007) 'Cooperation and human cognition: The Vygotskian intelligence hypothesis.' *Philosophical Transactions of the Royal Society of London. Series B, Biological Sciences, 362* (1480), 639–648. https://doi.org/10.1098/rstb.2006.2000.

Mora-Guiard, J., Crowell, C., Pares, N. & Heaton, P. (2016) 'Lands of Fog: Helping Children with Autism in Social Interaction through a Full-Body Interactive Experience.' *Proceedings of IDC 2016 – The 15th International Conference on Interaction Design and Children* (pp.262–274). New York, NY: Association for Computing Machinery. https://doi.org/10.1145/2930674.2930695.

Murray, D. (1997) 'Autism and Information Technology: Therapy with Computers.' In S. Powell & R. Jordan (eds) *Autism and Learning: A Guide to Good Practice* (pp.100–117). London: David Fulton Publishers.

Parsons, S. (2005) 'Use, understanding and learning in virtual environments by adolescents with autism spectrum disorders.' *Annual Review of Cybertherapy and Telemedicine, 3*, 207–215.

Parsons, S. & Mitchell, P. (2002) 'The potential of virtual reality in social skills training for people with autistic spectrum disorders.' *Journal of Intellectual Disability Research, 46*, 430–443.

Parsons, S., Kovshoff, H. & Ivil, K. (2020) 'Digital stories for transition: Co-constructing an evidence base in the early years with autistic children, families and practitioners.' *Educational Review*, 1–19. https://doi.org/10.1080/00131911.2020.1816909.

Piper, A.M., O'Brien, E., Morris, M.R. & Winograd, T. (2006) 'SIDES: A Cooperative Tabletop Computer Game for Social Skills Development.' In *Proceedings of the 2006 20th Anniversary Conference on Computer Supported Cooperative Work* (pp.1–10). New York, NY: Association for Computing Machinery.

Ragone, G., Good, J. & Howland, K. (2020) 'OSMoSIS: Interactive Sound Generation System for Children with Autism.' In *Proceedings of the 2020 ACM Interaction Design and Children Conference: Extended Abstracts* (pp.151–156). New York, NY: Association for Computing Machinery. https://doi.org/10.1145/3397617.3397838.

Rao, P.A., Beidel, D.C. & Murray, M.J. (2008) 'Social skills interventions for children with Asperger's syndrome or high-functioning autism: A review and recommendations.' *Journal of Autism and Developmental Disorders, 38*(2), 353–361.

Ringland, K.E., Wolf, C.T., Faucett, H., Dombrowski, L. & Hayes, G.R. (2016) '"Will I Always be Not Social?" Re-Conceptualizing Sociality in the Context of a Minecraft Community for Autism.' In *Proceedings of the 2016 CHI Conference on Human Factors in Computing Systems* (pp.1256–1269). New York, NY: Association for Computing Machinery.

Rogers, Y. & Lindley, S. (2004) 'Collaborating around vertical and horizontal large interactive displays: Which way is best?' *Interacting with Computers, 16*(6), 1133–1152. https://doi.org/10.1016/j.intcom.2004.07.008.

Roschelle, J. & Teasley, S.D. (1995) 'The construction of shared knowledge in collaborative problem solving.' *Computer Supported Collaborative Learning, 128*, 69–97. https://doi.org/10.1007/978-3-642-85098-1_5.

Sabey, C., Ross, S. & Goodman, J. (2020) 'Beyond topography: Addressing the functional impact of social skills training for students with autism.' *Educational Psychology in Practice, 36*(2), 133–148.

Shepherd, J. & Hancock, C. (2020) *Education and Covid: Perspectives from Parents of Children with SEND.* Retrieved from www.sussex.ac.uk/webteam/gateway/file. php?name=education-and-covid-19-perspectives-from-parent-carers-of-children-with-send-392020.pdf&site=319.

Shic, F. & Goodwin, M. (2015) 'Introduction to technologies in the daily lives of individuals with autism.' *Journal of Autism and Developmental Disorders, 45*(12), 3773–3776.

Shukla-Mehta, S., Miller, T. & Callahan, K.J. (2010) 'Evaluating the effectiveness of video instruction on social and communication skills training for children with autism spectrum disorders: A review of the literature.' *Focus on Autism and Other Developmental Disabilities, 25*(1), 23–36.

Shurr, J., Bouck, E.C., Bassette, L. & Park, L. (2021) 'Virtual versus concrete: A comparison of mathematics manipulatives for three elementary students with autism.' *Focus on Autism and Other Developmental Disabilities, 36*(2), 72–81.

Sobel, K., Rector, K., Evans, S. & Kientz, J.A. (2016) 'Incloodle: Evaluating an Interactive Application for Young Children with Mixed Abilities.' In *Proceedings of the 2016 CHI Conference on Human Factors in Computing Systems* (pp.165–176). New York, NY: Association for Computing Machinery.

Trevarthen, C. (1998) 'The Concept and Foundations of Infant Intersubjectivity.' In S. Braten (ed.) *Intersubjective Communication and Emotion in Early Ontogeny* (pp.15–46). Cambridge: Cambridge University Press.

Valencia, K., Rusu, C., Quiñones, D. & Jamet, E. (2019) 'The impact of technology on people with autism spectrum disorder: A systematic literature review.' *Sensors, 19*(20), 4485.

Villafuerte, L., Markova, M. & Jorda, S. (2012) 'Acquisition of Social Abilities through Musical Tangible User Interface: Children with Autism Spectrum Condition and the Reactable.' In *CHI'12 Extended Abstracts on Human Factors in Computing Systems* (pp.745–760). New York, NY: Association for Computing Machinery.

Vygotsky, L.S. (1930–34/1978) *Mind in Society: The Development of Higher Psychological Processes* (eds) M. Cole, V. John-Steiner, S. Scribner & E. Souberman. Cambridge, MA: Harvard University Press.

Whyte, E.M., Smyth, J.M. & Scherf, K.S. (2015) 'Designing serious game interventions for individuals with autism.' *Journal of Autism and Developmental Disorders, 45*(12), 3820–3831.

Yuill, N. (2021) *Technology to Support Children's Collaborative Interactions: Close Encounters of the Shared Kind.* London: Palgrave MacMillan.

Yuill, N. & Martin, A. (2016) 'Curling up with a good e-book: Mother–child shared story reading on screen or paper affects embodied interaction and warmth.' *Frontiers in Psychology, 7,* 1951. https://doi.org/10.3389/fpsyg.2016.01951.

Yuill, N., Strieth, S., Roake, C., Aspden, R. & Todd, B. (2007) 'Brief Report.' In N. Yuill (2021) *Technology to Support Children's Collaborative Interactions: Close Encounters of the Shared Kind.* London: Palgrave MacMillan.

Yuill, N., Hinske, S., Williams, S. & Leith, G. (2014) 'How getting noticed helps getting on: Successful attention capture doubles children's cooperative play.' *Frontiers in Psychology, 27*(5), 418. https://doi.org/10.3389/fpsyg.2014.00418.

Zervogianni, V., Fletcher-Watson, S., Herrera, G., Goodwin, M. *et al.* (2020) 'A framework of evidence-based practice for digital support, co-developed with and for the autism community.' *Autism, 24*(6), 1411–1422.

CHAPTER 11

Concluding Thoughts

Judith Gainsborough

The process of sifting through the content of each EP-ASIG study day since 2007 has been very enjoyable. The sub-editors and I can see that over the last 14 years our knowledge and understanding of autism has developed significantly, our attitudes and use of language to describe autistic individuals has changed, and there is a new focus of priorities for the work of professionals and in the aims of many researchers. One of the objectives of this book was to facilitate the voices of a number of autistic individuals as well as the parents of autistic children, and this is very much part of a widespread growing commitment not only to listen to the autism community but also to work within it in equal partnership. Thus, researchers can begin to plan research that has true relevance and usefulness to the lives of autistic individuals. In fact, there are some recent 'participant-led' research paradigms that allow the participant to co-design the research topic. Similarly, professionals can begin to support autistic individuals to identify their strengths and plan their life choices accordingly as well as to try to find solutions to any obstacles in the way of achieving those aims. It is clear from many of the contributions in this book that there remains much more work to be done before the skills and strengths of autistic people are valued by all and the community has an equal footing in society without discrimination and disadvantage.

Many themes and threads have emerged during the compilation of this book and it seems important to us to identify some concepts which may help all of us to clarify priorities and a focus for the future. Such a focus might help us to achieve a much more inclusive and positive life experience for autistic individuals as we move forward.

Inclusivity

We have begun to notice a welcome shift in schools and colleges in conceptual thinking away from the term 'behaviour' and towards the use of terms such as 'regulation' and 'emotional regulation'. We hope that this will lead to a more constructive approach to explaining and understanding 'behaviour' and looking for appropriate modifications to environments and policies in order to support a more successful inclusion of autistic students. There remains a great deal of concern about the exclusion rate for autistic students and we have learned of the strong link between school exclusions of autistic students and later involvement with the criminal justice system. More widely, there is increasing recognition of anxiety as a predominant feature in the lives of many autistic individuals and their families. Anxiety is often at the root cause of many behaviours which are perceived to be challenging. It is hugely important that anxiety and the reasons for it are recognized as a significant barrier to the inclusion of autistic individuals in all aspects of society – in school classrooms and playgrounds, public spaces and public transport, and in the arena of employment. There is much that we all need to do to raise awareness of these issues and encourage more thought and planning to reduce the anxiety-inducing features of our social and physical environments, and therefore break down those barriers to more effective inclusion.

Equality

We have learned about the continued disadvantages experienced by minority ethnic communities and the complexity of difficulties experienced by families belonging to such communities when they have an autistic child. Not only is there an inequality of access to services and assessment opportunities, but there are also concerns about inappropriate assessment practices and a disregard of cultural differences in parenting. More generally, the theme of building trusting relationships with autistic individuals and their families, with mutual respect, is a recurrent one throughout the book and is a basic foundation for understanding and supporting positive outcomes.

When thinking about sexuality, autistic youngsters require a different kind of support to their neurotypical peers so that they can understand and rationalize their own sexual development and be supported to have opportunities for healthy, happy and safe relationships if they should choose to do so. This requires a great deal of sensitive preparation in partnership with families. Historically, there has not been acknowledgement of the different profile of autistic women and girls, and much more needs to be done to ensure that their needs are more widely understood and that they are identified early for appropriate intervention.

We have learned a great deal in this book from the contributions of parents and from autistic people themselves about their own personal journeys. There are clear messages about the need for professionals to listen actively to parental voices and the voices of autistic children and young people, in order to learn about their individual needs and preferences and to work in equal partnership to find ways forward. This is particularly vital in terms of supporting transitions to adulthood. There are no 'off the shelf' solutions, only a need for acknowledgement that none of us has all the answers and we need to take time to listen and collaborate as an integral part of any assessment. Furthermore, more work needs to be done to elicit the child's voice in any assessment, especially the voice of autistic children with severe cognitive and communication needs.

Advocacy

The advocacy role is key both to explaining behaviour that might be perceived to be challenging in a range of environments, and to ensuring that account is taken of the autistic person's voice.

Considering the roles of educators and professionals involved with autistic children and young people, it is clear that there are many situations where being an advocate is crucial in effecting positive experiences of inclusion at different levels. This might include actively explaining behaviour that is perceived to be challenging, or developing and sharing a detailed profile of the child in order to understand their needs. At a group level, advocacy might include the provision of school staff training opportunities so that all those working in the school can respond appropriately to their autistic students. At an organizational level, there remains a role for us all in promoting autism awareness and championing the development of autism provision in all sectors of society.

Advocacy might also extend outside a school environment in order to find the best opportunities for college placement, employment or, indeed, where a young person has encountered difficulties and has become involved with the CJS. Later on, autistic adults encountering difficulties in employment may benefit from the involvement of a professional acting as an advocate for them.

Adaptability

We all need to be reflecting constantly on our knowledge base and practice, the language we use, the assessment techniques we favour, and the extent to which there is equality of access to our services. Everyone working in the field of autism should be considering what needs to change to ensure that every autistic individual receives the service and support that will enable them to fulfil their potential. We need to be open to changing the way we do things and introducing much more flexibility into our own practices. We need to work in equal partnership not only with families, but also with schools and a range of other professionals to ensure an optimum experience for service users. Mutual respect, good communication and creative partnerships when collaborating with other professionals are vital for ensuring the best outcomes for autistic children and young people and their families.

The use of profiles to understand and explain an autistic individual's presentation of behaviours, and also to inform decision-making about the most appropriate interventions, is clearly something which should be deeply embedded in professional practice. Similarly, it is hoped that the developing use of formulation as a tool for providing a working hypothesis about a child or young person's needs and the most appropriate way forward will be beneficial for all those working in the field of autism.

Creativity

The Covid-19 pandemic and subsequent lockdowns have made all of us find new and unfamiliar solutions to everyday working and communication. There have been numerous examples of extraordinary creativity in the way schools and professionals have offered support to the autistic community. Information technology has sparked a multitude of creative and innovative ideas to support autistic people and their families, and sets the scene for the continued development of a wealth of software which can support autistic people in their lives.

Subject Index

'translational gap' 49
trust 140–2, 149

unconscious bias 246

video feedback (in PCI
    interventions) 81–5
Video Interaction for Promoting
    Positive Parenting (VIPP PCI) 84
virtual environments (for social
    skills training) 288–93
voice see parents/carers; pupil voice
voice-output communication
    aids (VOCAs) 271

vulnerability to exploitation 166, 189

'witness-aimed first account'
    interviewing technique 197

young offender institutions 202
Youth Justice Liaison and
    Diversion scheme 194
youth offending teams 201
    see also criminal justice system

zero tolerance behaviour systems
    100

Author Index

CPI Antony Rowe
Eastbourne, UK
May 24, 2025